...FOR DUMMIES

References for the Rest of Us!

COMPUTER BOOK SERIES FROM IDG

Are you intimidated and confused by computers? Do you find that traditional manuals are overloaded with technical details you'll never use? Do your friends and family always call you to fix simple problems on their PCs? Then the *...For Dummies®* computer book series from IDG Books Worldwide is for you.

...For Dummies books are written for those frustrated computer users who know they aren't really dumb but find that PC hardware, software, and indeed the unique vocabulary of computing make them feel helpless. *...For Dummies* books use a lighthearted approach, a down-to-earth style, and even cartoons and humorous icons to diffuse computer novices' fears and build their confidence. Lighthearted but not lightweight, these books are a perfect survival guide for anyone forced to use a computer.

> *"I like my copy so much I told friends; now they bought copies."*
>
> **Irene C., Orwell, Ohio**

> *"Quick, concise, nontechnical, and humorous."*
>
> **Jay A., Elburn, Illinois**

> *"Thanks, I needed this book. Now I can sleep at night."*
>
> **Robin F., British Columbia, Canada**

Already, hundreds of thousands of satisfied readers agree. They have made *...For Dummies* books the #1 introductory level computer book series and have written asking for more. So, if you're looking for the most fun and easy way to learn about computers, look to *...For Dummies* books to give you a helping hand.

IDG
BOOKS
WORLDWIDE

MORE

WINDOWS® 98
FOR
DUMMIES®

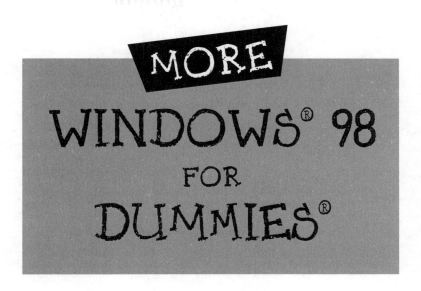

MORE
WINDOWS® 98
FOR
DUMMIES®

by Andy Rathbone

IDG Books Worldwide, Inc.
An International Data Group Company

Foster City, CA ♦ Chicago, IL ♦ Indianapolis, IN ♦ New York, NY ♦ Southlake, TX

MORE Windows® 98 For Dummies®

Published by
IDG Books Worldwide, Inc.
An International Data Group Company
919 E. Hillsdale Blvd.
Suite 400
Foster City, CA 94404
www.idgbooks.com (IDG Books Worldwide Web site)
www.dummies.com (Dummies Press Web site)

Copyright © 1998 IDG Books Worldwide, Inc. All rights reserved. No part of this book, including interior design, cover design, and icons, may be reproduced or transmitted in any form, by any means (electronic, photocopying, recording, or otherwise) without the prior written permission of the publisher.

Library of Congress Catalog Card No.: 98-85132

ISBN: 0-7645-0234-4

Printed in the United States of America

10 9 8 7 6 5 4 3 2 1

1B/SR/QU/ZY/IN

Distributed in the United States by IDG Books Worldwide, Inc.

Distributed by Macmillan Canada for Canada; by Transworld Publishers Limited in the United Kingdom; by IDG Norge Books for Norway; by IDG Sweden Books for Sweden; by Woodslane Pty. Ltd. for Australia; by Woodslane Enterprises Ltd. for New Zealand; by Longman Singapore Publishers Ltd. for Singapore, Malaysia, Thailand, and Indonesia; by Simron Pty. Ltd. for South Africa; by Toppan Company Ltd. for Japan; by Distribuidora Cuspide for Argentina; by Livraria Cultura for Brazil; by Ediciencia S.A. for Ecuador; by Addison-Wesley Publishing Company for Korea; by Ediciones ZETA S.C.R. Ltda. for Peru; by WS Computer Publishing Corporation, Inc., for the Philippines; by Unalis Corporation for Taiwan; by Contemporanea de Ediciones for Venezuela; by Computer Book & Magazine Store for Puerto Rico; by Express Computer Distributors for the Caribbean and West Indies. Authorized Sales Agent: Anthony Rudkin Associates for the Middle East and North Africa.

For general information on IDG Books Worldwide's books in the U.S., please call our Consumer Customer Service department at 800-762-2974. For reseller information, including discounts and premium sales, please call our Reseller Customer Service department at 800-434-3422.

For information on where to purchase IDG Books Worldwide's books outside the U.S., please contact our International Sales department at 650-655-3200 or fax 650-655-3295.

For information on foreign language translations, please contact our Foreign & Subsidiary Rights department at 650-655-3021 or fax 650-655-3281.

For sales inquiries and special prices for bulk quantities, please contact our Sales department at 650-655-3200 or write to the address above.

For information on using IDG Books Worldwide's books in the classroom or for ordering examination copies, please contact our Educational Sales department at 800-434-2086 or fax 817-251-8174.

For press review copies, author interviews, or other publicity information, please contact our Public Relations department at 650-655-3000 or fax 650-655-3299.

For authorization to photocopy items for corporate, personal, or educational use, please contact Copyright Clearance Center, 222 Rosewood Drive, Danvers, MA 01923, or fax 978-750-4470.

is a trademark under exclusive license to IDG Books Worldwide, Inc., from International Data Group, Inc.

About the Author

Andy Rathbone started geeking around with computers in 1985 when he bought a boxy CP/M Kaypro 2X with lime-green letters. Like other budding nerds, he soon began playing with null-modem adapters, dialing up computer bulletin boards, and working part-time at Radio Shack.

In between playing computer games, he served as editor of the *Daily Aztec* newspaper at San Diego State University. After graduating with a comparative literature degree, he went to work for a bizarre underground coffee-table magazine that sort of disappeared.

Andy began combining his two interests, words and computers, by selling articles to a local computer magazine. During the next few years, he started ghostwriting computer books for more-famous computer authors, as well as writing several hundred articles about computers for technoid publications like *Supercomputing Review, CompuServe Magazine, ID Systems, DataPro,* and *Shareware.*

In 1992, Andy and *DOS For Dummies* author/legend Dan Gookin teamed up to write *PCs For Dummies,* which was a runner-up in the Computer Press Association's 1993 awards. Andy subsequently wrote *Windows For Dummies, OS/2 Warp For Dummies, Upgrading & Fixing PCs For Dummies,* and *Multimedia & CD-ROMs For Dummies.* He also cowrote *Windows NT 4 For Dummies* with Sharon Crawford.

Andy lives with his most-excellent wife, Tina, and their cat in Southern California. When not writing, Andy fiddles with his MIDI synthesizer and tries to keep the cat off both keyboards.

ABOUT IDG BOOKS WORLDWIDE

Welcome to the world of IDG Books Worldwide.

IDG Books Worldwide, Inc., is a subsidiary of International Data Group, the world's largest publisher of computer-related information and the leading global provider of information services on information technology. IDG was founded more than 25 years ago and now employs more than 8,500 people worldwide. IDG publishes more than 275 computer publications in over 75 countries (see listing below). More than 60 million people read one or more IDG publications each month.

Launched in 1990, IDG Books Worldwide is today the #1 publisher of best-selling computer books in the United States. We are proud to have received eight awards from the Computer Press Association in recognition of editorial excellence and three from *Computer Currents'* First Annual Readers' Choice Awards. Our best-selling *...For Dummies*® series has more than 30 million copies in print with translations in 30 languages. IDG Books Worldwide, through a joint venture with IDG's Hi-Tech Beijing, became the first U.S. publisher to publish a computer book in the People's Republic of China. In record time, IDG Books Worldwide has become the first choice for millions of readers around the world who want to learn how to better manage their businesses.

Our mission is simple: Every one of our books is designed to bring extra value and skill-building instructions to the reader. Our books are written by experts who understand and care about our readers. The knowledge base of our editorial staff comes from years of experience in publishing, education, and journalism — experience we use to produce books for the '90s. In short, we care about books, so we attract the best people. We devote special attention to details such as audience, interior design, use of icons, and illustrations. And because we use an efficient process of authoring, editing, and desktop publishing our books electronically, we can spend more time ensuring superior content and spend less time on the technicalities of making books.

You can count on our commitment to deliver high-quality books at competitive prices on topics you want to read about. At IDG Books Worldwide, we continue in the IDG tradition of delivering quality for more than 25 years. You'll find no better book on a subject than one from IDG Books Worldwide.

John Kilcullen
CEO
IDG Books Worldwide, Inc.

Steven Berkowitz
President and Publisher
IDG Books Worldwide, Inc.

*Eighth Annual
Computer Press
Awards ≥ 1992*

*Ninth Annual
Computer Press
Awards ≥ 1993*

*Tenth Annual
Computer Press
Awards ≥ 1994*

*Eleventh Annual
Computer Press
Awards ≥ 1995*

IDG Books Worldwide, Inc., is a subsidiary of International Data Group, the world's largest publisher of computer-related information and the leading global provider of information services on information technology. International Data Group publishes over 275 computer publications in over 75 countries. Sixty million people read one or more International Data Group publications each month. International Data Group's publications include: **ARGENTINA:** Buyer's Guide, Computerworld Argentina, PC World Argentina; **AUSTRALIA:** Australian Macworld, Australian PC World, Australian Reseller News, Computerworld, IT Casebook, Network World, Publish, Webmaster; **AUSTRIA:** Computerwelt Osterreich, Networks Austria, PC Tip Austria; **BANGLADESH:** PC World Bangladesh; **BELARUS:** PC World Belarus; **BELGIUM:** Data News; **BRAZIL:** Annuário de Informática, Computerworld, Connections, Macworld, PC Player, PC World, Publish, Reseller News, Supergamepower; **BULGARIA:** Computerworld Bulgaria, Network World Bulgaria, PC & MacWorld Bulgaria; **CANADA:** CIO Canada, Client/Server World, ComputerWorld Canada, InfoWorld Canada, NetworkWorld Canada, WebWorld; **CHILE:** Computerworld Chile, PC World Chile; **COLOMBIA:** Computerworld Colombia, PC World Colombia; **COSTA RICA:** PC World Centro America; **THE CZECH AND SLOVAK REPUBLICS:** Computerworld Czechoslovakia, Macworld Czech Republic, PC World Czechoslovakia; **DENMARK:** Communications World Danmark, Computerworld Danmark, Macworld Danmark, PC World Danmark, Techworld Denmark; **DOMINICAN REPUBLIC:** PC World Republica Dominicana; **ECUADOR:** PC World Ecuador; **EGYPT:** Computerworld Middle East, PC World Middle East; **EL SALVADOR:** PC World Centro America; **FINLAND:** MikroPC, Tietoverkko, Tietoviikko; **FRANCE:** Distributique, Hebdo, Info PC, Le Monde Informatique, Macworld, Reseaux & Telecoms, WebMaster France; **GERMANY:** Computer Partner, Computerwoche, Computerwoche Extra, Computerwoche FOCUS, Global Online, Macwelt, PC Welt; **GREECE:** Amiga Computing, GamePro Greece, Multimedia World; **GUATEMALA:** PC World Centro America; **HONDURAS:** PC World Centro America; **HONG KONG:** Computerworld Hong Kong, PC World Hong Kong, Publish in Asia; **HUNGARY:** ABCD CD-ROM, Computerworld Szamitastechnika, Internetto online Magazine, PC World Hungary, PC-X Magazin Hungary; **ICELAND:** Tolvuheimur PC World Island; **INDIA:** Information Communications World, Information Systems Computerworld, PC World India, Publish in Asia; **INDONESIA:** InfoKomputer PC World, Komputek Computerworld, Publish in Asia; **IRELAND:** ComputerScope, PC Live!; **ISRAEL:** Macworld Israel, People & Computers/Computerworld; **ITALY:** Computerworld Italia, Macworld Italia, Networking Italia, PC World Italia; **JAPAN:** DTP World, Macworld Japan, Nikkei Personal Computing, OS/2 World Japan, SunWorld Japan, Windows NT World, Windows World Japan; **KENYA:** PC World East African; **KOREA:** Hi-Tech Information, Macworld Korea, PC World Korea; **MACEDONIA:** PC World Macedonia; **MALAYSIA:** Computerworld Malaysia, PC World Malaysia, Publish in Asia; **MALTA:** PC World Malta; **MEXICO:** Computerworld Mexico, PC World Mexico; **MYANMAR:** PC World Myanmar; **NETHERLANDS:** Computer! Totaal, LAN Internetworking Magazine, LAN World Buyers Guide, Macworld Netherlands, Net, WebWereld; **NEW ZEALAND:** Absolute Beginners Guide and Plain & Simple Series, Computer Buyer, Computer Industry Directory, Computerworld New Zealand, MTB, Network World, PC World New Zealand; **NICARAGUA:** PC World Centro America; **NORWAY:** Computerworld Norge, CW Rapport, Datamagasinet, Financial Rapport, Kursguide Norge, Macworld Norge, Multimediaworld Norge, PC World Ekspress Norge, PC World Nettverk, PC World Norge, PC World ProduktGuide Norge; **PAKISTAN:** Computerworld Pakistan; **PANAMA:** PC World Panama; **PEOPLE'S REPUBLIC OF CHINA:** China Computer Users, China Computerworld, China InfoWorld, China Telecom World Weekly, Computer & Communication, Electronic Design China, Electronics Today, Electronics Weekly, Game Software, PC World China, Popular Computer Week, Software Weekly, Software World, Telecom World; **PERU:** Computerworld Peru, PC World Profesional Peru, PC World SoHo Peru; **PHILIPPINES:** Click!, Computerworld Philippines, PC World Philippines, Publish in Asia; **POLAND:** Computerworld Poland, Computerworld Special Report Poland, Cyber, Macworld Poland, Networld Poland, PC World Komputer; **PORTUGAL:** Cerebro/PC World, Computerworld/Correio Informático, Dealer World Portugal, Mac*In/PC*In Portugal, Multimedia World; **PUERTO RICO:** PC World Puerto Rico; **ROMANIA:** Computerworld Romania, PC World Romania, Telecom Romania; **RUSSIA:** Computerworld Russia, Mir PK, Publish, Seti; **SINGAPORE:** Computerworld Singapore, PC World Singapore, Publish in Asia; **SLOVENIA:** Monitor; **SOUTH AFRICA:** Computing SA, Network World SA, Software World SA; **SPAIN:** Communicaciones World España, Computerworld España, Dealer World España, Macworld España, PC World España, PC World España; **SRI LANKA:** Infolink PC World; **SWEDEN:** CAP&Design, Computer Sweden, Corporate Computing Sweden, Internetworld Sweden, it branschen, Macworld Sweden, MaxiData Sweden, MikroDatorn, Nätverk & Kommunikation, PC World Sweden, PCaktiv, Windows World Sweden; **SWITZERLAND:** Computerworld Schweiz, Macworld Schweiz, PCtip; **TAIWAN:** Computerworld Taiwan, Macworld Taiwan, NEW ViSiON/Publish, PC World Taiwan, Windows World Taiwan; **THAILAND:** Publish in Asia, Thai Computerworld; **TURKEY:** Computerworld Turkiye, Macworld Turkiye, Network World Turkiye, PC World Turkiye; **UKRAINE:** Computerworld Kiev, Multimedia World Ukraine, PC World Ukraine; **UNITED KINGDOM:** Acorn User UK, Amiga Action UK, Amiga Computing UK, Apple Talk UK, Computing, Macworld, Parents and Computers UK, PC Advisor, PC Home, PSX Pro, The WEB; **UNITED STATES:** Cable in the Classroom, CIO Magazine, Computerworld, DOS World, Federal Computer Week, GamePro Magazine, InfoWorld, I-Way, Macworld, Network World, PC Games, PC World, Publish, Video Event, THE WEB Magazine, and WebMaster; online webzines: JavaWorld, NetscapeWorld, and SunWorld Online; **URUGUAY:** InfoWorld Uruguay; **VENEZUELA:** Computerworld Venezuela, PC World Venezuela; and **VIETNAM:** PC World Vietnam. 3/24/97

Dedication

To Windows users around the world.

Author's Acknowledgments

Special thanks to Tina Rathbone, Matt Wagner, Dan and Sandy Gookin, Pam Mourouzis, Ted Cains, and Mike Kelly.

Publisher's Acknowledgments

We're proud of this book; please register your comments through our IDG Books Worldwide Online Registration Form located at http://my2cents.dummies.com.

Some of the people who helped bring this book to market include the following:

Acquisitions, Development, and Editorial

Project Editors: Pamela Mourouzis, Colleen Rainsberger

Acquisitions Manager: Michael Kelly

Copy Editors: Ted Cains, Suzanne Thomas, Kelly Ewing

Technical Editor: Jim McCarter

Editorial Manager: Leah P. Cameron

Editorial Assistant: Darren Meiss

Production

Project Coordinator: Regina Snyder

Layout and Graphics: Cameron Booker, Lou Boudreau, Angela F. Hunckler, Drew Moore, Anna Rohrer, Brent Savage, M. Anne Sipahimalani

Proofreaders: Christine Berman, Kelli Botta, Laura L. Bowman, Vickie Broyles, Rebecca Senninger

Indexer: Carol Burbo

Special Help

Brian Kramer

General and Administrative

IDG Books Worldwide, Inc.: John Kilcullen, CEO; Steven Berkowitz, President and Publisher

IDG Books Technology Publishing: Brenda McLaughlin, Senior Vice President and Group Publisher

Dummies Technology Press and Dummies Editorial: Diane Graves Steele, Vice President and Associate Publisher; Mary Bednarek, Director of Acquisitions and Product Development; Kristin A. Cocks, Editorial Director

Dummies Trade Press: Kathleen A. Welton, Vice President and Publisher; Kevin Thornton, Acquisitions Manager

IDG Books Production for Dummies Press: Beth Jenkins Roberts, Production Director; Cindy L. Phipps, Manager of Project Coordination, Production Proofreading, and Indexing; Kathie S. Schutte, Supervisor of Page Layout; Shelley Lea, Supervisor of Graphics and Design; Debbie J. Gates, Production Systems Specialist; Robert Springer, Supervisor of Proofreading; Debbie Stailey, Special Projects Coordinator; Tony Augsburger, Supervisor of Reprints and Bluelines; Leslie Popplewell, Media Archive Coordinator

Dummies Packaging and Book Design: Patti Crane, Packaging Specialist; Kavish + Kavish, Cover Design

♦

The publisher would like to give special thanks to Patrick J. McGovern, without whom this book would not have been possible.

♦

Contents at a Glance

Cartoons at a Glance

By Rich Tennant

page 7

page 87

page 157

page 219

page 297

Fax: 978-546-7747 • *E-mail:* the5wave@tiac.net

Table of Contents

Introduction

● ●

Welcome to *MORE Windows 98 For Dummies,* the book for people who find themselves doing more with Windows 98 than they ever wanted to.

The Windows point-and-click lifestyle never retires. No matter how long those buttons and boxes live on your computer, they still hurl fresh bits of confusion at regular intervals. You constantly find yourself needing to make Windows do just a little bit more than it did before. . . .

That's where this book comes in. Don't worry — it doesn't try to turn you into a card-carrying Windows 98 wizard. No, this book merely dishes out the information that you need to make Windows 98 do your latest bidding. And — if possible — to make Windows do it a little more quickly than before.

About This Book

Are computers complicated? You bet. And Windows 98 is more complicated than ever, choking its users with hundreds of options, switches, buttons, and sliding levers. No one can specialize in all portions of it, because so many things can go wrong.

How do you tweak Windows 98 so that it works best with the particular programs and brands of hardware on *your* computer, for example? Does everybody know the step-by-step process for getting a new program off a floppy disk or CD and onto the Start menu?

Or perhaps you want to spark up a newsletter or report with a fun new font. How? Or maybe you upgraded your computer to make Windows 98 run faster and smoother — but now, unfortunately, Windows refuses to work at all. What do you do?

This book answers those types of questions and tosses in a well-beaten guide to the Internet: You discover how to browse the world's odd and mysterious cyber-library by flipping through animated Web pages packed with information.

All the while, the book tackles Windows 98 chores such as these:

- ✔ Installing a new program
- ✔ *Un*installing an old program
- ✔ Making the mouse work right
- ✔ Deciding which Windows 98 files you can delete
- ✔ Using Windows 98 on a laptop
- ✔ Browsing the Internet with Internet Explorer
- ✔ Creating your own Web page with FrontPage Express
- ✔ Installing a small network in your home or office
- ✔ Turning your computer into a television through multimedia
- ✔ Figuring out why everybody else's version of Windows 98 has more programs than yours

The information in this book comes in easy-to-read packets, just like the notes you saw being passed around in math class.

How to Use This Book

This book doesn't force you to *learn* anything about Windows 98. Save your brain cells for the important things in life. Instead, treat this book as your favorite reference. When you find yourself facing a particularly odious new Windows chore, find that subject in the index or table of contents. Flip to the appropriate page and follow the step-by-step instructions. Done? Then close the book and finish your Windows work, most likely a little more quickly than before.

You — Yes, You

Chances are, you've used Windows 98 for a little while — at least a month or two. You've figured out how to make Windows 98 do *some* things. It may take all day, but you can usually convince Windows 98 to do more or less what you want. But you're getting a little less tolerant of how Windows 98 keeps tossing new obstacles in your path.

If *everything* about Windows 98 looks new and confusing, check out this book's parent, *Windows 98 For Dummies* (also published by IDG Books Worldwide, Inc.). It explains how to start moving around in Windows 98 without breaking anything.

But if you're looking to solve those *new* problems that Windows 98 keeps bringing up, this book is for you.

How This Book Is Organized

Everything is easier to find when it's stored in its own well-marked bin, and the information in this book is no exception. This book contains five main parts, with each part divided into several chapters. You don't have to read Chapters 1 through 4, however, before you can figure out what's going on in Chapter 5.

So treat this book like the candy bins at the grocery store. Just reach straight in and grab the piece of information you want when you want it. You don't need to taste *everything* before you reach for the candy in the middle bin. In fact, the guy at the deli counter may yell if you even try.

Instead, just look up your particular problem and find the answer: a self-contained nugget that explains your particular situation and, what's more important, its particular solution.

Here are the book's main parts.

Part I: More on Everyday Stuff

Here you can find answers to those Windows 98 questions that pop up every day. Part I is stuffed with the information you didn't know you needed to know — until you'd used Windows 98 for a while.

First-timers may want to linger in Chapter 1, the "basics" chapter. It explains how to start Windows 98, push its menus around, and shut it down for the day. Chapter 1 is also a handy reference for Windows 98 users who suddenly realize that they need to know the difference between the Save command and the Save As command.

Part II: Entering the Internet with Windows 98

Face it, it doesn't matter whether everybody in the world's using the Internet, because you already *feel* that way. Are you the only person without e-mail? (Chapter 6 fixes that problem.) Are you confused by those `http://www.com` symbols on fast-food packages and TV shows? (Chapter 5 explains why they're there and what to do with them.)

Finally, once you enter the Internet's cyberworld and grow comfortable on its freeways, you may be tempted to put up your own billboards. (Chapter 8 shows how to create your own Web pages by using the software that comes with Windows 98.)

Part III: Getting More Out of Windows 98

Believe it or not, normal, everyday people have tricked Windows 98 into doing what they want it to do. This part of the book shares the secrets needed for stuffing Windows 98 onto laptops; it shows you how to play background music from CDs or the Internet, as well as tweaking Windows 98 for watching TV and playing back Internet news videos.

Best yet, this section contains clear-cut instructions on how to keep the mouse — and the rest of the computer — scurrying in the right direction.

Part IV: More Advanced Ugly Tasks Explained Carefully

Windows 98 eventually asks you to do something you'd just as soon not do. This part of the book tackles the most torturous Windows tasks and turns them into simple, step-by-step procedures. Large signposts carefully mark all the areas that are most likely to collapse first. You even get information on how to use Windows 98 to create your own network.

Part V: More Shortcuts and Tips Galore

Finally, you don't need to work harder than necessary. This part of the book explains the easiest ways to make Windows 98 do the most work — all with the least amount of effort on your part.

Icons Used in This Book

A picture is worth a thousand words. I'm being paid by the word for this book, so it has lots of *icons* — pictures that say "Look here!" Here's what the icons say:

Swerve past these signposts and don't bother slowing down. These icons point out boring pieces of extraneous technical information. (In fact, this technical stuff is only in the book so that your kids have something to read, too.)

 Keep an eye out for these icons. They point out a quick way of doing something. It's the kind of information that belongs on a note next to the monitor — if you have any room left.

 When you need a friendly reminder to do something, you see this icon.

 When you need a cautious tap on the shoulder to warn you not to do something, this icon is nearby.

Where to Go from Here

If you're looking for the most base-level Windows information, head for Chapter 1. If you're still stumped, head back to the bookstore for *Windows 98 For Dummies.*

But if you're looking for just a little more information to get you through the day, you've got the right book right now. Grab it with both hands, and you're ready to start striking back with full force. Good luck!

Part I

More on Everyday Stuff

It happens at every Windows show — group air-mousing.

In this part . . .

This part of the book covers the stuff that Windows 98 tosses at you every day: bunches of boxes that pile up on-screen like junk mail after a vacation. The first chapter explains how to shovel those boxes around so that you can find the good stuff.

The next few chapters talk about how to customize the world of Windows 98. You find out how to install new programs, add wallpaper, change fonts, install new screen savers, switch to new icons, record sounds, and use those other Windows 98 goodies that are flooding the market.

Finally, you find out the answer to that burning question: What the heck are all those other Windows versions supposed to do? Which is best? Should I use Windows 3.1, Windows for Workgroups, Windows 95, Windows 98, Windows NT, or Windows with a View?

Chapter 1
A Bit o' the Basics

● ●

In This Chapter

▶ Understanding the Windows 98 routine

▶ Starting Windows 98

▶ Using a mouse

▶ Moving windows

▶ Starting a program

▶ Opening a file

▶ Saving a file

▶ Printing a file

▶ Exiting a program

▶ Exiting Windows 98

● ●

*N*ew to Windows 98 or need a refresher? Then you're ready for this chapter. If you've never used Windows 98, you should read *Windows 98 For Dummies,* not this sequel. But if you're an extremely fast learner, this chapter may be all that you need to get up to speed.

Here, you find out how to get some work done, despite the computer's fancy *window* metaphor. You figure out how all those little menus are supposed to work and how you can make that little mouse arrow jump to the right places at the right times.

Finally, this chapter makes sure that *you* have the last word: You find out how to shoo Windows 98 off the screen when you've had enough pointing and clicking for one day.

The Windows 98 Computing Routine

Like government bureaucrats, computer users soon learn to follow the same steps over and over. That's the only way to make computers do your bidding.

Windows 98 expects — demands, in fact — that you complete each of the steps in the following list to accomplish just about anything. The rest of this chapter covers each of these steps in full, gory detail.

1. **Start Windows.**

   After you flip the computer's on switch, Windows 98 jumps onto the computer screen. This task is called *starting, running,* or *loading* Windows. Luckily, Windows 98 loads itself automatically. (You had to call some of the lazy, earlier versions of Windows to the screen by hand.)

2. **Create a new document.**

   In the old versions of Windows (if you're old enough to remember them), you opened a program and then created a file. Windows 98 lets you reverse matters. You first tell Windows 98 what *type* of file you'd like to create — a text file, a graphics file, a spreadsheet, or another sort of file — and Windows 98 obediently loads the program you need for creating that particular file.

   Then you use that program to add your numbers, organize your words, deal your playing cards, or help you perform any other computing chores. (*Programs* — the files that store computerized instructions — are often called *software* or *applications*. The stuff you create — text, spreadsheets, and other goodies — is usually called *data*.)

3. **Name and save your file.**

   Done diddling with your data? Then tell the program to *save* your newly mingled mixture of numbers or words so that you can play with them another day. When you choose a name for your work, the program saves your creation in a computerized container called a *file*.

4. **Exit the program.**

   When you finish using a particular program, close it down. That process is called *exiting* a program. (It's different from *exciting* a program, which appeals only to a few eccentric programmers.)

5. **Exit Windows.**

   Finally, when you're done with Windows, you can make it leave — *exit* — the screen.

Don't just flip the computer's off switch when you finish working in Windows 98. You need to use the Start button's Sh<u>u</u>t Down command so that Windows 98 has time to pack its bags before you shut down the computer.

That's it! The rest of this chapter shows you how to perform those same five steps over and over again. Welcome to computers!

Start Here

Although some people claim that Windows 98 is easy to use, Windows 98 isn't listening. No, Windows 98 usually listens to only two things: the mouse and the keyboard. You can boss Windows 98 around by moving the mouse across your desk and pushing those little buttons on the mouse's back.

The first thing Windows 98 listens for, however, is the click of your computer's on switch, as described in the next section.

Starting Windows 98

This part's easy: Simply turn on your computer, and Windows 98 leaps to the screen. Unfortunately, a few exceptions occasionally occur, and I describe them here.

If the screen is blank . . . If your computer and monitor are turned on but Windows 98 isn't on the screen, try tapping your spacebar. Chances are, Windows 98 is up and running but has turned on its *screen saver* to keep from wearing out your monitor. Tapping the spacebar tells Windows that you've grabbed a soda from the fridge, returned to the keyboard, and are ready to resume working.

If the screen says C:\> **or something similar . . .** The little C:\> symbol means that your computer is in MS-DOS mode — an antique method of using computers that some programs (and their users) still cling to. To bring Windows 98 back to the screen, type the word **exit** at the C:\> symbol, as shown below, and press the Enter key:

```
C:\> exit
```

If Windows keeps asking for your user name and password . . . Always suspicious, Windows prefers its users to *log in* by typing in a name and password. Windows recognizes people this way and keeps track of who's tapping at the keyboard. Networked computers, dissected in Chapter 17, often show the least pity for forgotten passwords.

Want to make Windows 98 load itself in a certain way — with your favorite programs already set up and running, for example? Then head for Chapter 21. It's loaded with ways to make Windows 98 start doing your bidding the instant it hits the screen.

Mouse mechanics

Nine out of ten German philosophers agree: Windows 98 prefers computers that have a mouse. Unlike the whiskered variety, a computer mouse looks like a little plastic bar of soap with a tail that plugs into the back of the computer.

When you nudge the mouse across your desk, Windows 98 responds by nudging a tiny arrow — officially called a mouse *pointer* — across the screen.

When the mouse's arrow points to a button on-screen, push one of the buttons on the mouse's back — usually the left one — to magically push the on-screen button.

- Don't pick up the mouse and point it at the screen. The little on-screen arrow won't budge, not even if you make spaceship noises. The mouse's belly needs to rub around on your desk.

- In fact, the mouse works best when it rolls around on a *mousepad,* a flat piece of rubber that looks like a child's placemat.

- If the mouse has reached the end of its rope and the arrow *still* isn't pointing to the right spot, lift the mouse off the desk. Then set it back down again, giving the cord some slack before nudging it around your desk again. In fact, picking up and repositioning a mouse is a major form of exercise for many computer aficionados.

- Sometimes, unfortunately, moving the mouse doesn't move the arrow. This heartbreaking predicament is solved in Chapter 11.

- A mouse has its own mouse language; the major terms are demystified in the following sections.

What's a click?

Pushing a button on the back of a mouse makes a clicking noise. So the engineers behind mouse movements dubbed the press of a button a *click.*

- You perform a click by pushing and quickly *releasing* the mouse button just as you use a button on a telephone. Pushing and *holding down* the mouse button is a completely different procedure. Computers and their mice take everything very literally.

 ✔ Clicking on something *selects* it for further action. You'll find yourself clicking on lots of things in Windows 98 — buttons, icons, words, edges of squares — even worms in some of the latest Windows 98 screen savers.

What's a double-click?

You perform a double-click by pushing and releasing the mouse button twice to make two clicks. But here's the catch to double-clicking: You have to press the mouse button *twice in rapid succession.*

If your clicks aren't fast enough, Windows 98 thinks that you're just fooling around and making two single-clicks, not a bona fide double-click.

 ✔ After a little practice, you should be able to double-click or click in the right place at the right time. After all, finding reverse gear the first time took a little practice, too.

 ✔ Contrary to the feeble single-click, the double-click makes an action. Single-clicking on a file to select it, for example, lets you check its size or creation date. Double-click on that file, however, and Windows loads it into the program that created it and brings them both to the top of the screen for further action.

 ✔ Windows 98 lets you beef up its single-clicks, however, so you never need to double-click. (After all, that's the way mice work on the Internet, modem users are quick to point out.) Chapter 11 facilitates the click fiddlers.

 ✔ If Windows 98 has trouble telling the difference between your clicks and double-clicks, head for Chapter 11 as well. That chapter shows you how to fine-tune the Windows 98 *mouse click recognition* areas.

Which mouse button do I use?

Most mice have two buttons. Some have three, and some real chunky NASA models have a dozen or more. Windows 98 listens to only two mouse buttons — the left one and the right one.

 ✔ The button on the left is for immediate actions. Click or double-click the left button on icons or menus to highlight them or to make them jump into action.

 ✔ The button on the right, by contrast, performs more cautious acts. Click the right mouse button on an object — an icon, for example — and Windows 98 brings up a menu listing the things you can do to that object.

 ✔ Whenever you see the nonspecific phrase *click the mouse,* click the left mouse button to remain safely above the high-water mark.

> ✔ If your right mouse button performs like your left mouse button should perform, then see Chapter 11. Some left-hander may have swapped your mouse buttons.

What's a drag 'n' drop?

The *point and click* concept stunned computer scientists with its inherent simplicity. So they took a vote and decided to complicate matters by adding the *drag and drop*.

Here's how drag and drop looks with your mouse on the dance floor:

1. **Nudge the mouse on your desk until the on-screen arrow points at something on-screen that you want to move — an icon, for example.**

2. **Hold down the left mouse button and *don't* release it. Then, while still holding down the button, subtly move the mouse.**

   The object you point at glues itself to the mouse pointer. As you move the mouse, the pointer moves and *drags* the object along with it.

3. **Drag the object to a new position — a different place on the desktop, for example — and release the mouse button.**

The pointer subsequently lets go of the object and *drops* it in its new location.

> ✔ Dragging and dropping can be a quick way to move stuff around on the screen. If you're not using a mouse with Windows 98, however, you're left out — no dragging and dropping for you.
>
> ✔ Windows 98 doesn't tell you which things you can drag and drop. Some items drag willingly, but others hold on for dear life.
>
> ✔ You can drag most of the icons on your desktop, as well as the icons, filenames, and folders in the My Computer and Windows Explorer programs.
>
> ✔ In Microsoft Word for Windows and some other programs, you can drag around words, paragraphs, and large chunks of text.

Window mechanics

The designers of Windows 98 had to know that they were asking for trouble. How could anybody possibly work on a monitor-sized desktop that's barely larger than one square foot?

When you work in Windows, everything piles up on top of everything else. You're not doing anything wrong — everything is *supposed* to pile up. This section explains how to move extraneous windows out of the way and make the important ones rise to the top.

You also discover how to find that window that was there just a second ago. . . .

Finding a misplaced window

Windows 98 offers as many ways to retrieve windows as it does ways to lose them. To extract your favorite window from the on-screen pile, try these methods until one of 'em works:

TIP

- Can you see any part of the window that you're after? Then click on any part of it. The window instantly rises to the top. Whew!

- If the window is completely hidden, hold down Alt and press Tab. A little window pops up, as shown in Figure 1-1. Keep pressing Tab until a box surrounds the icon for your missing window, and then let go of the Tab key. Your window rises to the top.

Figure 1-1:
Hold down Alt and press Tab to see a list of currently open windows, folders, and programs; press Tab to move from window to window.

- Right-click on a blank area of your desktop's *taskbar* — the bar that holds your Start button — and choose the Cascade Windows option from the pop-up menu. Windows 98 deals all the open windows across the screen like playing cards.

- Or if you choose either of the Tile options from that same pop-up menu, Windows 98 rearranges all your open windows across your desktop like tiles on a patio.

Almost any of the preceding techniques can round up and lasso runaway windows.

Changing a window's size or location

Open windows rarely appear on-screen in just the right size. Either they're too big and cover up everything else, or they're too small to play with.

To change a window's size, try any of the following tricks.

Double-click on the title bar

See the bar running across the top of the window in Figure 1-2? A window's title appears in that bar, which is why it's called the *title bar*.

Double-click on the title bar, and the window grows as big as it can. Or if the window *already* is as big as it can get, a deft double-click on the title bar shrinks it back down to its previous size.

To move a window around on the screen, drag its title bar. The window turns into a little outline as you drag it around the screen with the mouse. When you like the window's new location, let go of the mouse button to drop the window in the new spot. (However, you can't move windows that fill the entire screen.)

Figure 1-2:
Double-click on a window's title bar to toggle a window's size from large to small.

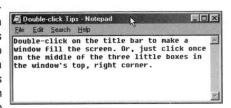

Drag its borders

For pinpoint accuracy in changing a window's size, drag its *borders* — the window's edges — in or out and drop them in their new location. The trick works like this:

1. Move the mouse arrow until it points at the side or corner of a window, as shown in Figure 1-3.

Figure 1-3:
A double-headed arrow shows the directions you can drag.

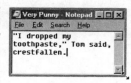

2. **While holding down the mouse button, nudge the mouse to move the window inward or outward (see Figure 1-4).**

Figure 1-4:
As you move the mouse, you move the border.

3. **When the window is the size you want, release the mouse button.**

The window snaps to fit its new size, as shown in Figure 1-5.

Figure 1-5:
Release the mouse button at the window's desired new size.

You can change a window's size by dragging either its borders or its corners.

Click on the little corner symbols

You can shrink or expand a window by clicking on the little symbols in its upper-right corner (see Figure 1-6).

Click here to shrink the window onto the taskbar.

Click here to make the window a little smaller.

Figure 1-6:
Click on the little box symbol to make the window a little smaller.

Click here to close the window.

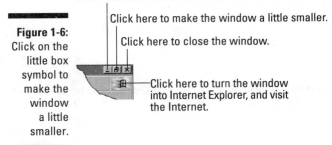

Click here to turn the window into Internet Explorer, and visit the Internet.

After you click on the symbol containing the two overlapping squares, for example, the window gets a little smaller, and the two overlapping squares symbol turns into a symbol with one square. That symbol with the square is called the Maximize button because it maximizes the window.

✔ When a window fills the screen, click on the symbol in the upper-right corner — the one with two overlapping squares — to toggle back to the window's regular size. That symbol is called the Restore button.

✔ To shrink a window — turn it into a little icon at the bottom of the screen — click on the symbol with the little bar in the window's upper-right corner. That little symbol is called the Minimize button.

✔ Double-clicking on the window's title bar does the same thing as clicking on the symbol with the square in it — it toggles the window between full-screen and normal-sized.

Starting Your Work

You do all your Windows 98 work in *programs*. The words *load, launch, start,* and *run* all describe the same thing: making a program come to the screen so that you can get some work done.

The programs appear on your computer's screen — your computerized *desktop* — while you move information around and get your work done.

Windows 98 offers several ways to start a program. The following sections describe the least cumbersome.

Starting a program from the desktop

The best way to start a program is to simply grab it off the desktop. First, decide what type of file you want to create: a sound, a graphic, a simple text file, a more elaborate word-processed document, a spreadsheet, or some other type of document.

Then follow these steps:

1. **Slide your mouse across the desktop until the little arrow points at a blank area.**

2. **Click on the right mouse button.**

   A menu pops up out of nowhere.

3. **Click on New from the menu, as shown in Figure 1-7.**

Figure 1-7:
Click on the desktop with your right mouse button, choose New, and click on the type of document that you want to create.

A menu pops up, listing all the types of new files Windows 98 lets you create. The menu is personalized — it's set up for the programs on your particular computer — so it looks different on different computers.

4. **Click on the type of file you want to create.**

   The program that's responsible for creating that file comes to the screen, ready for you to work. If you choose WordPad Document, for example, the Windows 98 WordPad program appears, ready to create a letter.

   • If this mouse arrow and double-click stuff sounds a little confusing, head for the "Mouse mechanics" section, earlier in this chapter.

   • If this basics chapter seems like old hat, however, then skip it. All the new stuff is in the later chapters.

- Although Microsoft may think that Windows 98 is easy to use, most people don't think of the phrase *WordPad document* when they think of *letter.*

- If you don't see the type of file you'd like to create listed on the desktop's pop-up menu, then you may not have a program that can create that type of file. Time to head to the software store. Or if you're pretty sure that you have that program on your hard drive somewhere, move along to the next section, which explains how to load a program listed on your Start menu.

- Do you see your program's icon sitting right on your desktop? If that icon has a little arrow embedded in its bottom-left corner, then you found your program's *shortcut.* Double-click on the shortcut, and the program comes to the screen. Shortcuts are an essential part of Windows 98, as you see throughout this book.

Starting a program from the Start button

An easy way to start a program is to launch it from the *Start button,* a button usually seen in the corner of your computer's taskbar. On most desktops, the Start button appears in the bottom-left corner, as shown in Figure 1-8.

Figure 1-8:
Click on the
Start button
to see a
menu of
programs
to launch.

If you don't see the Start button immediately, it may be hiding: Move your mouse pointer slowly to all four edges of your monitor's screen. Eventually, the taskbar leaps out from one edge, revealing the Start button. Once you spot the Start button, follow these steps to launch a program.

1. **Slide the mouse across your desk until the little arrow points at the Start button.**

2. **Click the left mouse button.**

   The Start menu appears, as shown in Figure 1-9.

Figure 1-9:
Clicking on
the Start
button
reveals the
Start menu.

3. Click on the word Programs.

A new menu squirts out to the side, this time listing programs and types of programs.

4. Click on the name or type of program you'd like to use.

Windows 98 either loads the program you chose or delves deeper into its menus, displaying names of programs that match the types of programs you chose. Keep repeating Step 4 until your program appears on-screen.

- Want to reload a document you used recently? Click on Documents — not Programs — and you see a fairly accurate list of the past 15 documents you used. Click on the name of the document you want, and Windows 98 obediently loads that document into the program that created it and places them both on the screen for your perusal.

- Want to put an icon for a favorite program onto the Start menu? Then forge ahead to Chapter 2. There, you also can find out how to install a program — even if that program didn't come with a quick 'n' easy installation program.

Starting a program from My Computer

The My Computer icon — a picture of a computer, as shown in Figure 1-10 — represents your computer and its contents. Double-click on the My Computer icon, and a window appears, listing various programs and *disk drives* — areas where your computer stores its files.

Figure 1-10: The My Computer icon.

Starting a program from within My Computer works like starting a program from within the Start menu: Keep moving from area to area until you spot the program's name and icon and then give the program's icon a double-click. The My Computer icon is a little harder to use than the Start button, however: My Computer displays nearly every file on your computer and doesn't bother filtering out extraneous files for easy viewing. Anyway, My Computer works like this:

1. **Slide the mouse across your desk until the little arrow points at the My Computer icon.**

   Double-click on the icon, and My Computer opens, revealing your computer's disk drives and a few other goodies.

2. **Double-click on the disk drive where your program lives.**

   You *do* know what disk drive your program lives on, don't you? If you don't, you'd best stick with the Start button method of launching programs.

   When you double-click on the disk drive, a new window reveals all the folders and programs living on that disk drive.

3. **Double-click on the program's name or on the folder where it's located.**

   If you double-click on the program's name, the program comes to life, ready for use. If you double-click on the folder, the folder opens to reveal its contents.

   Because folders often contain more folders, you often have to double-click on several folders to get to the one containing your desired program.

Tired of double-clicking on folders to get to the program you're after? Make a shortcut to that program, as described in Chapter 2, and put that shortcut in a handy corner of the desktop.

Starting a program from Windows Explorer

Some folks don't like My Computer's window full of picture buttons. They prefer the more rectilinear Windows Explorer program. Windows Explorer lets you manipulate programs, files, and folders by pointing and clicking on their names.

Next to the names, you see miniature versions of the icons you spotted in My Computer, as well as minute details like file sizes, file types, and the dates the files were created. Figure 1-11 shows a picture of Windows Explorer.

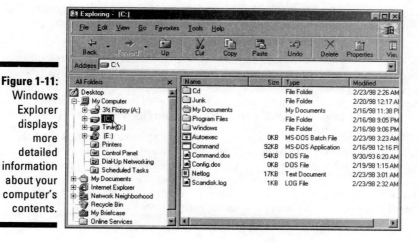

Figure 1-11:
Windows
Explorer
displays
more
detailed
information
about your
computer's
contents.

You start a program in Windows Explorer the same way that you start one in My Computer. Just follow these steps.

1. **Click on the Start button and choose Windows Explorer from the Programs menu.**

   Explorer rises to the screen, as shown earlier in Figure 1-11.

2. **Double-click on the disk drive where your program lives.**

   Like the My Computer program, Windows Explorer requires that you already know what disk drive your program lives on. If you don't know, stick with the Start button method of launching programs.

   When you double-click on the disk drive, Explorer reveals folders and programs living on that disk drive. Or if Explorer was already showing all the goodies on that drive, it hides all the goodies, leaving more room on the screen for you to see other disk drives.

3. **Double-click on the program's name or on the folder where the program is located.**

   If you double-click on the program's name, the program comes to life, ready for use. If you double-click on the folder, the folder opens to reveal its contents.

   Because folders often contain more folders, you often have to double-click on several folders to get to the one containing your desired program.

 ✔ Unlike My Computer, which usually displays one view of your computer's contents at a time, Windows Explorer shows the contents of several disk drives at the same time. What are all those other files? Chapter 16 contains a handy chart to help you identify them.

 ✔ My Computer and Explorer can do much more than load programs. For example, you can use them to move files around on the hard drive. (Chapter 2 describes the procedure.)

 ✔ Also, try pointing the mouse arrow at one of the filenames, programs, folders, or disk drives and clicking the right mouse button. The filename darkens, and a menu appears, listing all the things you can do to that object: Change its name, make a copy of it, delete it, create a shortcut, or perform other computer-like activities.

 ✔ Confused about My Computer or Windows Explorer? Then press the key labeled F1. (It's usually located near the keyboard's upper-left corner.) The Windows 98 Help program appears, ready to answer your questions. In fact, press F1 anytime Windows 98 leaves you tugging at your hair in exasperation. The Help program pops up, usually bringing helpful information that pertains to your current dilemma.

Opening a File

A *file* is a computer's container for holding *data* — bits of important information — on disk. So whether you want to create something on a computer or touch up something that you created earlier, you need to snap open its container. That little task is called *opening the file*.

Opening a file from within a program

In a refreshing change of pace, all Windows 98 programs let you open a file by following the same steps:

1. **Click on File in the program's menu bar, as shown in Figure 1-12.**

2. **When the menu falls down, click on the word Open.**

Figure 1-12:
Click on File to expose a menu with file-oriented choices.

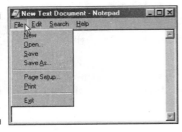

The Open box appears, as shown in Figure 1-13. By clicking on the words in this box, you can search for files in different locations.

Figure 1-13:
Clicking on
various
filenames,
shortcuts,
or disk
drives in
this box lets
you find and
choose the
file that
you want
to open.

3. **If you see the name of the file you're after in the box, double-click on it.**

   You're lucky. The program immediately opens that file. If you don't see your file right off the bat, though, you have to do a little hunting — and that means moving to Step 4.

4. **Double-click on the little My Computer icon listed in the Open box.**

   Don't confuse this icon with the big My Computer icon on your desktop; this is the little My Computer icon, shown earlier in Figure 1-13, that's mixed in with the filenames listed in your program's Open box.

   The program's Open box switches to a view of your computer's disk drives.

   Don't spot the My Computer icon in your program's Open box? Then click on the arrow next to the box marked Look in and choose My Computer from the menu that drops down. That also brings you to Step 5.

5. **Double-click on the disk drive where your desired file lives.**

   The Open window displays the folders stored on that particular disk drive. Spot your file? Double-click on it. Otherwise, move to Step 6.

6. **Double-click on the folder where your desired file lives.**

   The folder opens to reveal the files inside. Spot your file? Double-click on it to bring it to life. Otherwise, keep searching through your disk drives and folders until you find your file. Or if you don't know where the heck that file could be, you need to use the file finder program. (Click on Find from the Start menu and choose Files or Folders to search for missing files. Or head for Chapter 7 of *Windows 98 For Dummies* for further instructions on the file finder.)

Viewing different types of files

Sometimes the Open type box doesn't display all the files in a particular folder or drive. For example, the Files of type box in the Open box (shown earlier in Figure 1-13) says that it currently displays all Text Documents (files ending in TXT).

To see other types of files, click on the downward-pointing arrow in the Files of type box. Then use the menu that drops down to choose a different type of file — or even *all* the files — that live in that folder.

 ✔ By looking in different directories and on different disk drives in the Open box, you eventually stumble across the file you're after.

 ✔ The Files of type box normally displays the types of files you're interested in. For example, when you try to open a file in Notepad, the box displays Text files. In Paint, the box displays Paint files.

 ✔ This Files of type stuff can be a little dizzying at first. To find out which Windows 98 program creates which type of file, head for Chapter 16.

 ✔ See how some words in a menu have an underlined letter, like the F in File and the O in Open? That letter is a shortcut. You can press and release the Alt key and then press that underlined letter to trigger that menu item. For example, you press Alt, F, and O to make the Open box pop up without any urging from the mouse.

Opening a file in Windows Explorer or My Computer

Finally, something easy. The Windows Explorer and My Computer programs can open a file the same way that they load a program, and they both work the same way: You just double-click on the name of the file you're hungry for, and that file pops to the screen. It works like this:

 1. Find the name of the file that you want to open.

 2. Move the mouse until the little arrow points at the filename.

 3. Without moving the arrow away, double-click the mouse button.

That's it. If you're working in Windows Explorer, Explorer first loads the program that created the file you clicked on. Then Explorer loads the file into that program. For example, if you double-click on a file that you created in Windows 98 Notepad, Explorer first loads Notepad and then loads the file into Notepad, leaving them both on-screen.

Opening a file in Windows Explorer is easier than making a sandwich — especially if the mustard lid has dried closed.

Saving a File

Talk about lack of foresight. Even after you spend all morning painstakingly calculating the corporate cash flow, Windows 98 sometimes thinks that you've been goofing around.

You see, some computer programs don't know that you want to *save* your work. Unless you specifically tell the program to save it, the program just dumps it. And you can never retrieve unsaved files, not even with reinforced tongs.

To make a program save a file, do this:

1. **Click on File from the program's menu bar.**

   A menu of file-oriented chores appears, the same menu you saw a few pages earlier in Figure 1-12.

2. **After the menu falls down, click on Save.**

   A box pops up, looking much like the one you saw a bit earlier in Figure 1-13.

3. **Type a name for the newly created file.**

   If Windows 98 freaks out over the newly created file's name, you're probably trying to use one of the Forbidden Filename Characters described in Chapter 2.

4. **Click on the folders in the Save As window until you open the folder where you want to store the file.**

   Want to create a new folder? Then click on the folder near the box's top that has the little sparkling star in its upper-right corner. Or if you want to save the file in a folder that's on a different drive, click on the little arrow in the Save in box to move to one of your computer's other drives.

5. **Press Enter.**

   Typed in the name? Chosen the right folder and drive? Then press the Enter key, and the program saves the file using the name, folder, and disk drive that you've chosen.

   • After you save a file for the first time, you won't have to repeat Steps 3 through 5. Instead, the program just saves the file, using the same name, folder, and disk drive. Kind of anticlimactic, actually.

   • If you want to use a different name or location to save a file, then choose the Save As option. That option comes in handy when you want to open a file, change a few numbers or paragraphs, and save the file under a new name or folder.

- The easiest way to save a file in any Windows 98 program is to press these three keys, one after the other: Alt, F, S. The little light on the computer blinks, and the program saves the file. Quick and easy, as long as you can remember Alt, F, S.

Printing a File

Printing a file works the same way as opening or saving one. Click on the right spots and grab the piece of paper as it slides out of the printer. If the printer is turned on and plugged in and the paper doesn't jam, you print a file this way:

1. **Click on File from the program's menu bar.**

    Once again, a menu of file-oriented tasks appears, just as you saw in Figure 1-12.

2. **After the menu falls down, click on Print.**

    The program dutifully sends the information to the printer.

    - Some programs toss a Print box in your face, asking for more information. For example, Paint asks how many copies you want to print, and Word asks whether you want to print all the pages or just a select few.

        Notepad, on the other hand, merely whisks the text straight to the printer. Whoosh! No stopping that program.

    - People with more than one printer may want to choose the program's Print Setup option if it's listed on the menu. That option lets them choose which printer they want the information routed to. Then choose the program's Print command.

    - The quickest way to tell a program to print something is to press Alt, F, P. That method is faster than fumbling around with menus.

Done for the Day

When you finish working, you haven't *really* finished working. No, the computer still demands a little more of your time. Before you can turn off the computer, you need to follow the steps described in the rest of this section.

Don't simply turn off the computer when Windows 98 is on-screen, no matter how frustrated you are. You must save your work and exit Windows 98 the right way. Doing anything else can cause problems.

Saving your work

As described in "Saving a File" earlier in this chapter, you save your work by telling the program to save it in a file so that you can return to it another day.

Exiting any running DOS programs

Are you running any DOS programs? You need to exit them before Windows 98 lets you leave. If you're running a DOS prompt (that little C:\> thing) in a window, type **exit** and press Enter:

```
C:\> exit
```

Some DOS programs make you press several keys before they disappear. Try pressing F10 and Alt+X or, if you're really stumped, check the program's manual. When you press the correct keys, the program shrivels up, disappears from the screen, and leaves you back at Windows.

Exiting any Windows 98 programs

Unlike DOS programs, Windows 98 programs shut themselves down automatically when you shut down Windows. They even ask whether you want to save your work. Still, you can use one of these methods to exit a Windows 98 program:

✔ Click on the little X in the program's upper-right corner, shown in Figure 1-14.

The program disappears. If you haven't saved your work first, however, the program cautiously asks whether you're *sure* that you don't want to save your work.

Figure 1-14:
Click on this button to close this window or program.

✔ Hold down Alt and press F4 (known in Windows 98 parlance as pressing Alt+F4).

✔ Click on File in the menu bar and then click on Exit from the little menu that pops down.

✔ Press Alt, F, X, one after the other. That sequence quickly calls up the little File menu and presses the Exit button, all without the help of a mouse.

Exiting a program isn't a four-step procedure. You can use any of these methods to shut down a program.

Windows 98 offers bunches of ways to do the same thing. Some folks say that the alternatives offered by Windows 98 make it easier to use. Others say that the alternatives just complicate matters.

Exiting Windows

Strangely enough, the way to stop using Windows 98 is to use the Start button. Click on the Start button and choose Shut Down, the option at the bottom of the menu. A menu pops up with three options, all described in the following list:

✔ **Standby:** Found on some laptops, this puts your computer in a low-power mode while you take off for a few minutes. Sure, you'd save more power by just turning the computer off, but then Windows 98 takes a long time to come back to life; Standby mode jumps back to life much more quickly.

✔ **Shut down:** Click here, and Windows 98 shuts itself down. Turn your computer off when a message appears on the screen saying that it's okay, and you're ready to leave your desk and get some dinner.

✔ **Restart:** If your computer has been acting weird (or you've just installed some new software), choosing this option often comes into play. This option *reboots* your computer, making Windows 98 shut itself down and start itself back up from scratch.

✔ **Restart in MS-DOS mode:** Some picky MS-DOS programs prefer this mode, which leaves your computer with a C:\> prompt. (Type **exit** at the C:\> prompt and press Enter to return to Windows.)

✔ Windows 98's multiple-user setup enables several people to use the same computer, but each with his or her own account. Choose the Log Off feature, found on the Start menu right above Shut Down. Then log back in, typing in your name and personalized password. Windows keeps track of your likes and dislikes, automatically loading your desktop setup and wallpaper when you log in. Double-click on the Control Panel's Passwords icon to get started with this setup.

Chapter 2

Installing New Software

● ●

In This Chapter

▶ Installing Windows 98 and DOS programs

▶ Using installation programs

▶ Working without installation programs

▶ Copying files

▶ Creating folders

▶ Adding programs to the Start menu

● ●

*I*magine buying a toothbrush, opening the package, and finding a packet of loose little bristles, plus instructions on fastening them to the brush's plastic handle. And you just wanted to brush your teeth!

A new Windows 98 program can bring similar complications. You don't always find the new program's icon waiting for you on the Start menu. Instead, you find a floppy disk with a bunch of strange files on it. Which file does what? Where do they go?

Some programs come with an installation program that simplifies the whole process. Other programs leave it all up to you. To keep things simple, this chapter shows how to pry a program off a floppy disk, stick it on your computer's hard drive, and put its name and icon on the Start button menu where it belongs.

The Installation Nirvana for Windows

Windows 98 finally makes it easy to install programs if the program's creator took advantage of these good graces. To find out whether your new program is easy to install, just follow these steps:

1. **Click on the Start button, click on <u>S</u>ettings, and choose <u>C</u>ontrol Panel from the menu that appears.**

   The Control Panel appears, as shown in Figure 2-1, displaying a plethora of icons.

Figure 2-1:
Double-click on the Control Panel's Add/Remove Programs icon to install programs.

2. **Double-click on the Add/Remove Programs icon.**

3. **Click on the Install button at the top of the Add/Remove Programs Properties box.**

   Follow the instructions that appear in the following boxes. Windows 98 asks you to insert the disk containing your program. If Windows 98 can't find an installation program, however, and it sends out the box shown in Figure 2-2, you have to struggle through the rest of this chapter, unfortunately. The programmer took the easy way out.

Figure 2-2:
This box means that Windows 98 couldn't find an installation program for your program, and you have to install the program yourself.

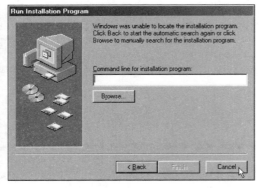

Still dallying with DOS?

Programs for IBM computers come in two main types: DOS programs (the *old* kind of programs) and Windows programs (the ones sold in the store today). Windows programs cause the fewest problems because they're designed to run under Windows 98.

DOS programs, on the other hand, don't know anything about Windows 98. They're as helpless as a tourist visiting Disneyland on Labor Day and trying to find a bathroom without using a map.

To help care for these confused DOS programs, Windows 98 often needs a *Properties* form — which works somewhat like a chart at the foot of a hospital patient's bed. The Properties form tells Windows 98 what that DOS program needs so that it can run most efficiently: memory limits, video expectations, and more trivia.

Windows 98 recognizes some DOS programs when they're installed and fills out the Properties form automatically. Other DOS programs come with their Properties forms already filled out. Still other DOS programs make you handle the dirty details of filling out Properties forms. And some DOS programs run fine without a Properties form at all. If a DOS program causes you problems, check out the Properties form tips in Chapter 14.

Windows 98 programs rarely need to have their Properties forms tweaked. They can automatically find the things that programs hold dear — sound cards, video cards, hard drives, and other treats.

The Installation Headache

Programs are merely little bits of instructions for the computer, telling it to do different things at different times.

Unfortunately, most programs don't store those instructions in a single, easy-to-handle file. Instead, they're often spread out over several files — sometimes spread out over several floppy disks.

Regardless of what program you install, the basic idea behind installation is the same. You copy the program's files from the floppy disk or compact disc onto the computer's hard drive. Then you place the program's "start-me button" — its icon — onto your computer's Start menu so that you can start using the program with a simple click.

What's an Installation Program?

Installing a program can be a long, tortuous process. So programmers handled the chore the best way they could. They wrote a second program designed specifically to install the first program.

Known as *installation programs,* these programs handle the chores of copying the main program to the computer's innards and making sure that it gets along with Windows 98.

- ✔ Most programs sold in software stores come with installation programs.

- ✔ Some programmers are lazy, however, and don't write an installation program. As a result, they leave the installation chores squarely in your hands.

- ✔ Many shareware programs don't come with an installation program, so you have to tackle their installation yourself.

- ✔ The secret to a successful marriage is to know when to nod your head earnestly and say, "Gosh, you may be right, dear."

How to Install a Program

The steps described from here to the end of the chapter transform a compact disc, disk, or massive bundle of floppy disks into a program that actually runs on your computer.

By following all these steps, you install your new program, whether you like it or not. (And if you *don't* like it, head for Chapter 13 for instructions on how to *un*install it.)

If you're stumped by only a few installation procedures — putting a new program's name and icon on the Start menu, for example — then jump ahead to that particular step. Pogo sticks are allowed here.

Finally, installing a program isn't as hard as it looks. This chapter describes every step in clinical detail — down to the last toe muscle twitch. After you install a program or two, you may find that it's as easy as walking and chewing gum at the same time.

If you only need a handrail while installing a new program, follow these steps:

1. **Find the program's disk.**

2. **Put the disk in the disk drive.**

3. **View the disk's contents in the My Computer program.**

What's shareware?

In the early 1980s, an iconoclastic programmer named Jim Button startled the software industry by simply giving away his database program, PC-File. The catch? Button asked any satisfied PC-File users to mail him a check.

Much to the surprise of everybody, Button included, this honor system has since grossed millions of dollars. The shareware concept matured into a healthy business.

By simply giving away their wares, shareware programmers can avoid the high costs of advertising, marketing, packaging, and distributing their products. They give away their programs on a trial basis, though. Users who discover a program, install it, and find it useful are obligated to mail the programmer a registration fee — usually somewhere between $5 and $30.

The price may be low, but the quality level is usually high. Only programs that really do the job convince grateful users to mail back that registration check.

4. **Find and load the installation program and read the README file.**

   No installation program? Then keep going:

5. **Create a new folder on the hard drive.**

6. **Copy the program's files to the new folder.**

7. **Put the program's name and icon on the Start menu.**

Finding the installation disk

If your software came in a big box, start rooting around for the floppy disks. Look for one labeled *Disk 1, Setup, Installation,* or something similar. If your program came on a compact disc, that's all you need — the installation program is usually on the disc.

While you rummage, look for a *cheat sheet.* Some companies offer a quick, one-page set of installation instructions. (Others hide the installation tips in the middle of the inch-thick manual.)

- ✔ If the software comes on a single disk, use that disk. The label doesn't matter.

- ✔ If you find a cheat sheet, give it a quick ogle. It may have some handy tips or pertinent warnings.

- ✔ If you find a registration card inside the box, fill it out and mail it in. Some companies make you register the program before they give you any technical support on the telephone. (Other companies just put you on a mailing list.)

Sliding a disk into the disk drive

On the rare occasion that the disk doesn't fit inside any of your computer's disk drives, troop back to the computer store and see whether the software comes in any other formats.

But face the facts: Your computer sounds like an oldster. Update it to work with 99 percent of today's software by adding a CD-ROM drive and a 3¹/₂-inch floppy drive. (You can find instructions in *Upgrading & Fixing PCs For Dummies,* 4th Edition, also published by IDG Books Worldwide, Inc.)

✔ Floppy disks slide into the drive with their label facing up. These disks have either a shiny metal edge or a small oval window — either way, slide that edge in first.

✔ Some disk drives make you slide down a little lever to hold the disk in place. Other drives swallow the disk with no special urging.

✔ Some programs that come on compact discs have an Autoplay feature: As soon as you insert the disc, the installation program comes to the screen. If you're this lucky, just click on the Install or Setup program, and the installation program takes over. You probably won't have to worry about the rest of this chapter.

Viewing a disk's contents in My Computer

Before working with a disk or CD-ROM, look at the files that live on it:

1. **Load the My Computer program by double-clicking on its little computer-shaped icon on your desktop.**

   My Computer's icon usually lives in the upper-left corner of your screen; a double-click brings its window to life.

2. **Find the little pictures of disk drives in the My Computer window.**

3. **Double-click on the little picture of the drive where you put the disk.**

   For example, if you put the floppy disk in drive A, double-click on the little picture of the drive labeled (A:).

   Or if you put the disk in drive B, double-click on the little drive labeled (B:).

   Or if you put the disc into your CD-ROM drive, double-click on your CD-ROM drive's icon.

   Either way, My Computer shows the disk's contents (see Figure 2-3).

Figure 2-3:
Click on the
icon for
the drive
where you
inserted the
program's
disk,
and My
Computer
displays
that disk's
contents.

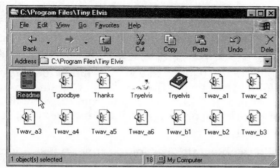

Finding a program's installation program

If you're lucky, your program came with a customized installation program
that automatically handles the awkward migration from floppy disk to Start
button menu. Here's how to tell for sure:

1. **After My Computer displays the disk's contents, look for a file named
   INSTALL.EXE, SETUP.EXE, or something similar.**

   See anything that looks like the SETUP program listed in Figure 2-3? If
   so, you've found the installation program.

2. **Double-click on that particular filename.**

3. **Follow the instructions that the SETUP program tosses on-screen, and
   you're home free.**

   The program copies itself to the hard drive and usually sticks its name
   and icon on the Start button's menu. (If it doesn't wind up on the Start
   menu, you can find instructions for putting it there yourself later in the
   chapter.)

Finding no installation program, however, means bad news: You have to
handle all the installation grunt work yourself. So practice grunting earnestly a few times before you move to the next section.

Copying a program's files to a folder on the hard drive

If the lazy programmers didn't write an installation program for you, you
have to install your new software onto the computer yourself. Following
these steps should do the trick:

1. Create a new folder on your hard drive and name it after the program.

From within My Computer, create a new folder where you'd like the new program's files to live. In this example, you're installing the Tiny Elvis program into a Program Files folder on drive C. So from within My Computer, open drive C by double-clicking on the drive C icon.

Next, from within the newly opened drive C window, double-click on the Program Files folder to open it. (Don't have a Program Files folder? Then create one: Click on <u>F</u>ile, choose <u>N</u>ew from the drop-down menu, and then choose <u>F</u>older. Type **Program Files** and press Enter, and the new folder appears.)

Then from within the Program Files folder, create a new folder called Tiny Elvis. Your screen looks something like Figure 2-4.

Try to keep your folders organized. For example, if you install the game Blasteroids onto drive C, create a folder called Games inside drive C's Program Files folder. Then create a folder called Blasteroids *inside* the Games folder. By keeping your games, utilities, and other types of programs grouped together, you can find programs easily when you need them.

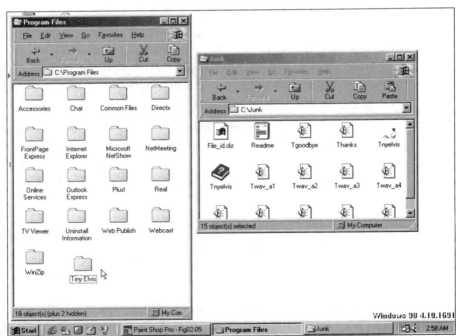

Figure 2-4: When creating a new folder for a new program, try to "nest" it with similar programs; put the Tiny Elvis program in the Program Files folder, for example.

2. **Move the program's file or files from its disk to its new folder.**

   The new program — the one without an installation program — should be sitting in the My Computer's drive A window. The program's upcoming home, drive C, should be in another window on your desktop. You may need to rearrange all the windows on your desktop until you can see them both clearly, like you can in Figure 2-4.

   Next, if you're installing the Tiny Elvis program from drive A, highlight all of its files. Then drag and drop those files onto the new Tiny Elvis folder in your drive C's Program Files folder, as shown in Figure 2-5.

   ✔ A quick way to highlight a large number of files is to lasso them: Point the mouse adjacent to the corner, hold down the mouse button, and move the mouse to the other corner. A "lasso" appears, highlighting all the files in between the mouse movements. Let go of the mouse button, and the files and folders stay highlighted.

   ✔ An even *quicker* way to highlight all the files in a window is to click in the window once and press Ctrl+A.

   ✔ The My Computer program can make your desktop look awfully crowded when it leaves more than two windows open. If the desktop starts looking crowded, you can get rid of the windows you don't need. Just click in the little box in the upper-right corner of each window that you don't want to see anymore. (The little box has an X in it.)

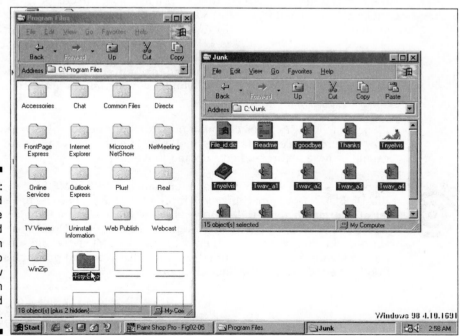

Figure 2-5: Drag and drop the highlighted files from the disk to their new folder on your hard drive.

Windows 98 can't digest these filenames

Windows 98 squirms uncomfortably if you try to use more than 255 letters or numbers in a filename or folder. (Earlier versions of Windows — and DOS — writhed in agony if you tried to use more than 8.) Windows 98 still won't let you use any of these forbidden characters, though:

" / \ : * | < > ?

The moral? Limit the names of files and folders to simple letters or numbers with no forbidden characters between them.

✔ You can use uppercase or lowercase letters when you name files and folders in Windows 98. This book tends to use uppercase letters so that it's easier for you to see what to type.

✔ When peeling a clove of garlic, give it a deft twist with both hands to break the tough outer covering and make the skin easier to remove.

Reading README files

When programmers notice a goof in the software manual, they don't grab the correction fluid. Instead, they type a list of all the corrections and store them in a file called README.TXT, README, README.DOC, or something similar.

In fact, Figure 2-4 shows a file called README. To view that file, double-click on its name. The Windows 98 Notepad text editor pops up to show the README.TXT file's contents, and you learn which parts of the manual may trip you up.

Also, some README files contain quick, stick-to-the-point instructions on how the program expects you to install it. They're always worth at least a casual browse before you give up and move on.

Sometimes a disgruntled programmer names the README file README!.NOW or something even more obtuse. Because the file ends in letters unrecognizable to Windows 98, double-clicking on the file's name doesn't automatically bring up Notepad. The solution? Open Notepad to a window on your screen, and then drag the README!.NOW file's icon from the My Computer program and drop it into the Notepad program's window. Poof! Notepad reveals the file's contents.

Putting a program's name and icon in the Start button's menu

After a Windows 98 program moves onto the hard drive, the program is ready to get its little button — or *icon* — and name placed in the Start button's menu. Windows 98 offers a bunch of ways to stick a new program's icon in the Start button's menu.

Here's the easiest way:

1. **Open the My Computer program.**

   It's that icon of a computer that usually rests in the upper-left corner of your screen. Or if you've been installing a program throughout this chapter, My Computer is probably already open and waiting for action on your desktop.

2. **Move to the folder where you installed your new program.**

   In this chapter's example, you point and click your way to the Tiny Elvis folder, which lives in the Program Files folder of drive C.

3. **Drag and drop the program's icon to the Start button.**

   The program's name appears on the top of the Start menu for easy pointing and clicking. It's that easy — unless you want to place the program's name more strategically inside the Start button's menu, a process covered in the next section.

Putting a program's name in a specific section of the Start button's menu

The preceding section shows how to put a program's name at the top of the Start menu, where it's easy to reach. But if you want a more professional look, you want to be more organized. For example, you may want to list your newly installed program in the Applications section of the Start button's Programs menu. Here's how:

1. **Decide where you want the program's listing to appear.**

   For example, do you want the program to appear as a new item under the Start menu's Programs area? Do you want it listed as an Accessory under the Programs area?

2. **Click on the Start button with your right mouse button and choose Open (see Figure 2-6).**

   The Start Menu window appears — looking suspiciously like the My Computer program. The icon called Programs stands for the Programs listing on the Start menu.

Figure 2-6:
Click on the
Start button
and choose
Open to
begin
adding
programs to
the menu.

3. Double-click on the Programs icon.

Yet another window appears, this time revealing the items listed under the Start menu's Programs area: Accessories, Applications, Startup, and a few others.

4. Open My Computer and open the folder where you installed your program.

If you want to move Tiny Elvis, for example, open the Tiny Elvis folder you created in the Program Files folder of drive C.

5. Drag and drop the program's icon into the appropriate icon in the Start menu's Programs window.

To move the Tiny Elvis program into the Applications section, drag and drop the Tiny Elvis program's icon into the Applications icon revealed in Step 3.

6. Close down all the windows you opened for the preceding five steps.

That's it; the next time you click on the Start button, you'll see the program waiting for you on the appropriate section of the Start button's Programs menu.

Dragging and dropping programs' icons into the Startup folder makes those programs load themselves automatically when you start Windows 98.

Putting a shortcut on the desktop

Find yourself using a program all the time? Then put an icon for the program right on your desktop, ready to be called into action with a double-click. Here's how to put one of those *shortcuts* onto your desktop.

1. Open My Computer and open the folder where you installed your program.

In this case, you want to open the Tiny Elvis folder you created in the Program Files folder of drive C.

2. **With your right mouse button, drag and drop the Tiny Elvis program's icon onto your desktop.**

    After you let go of the mouse button, a menu pops up. Choose the Create <u>S</u>hortcut(s) Here option, and a shortcut to your program appears on the desktop. From then on, just double-click on that shortcut icon, and Windows 98 pulls your program to the screen.

It Won't Install Right!

Occasionally, a widget falls into the wrong gear of the gatzoid, bringing everything to a resounding halt. This section tackles some of the more common problems that you can encounter while installing programs.

It's one big file ending in ZIP!

If your file ends in ZIP, like PICK.ZIP, you're holding a file that has been *zipped*. I'm not kidding.

The file has been compressed — shrunken like a dry sponge. You need an *unzipping* program to put water back into the sponge and turn the program into something you can use.

That unzipping program is called WinZip, and it's shareware. You can find a description of shareware earlier in this chapter, and Chapter 12 tells you how to unzip a file.

When I loaded my new program, it exploded into a bunch of little files!

Sometimes you create a new folder for your new program, drag and drop the new program's file into the folder, and double-click on the program's icon, expecting to start playing with the new program right away.

But instead of coming to the screen, the program's icon suddenly turns itself into a *bunch* of icons. What happened? Well, the program was probably in a *self-extracting compression program*. When you loaded it, it broke itself down into its *real* components.

So what do you do now? Well, look for an installation program, as described earlier in this chapter. If you don't see an installation program, just put the program's icon on your Start menu, as mentioned previously in this chapter.

Then copy the big file — the one that contained all the little ones — to a diskette for safe-keeping and delete the original one from your hard drive to save space.

It keeps asking for some VBRUN thing!

Like ungracious dinner guests, some Windows programs keep shouting for *more.* Some of them start asking for a file called VBRUN300.DLL or something with a similarly vague name.

The solution? Find that VBRUN.DLL file. It doesn't come with Windows 98, however. Instead, you can *download* it — copy it onto your computer — from the Internet. (Try heading for PC World's Web page at `www.pcworld.com/software_lib/data/articles/essential/1191.html` to download the file; if that dead-ends, head for plain ol' `www.pcworld.com` and follow the search menus.)

After you download it, copy it to the Windows folder and ignore it. The program shuts up and runs.

✔ The program may ask for VBRUN100.DLL, VBRUN200.DLL, VBRUN300.DLL — you get the idea. The different numbers stand for different version numbers. Make sure that you download the same version that the program asks for.

✔ You need the specific version of VBRUN that the program asks for. You can't just get VBRUN300.DLL and expect it to satisfy older programs that ask for the earlier versions of VBRUN. (Some VBRUN300.DLL packages come with the earlier versions, too, however.)

✔ A program that asks for VBRUN is written in a programming language called Visual Basic. Before the program can feel comfortable enough to run, it needs to find a special Visual Basic file, which is what the VBRUN300.DLL file is. Nothing really mysterious here.

My DOS program doesn't work!

DOS programs never expected to run under Windows 98. Some of them simply can't stand the lifestyle change.

It's as if somebody dropped you onto an ice-skating rink, and you were wearing slippery tennis shoes. You'd need ice skates to function normally.

A DOS program's ice skates come in the form of a *Properties form,* also discussed near the beginning of this chapter.

When you fill out the Properties form for a DOS program, Windows 98 knows how to treat it better, and it performs better. Unfortunately, filling out that form can be even harder than learning how to ice skate, so DOS Properties forms get their own chapter — Chapter 14.

There's no room on the hard disk!

Sometimes, Windows 98 stops copying files from the floppy disk to the hard disk because there's no room in the inn. The hard drive is full of files, with no room left for the stragglers.

You can install a bigger hard drive quickly. Or you can delete some of the files on the hard drive that you don't need. In fact, you can even delete some Windows 98 files that are on a hit list in Chapter 16.

Before installing a program, make sure that you have enough room. In My Computer, click on the drive's icon with your right mouse button and choose Properties from the menu. The Free Space area shows how many megabytes you have left on your hard drive.

Chapter 3

Wallowing in Wallpaper, Screen Savers, Icons, Fonts, Sounds, and Drivers

- -

In This Chapter

▶ Wallpaper

▶ Screen savers

▶ Icons

▶ Fonts

▶ Sounds

▶ Drivers

- -

Y ou've probably seen a wild new screen saver on a coworker's computer. Whenever she steps away from her computer for a few minutes, the screen turns black, and the little Grateful Dead bear starts kicking across the screen.

Or how about that guy down the street who uses all those weird fonts when he makes wild party fliers? Plus, he just upped his icon collection to 763 with that new Bart Simpson icon he found last week.

Or how about that guy whose computer lets loose with a different-sounding burp whenever he loads or exits Windows 98?

You can sprinkle hundreds of these little spices on the Windows 98 pie. Screen savers, icons, and sounds merely add new flavors. But the latest device drivers add necessary nourishment; Windows 98 probably can't work without them.

This chapter shows you how to keep Windows 98 up-to-date by adding the new stuff and trimming off the old. Plus, it shows you how to get the most out of the wallpaper, sounds, and Desktop Themes that come with Windows 98.

Where Can You Get These Things?

Windows 98 comes with a few screen savers, fonts, sounds, and icons. But where do people get all their new goodies? Chances are, they pull them from some of the following pots.

Off the shelf

Most software stores carry boxes of Windows 98 add-ons. Look in the Windows 98 software section for packages of fonts, sounds, screen savers, icons — even movies.

- **Good news:** The stuff you can buy in the software store usually comes with an installation program, making it simpler to set up and put to work.
- **Bad news:** The stuff costs money; but software purchased by mail-order can sometimes be a tad cheaper. (Keep reading — you can even grab some of these goodies for free. . . .)

From the manufacturer

Sooner or later you need a new *driver* — software that enables Windows 98 to hold an intelligible conversation with a mouse, sound card, video card, or other part of your computer's hardware.

Windows 98 comes with drivers for many computer parts. However, drivers often need to be updated to perform at their peak. Your best bet for a new, custom-written driver is to go straight to the company that made the gadget. Or you can sometimes get new drivers by using the Windows Update program on your Start menu.

If Windows 98 isn't working well with your sound or video card, call the tech support number of the company that made the card. Ask the techie who answers to send you the card's latest driver on a floppy disk. Some companies charge shipping costs, and others mail the drivers free of charge. Still other companies offer a third route: They let you grab the files through the phone lines, as described next.

Through the phone lines and the Internet

Today, nearly every computer company hooks up a computer or two to its telephone lines. Then you connect your computer to your phone lines by using a *modem*.

With the help of the modem, the Internet, and Windows 98's Internet Explorer, you can dial up the company's computer and get copies of the latest Windows 98 goodies. In fact, Microsoft's Internet Web page has the latest drivers for a huge assortment of printers, sound cards, video cards, and other toys.

Best yet, all that stuff is free for the taking (except for the Internet access charges that show up on your phone bill). Chapter 5 covers the Internet and its lifestyle.

Some people call up America Online or CompuServe — huge computers with their own services, as well as Internet access.

If you bought a modem and want to explore the Internet, head for Chapter 5.

User groups

Some folks can't stop talking about their computers. So their spouses send them to local *user groups*. A user group is simply a club, just like a Saturday Sewing Club or a '67 Corvette Lovers' Club. The members all meet, usually on a weekend or evening, and swap talk about the joy of computing.

If you're having trouble with Windows 98 or with locating some of its parts, ask your local computer store where the local Windows 98 user group meets. Chances are, one of the folks at the meeting can come up with the Windows 98 goodie you're after.

From friends

Some charity-minded programmers give away their work for free *(freeware)*. Knowing that people around the world use their flying eyeball screen saver makes them feel all warm inside. Other programmers offer their programs as *shareware,* which I describe in Chapter 2. You can try shareware programs for free; if you like them, you're obligated to mail the programmer a registration fee.

Many people swap these freeware and shareware programs with each other, and you can find lots of shareware screen savers, wallpaper, and other goodies through online services like America Online and CompuServe.

✔ An Internet site called www.tucows.com has one of the best selections of files for downloading.

✔ Shareware and freeware are in a different legal realm than that of the boxed software sold in stores. That boxed software is known as *commercial* software, and giving copies of commercial software to friends can cause big legal problems.

In fact, making a copy of Windows 98 and giving it to a friend is illegal.

✔ Feel free to give away, or even sell, old copies of commercial software. Just be sure to include the manual and don't keep a copy of the software for yourself.

Wallowing in Wallpaper

Windows 98 *wallpaper* is the pretty pictures that you can stick to the back of the screen; the wallpaper becomes the coating for your desktop, and all your icons and windows ride on top of it. When you first install Windows 98, it looks pretty forlorn, with a boring gray/green backdrop. Windows 98 comes with several sheets of wallpaper to spruce things up, but those offerings can get old pretty fast.

So people start adding their own wallpaper, like the stuff in Figure 3-1.

Adding wallpaper is the easiest way to make Windows 98 reflect your own personal computer style.

What are wallpaper files?

Wallpaper is a picture that is usually stored in a special format known as a *bitmap* or *BMP* file. For easy identification, bitmap files have an arty icon that looks like a little pencil cup, as shown in Figure 3-2.

For example, Straw Mat and Black Thatch are some of the wallpaper files included with Windows 98. (And if you didn't get those with your copy of Windows 98, flip ahead to the Control Panel's Add/Remove Programs icon and install Desktop Themes for a solution.)

Figure 3-1:
Windows 98
lets you
cover your
desktop
with your
own
personalized
graphics.

Figure 3-2:
You can use
files with
this type
of icon —
bitmap
files — for
wallpaper.

If you're tired of the wallpaper that came with Windows 98, create your own. You can use anything you draw in Windows 98 Paint as wallpaper.

✔ If somebody hands you a PCX file, you're stuck. Windows 98's Paint program doesn't handle that format very well anymore, so it can't save the file as a bitmap file. Sniff.

✔ However, Windows 98's Internet Explorer can download and display GIF files from the Internet. Plus, when you turn on Windows 98's Active Desktop and activate its View as <u>W</u>eb Page mode, discussed in Chapter 7, you can use GIF files as wallpaper both for your computer and for individual folders.

> ✔ See any fun graphics while on the Internet? Click on the object with
> your right mouse button and choose Set as <u>W</u>allpaper. The graphic
> immediately copies itself to your hard drive and decorates your screen.
>
> ✔ For best results, use 256-color BMP files for wallpaper. Larger files can
> eat up memory, slowing Windows down.

Where to put wallpaper

Windows 98 looks for its wallpaper — bitmap files — in only one place: the
computer's Windows folder. So if you have wallpaper named Hand Smears
on the floppy disk in drive A, copy the files from drive A into the hard drive's
Windows folder. (Chapter 2 covers copying files from a floppy drive to a
hard drive.)

Okay, I lied. You can click on the <u>B</u>rowse button to search other folders for
potential wallpaper, but it's a pain. Spreading wallpaper files around on your
hard drive makes them difficult to find later. That makes them harder to
delete when you no longer use them, so they tend to clog your hard drive.

How to display wallpaper

Follow these steps to display your new wallpaper (or any other wallpaper,
for that matter):

1. **Click on a blank area of the desktop with your right mouse button
   and choose P<u>r</u>operties from the pop-up menu.**

   An even bigger menu with buttons and tabs pops up, as shown in
   Figure 3-3. The window at the top of the box displays your current
   wallpaper; the box directly below it marked Wallpaper lists the graphics
   files that are available.

2. **Click on the desired graphics file from the Wallpaper box.**

   Windows 98 immediately shows a miniature view of what your choice
   looks like on the monitor.

3. **Click on the <u>A</u>pply button at the bottom of the box (optional).**

   To see what your choice looks like on the desktop itself, click on the
   <u>A</u>pply button. If you don't like it, head back to Step 2. When you finally
   find some wallpaper you like, move on to Step 4.

4. **Satisfied with the choice? Click on the OK button.**

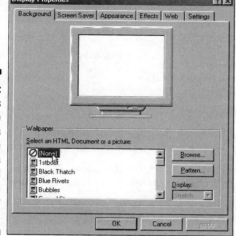

Figure 3-3:
This extensive menu lets you change the settings of all aspects of your desktop.

The box disappears, and your new wallpaper selection coats your desktop.

- If you didn't like any of the selections, click on the Cancel button. That gets rid of the box and lets you get back to work. (You are left with either your original wallpaper or the last wallpaper you used the Apply button on.)

- In the Display area, choose the Tile option to *tile* small images across the screen. Choose the Center option button to place one large image in the center of your screen. And choose the Stretch option to enlarge one picture so that it fills your monitor.

- Don't bother with the Pattern button. The patterns are pretty ugly, and they only show up when you select None as your wallpaper.

- Created something fantastic in the Paint program? Save the file and choose one of the two Set As Wallpaper options from Paint's File menu. Your creation immediately appears on the desktop.

How to get rid of wallpaper

Wallpaper files consume a great deal of space on the hard drive, so excess wallpaper can fill up a hard disk fast.

To get rid of old wallpaper, follow these steps:

1. **Choose Files or Folders from the Start button's Find menu.**

   The handy Windows 98 file finder comes to the screen, ready to prowl.

2. **Type *.bmp in the Named box, type** c:\windows **in the Look in box, and click in the Include subfolders box to make the check mark disappear.**

   The screen looks like Figure 3-4.

3. **Click on the Find Now button.**

   The file finder program finds all the bitmap files living in your Windows folder, which is the home of all your wallpaper files.

4. **With your right mouse button, click on the name of a file that you don't want anymore and choose Quick View from the menu.**

   The Quick View window pops up, showing you what the file looks like. No Quick View option on the menu? Troop ahead to Chapter 15 to find out how to add this valuable weapon to your Windows 98 arsenal. (Hint: It's one of the utility programs in Tweak UI.)

5. **Drag and drop the files that you don't want to the Recycle Bin.**

   The Recycle Bin erases those files from the hard drive. (If it asks for permission first, click on the Yes button.)

6. **Continue to drag and drop files to the Quick View window for quick viewing and continue to drag and drop them to the Recycle Bin if you no longer need them.**

   By dragging and dropping the filenames to the Quick View window, you can tell whether you want to keep them or not. Then just drag the rejects to the Recycle Bin.

Figure 3-4:
Fill out the dialog box to make the Windows 98 file finder seek out all the wallpaper files living on your hard drive.

What's the hard part?

Changing wallpaper or adding new wallpaper is pretty easy. You shouldn't go wild, though, for two reasons:

✔ First, huge, ornate wallpaper files take up a lotta memory, which can slow down Windows 98. If Windows 98 starts running sluggishly, stick with the boring gray backdrop. Or use a tiny piece of wallpaper and tile it across the screen.

✔ Second, huge wallpaper files take up a lotta space on a hard drive. Don't fill up the hard drive with frivolous wallpaper that you never use. When bitmaps get boring, delete them or copy them to a floppy disk to trade with friends.

✔ If you can't remember what a bitmap file looks like, click on its name with your right mouse button from within My Computer or Windows Explorer. Choose Quick View from the menu, and you can see the picture.

Adding or Changing a Screen Saver

If you've seen a dusty old monitor peering from the shelves at the Salvation Army store, you've probably seen WordPerfect, too. The popular word processor's faint outline still appears on many old monitors, even when they're turned off.

In the old days, frequently used programs burned an image of themselves onto the monitor's face. So to save the screens, a programmer invented a *screen saver*. When the computer's keyboard and mouse haven't been touched for a few minutes, the screen saver kicks in and turns the screen black to give the monitor a rest.

Burn-in isn't really a problem with today's color monitors, but screen savers persist — mainly because they're fun. Plus, turning on a screen saver when you go get a cup of coffee keeps other people from seeing what you're really doing on the computer.

What are screen saver files?

Screen savers aren't as simple as the files you use for wallpaper. You need to be a programmer to build a Windows 98 screen saver. A screen saver is a miniature program that does groovy things to your screen; the 3D Flower Box option, for example, places an animation on the screen that twists its shape from a box to a flower.

Windows 98 doesn't normally reveal a file's *extension* — three letters tacked onto a file's name that identify its purpose. However, bitmap files end in BMP (that's why you tell the file finder program to search for files ending in BMP in the wallpaper example earlier); screen saver files end in SCR.

Where to put screen savers

Just like wallpaper files, screen savers prefer to live in the Windows folder. So if you have a Grateful Dead Bear screen saver named DBEAR.SCR on the floppy disk in drive A, copy DBEAR.SCR from drive A onto the hard drive's Windows folder. Chapter 2 covers copying files from a floppy drive to the hard drive.

How to use screen savers

To try out a new screen saver, follow these steps:

1. **Copy the new screen saver to your Windows folder.**

   Some screen savers come with installation programs that put them in the right place. If you just have a single screen saver file, copy it to your Windows folder. (That folder is almost always on drive C.)

   Or if you just want to see what screen savers are currently on your system, move to Step 2.

2. **Click on a blank area of the desktop with your right mouse button and choose P**r**operties from the pop-up menu.**

   The desktop's Properties dialog box pops up, the same one you saw in Figure 3-3 when changing wallpaper.

3. **Click on the tab marked Screen Saver along the top of the box.**

   As shown in Figure 3-5, Windows 98 immediately shows a miniature view of what your currently selected screen saver choice looks like. If you don't have a screen saver set up, the miniature view is blank.

4. **Click on the downward-pointing arrow in the box that says S**creen Saver.**

   A menu drops down, revealing your current choices of screen savers.

5. **Click on one of the listed screen savers.**

   A miniature view of that new screen saver appears on the monitor inside the box.

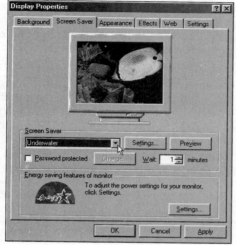

Figure 3-5:
Windows 98
provides a
preview
of your
currently
selected
screen
saver.

6. Click on the Preview button (optional).

To see what your choice would look like on the desktop itself, click on the Preview button. If you don't like it, press the spacebar to return to the desktop and head back to Step 4. When you finally find a screen saver you like, move on to Step 7.

7. Satisfied with the choice? Click on the OK button.

The box disappears, and your new screen saver selection starts counting down the minutes until it's set to kick in. (The number of minutes you choose in the Wait box determine how long the screen saver waits before kicking in.)

- Different screen savers have different settings — the speed the bears dance across the screen and so on. To change these settings, click on the Settings button.

- Click on the Password protected box if you want your screen saver to stay put until somebody types the right password. (If you forget the password, though, you're out of luck: You must reboot Windows by pressing Ctrl+Alt+Del, losing any unsaved work in the process. When Windows returns to life, return to the screen saver screen and turn off the password feature before the screen saver kicks back into life. Then read the next tip.)

- Desktop Themes, one of several hidden Windows 98 options, comes with a bunch of screen savers. To install Desktop Themes, head for the Control Panel's Add/Remove Programs icon, click the Windows Setup tab, and select Desktop Themes from the list of available programs. (Here's a secret: If you've forgotten your screen saver password and followed the steps in the preceding paragraph, install Desktop Themes. At press time, a Desktop Themes screen saver doesn't require you type in your *forgotten* password in order to receive a new, easier-to-remember password.)

- Some monitors can turn themselves off or go into "low-power" mode if you haven't used them for a while. If your monitor falls into one of these categories, click the <u>S</u>ettings box in the Energy saving features of monitor box. A variety of options help dole the least amount of energy to your computer as possible. The minutes you type into the first box determine how long the monitor waits before going blank; the second box decides how long the monitor stays powered up.

How to get rid of screen savers

When you're sick of the same old screen savers, delete the old ones to keep the hard drive from filling up.

To get rid of old screen savers, follow these steps:

1. **Choose <u>F</u>iles or Folders from the Start button's <u>F</u>ind menu.**

   The handy Windows 98 file finder comes to the screen, ready to prowl.

2. **Type *.scr in the <u>N</u>amed box, choose c:\windows in the <u>L</u>ook in box, and click in the Include <u>s</u>ubfolders box to make the check mark appear.**

   Clicking on the <u>B</u>rowse button makes it easy to switch the search to c:\windows. Eventually, the screen looks like Figure 3-6.

Figure 3-6:
Fill out the dialog box like this to make the Windows 98 file finder seek out all the screen saver files living on your hard drive.

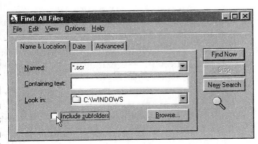

3. **Click on the F̲ind Now button.**

   The file finder program finds all the screen saver files living in your Windows folder, which is also the home of all your wallpaper files. The files with the little screen saver icons all contain little screen saver programs.

4. **With your right mouse button, click on the name of a file that you don't want anymore and choose T̲est from the menu.**

   The screen saver takes over the screen, showing you what the file looks like. (Wiggle the mouse slightly to get the screen saver off the screen.)

5. **Drag and drop the files you don't want to the Recycle Bin.**

   The Recycle Bin erases those files from the hard drive. (If it asks permission first, click on the Y̲es button.)

6. **Continue to test screen savers to remember what they look like, if needed, and then drag and drop them to the Recycle Bin if you don't want them any longer.**

   By testing the files, you can tell whether you want to keep them or not. Then just drag the rejects to the Recycle Bin.

What's the hard part?

Don't let too many screen savers pile up in your Windows 98 folder; they hog space, just as wallpaper does.

Finding decent screen savers can be hard because creating them takes some work. A programmer needs to sit down and create one, preferably while in a good mood. Expect to find a lot more wallpaper and icons floating around than screen savers.

All about Icons

Soon after Windows 98 hits a computer, the icon urge sets in. Face it; icons are cute. Pointing and clicking at a little picture of the Mona Lisa is a lot more fun than the old DOS computing method of typing **C:\UTILITY\ PAINT\ART.EXE** into a box and pressing Enter.

If you've ever collected anything — stamps, seashells, bubble-gum wrappers — you'll be tempted to start adding "just a few more" icons to your current crop.

What are icon files?

Icons — those little pictures you point at and click on — come embedded inside just about every Windows 98 program. Windows 98 reaches inside the program, grabs its embedded icon, and sticks the icon on its menus.

But DOS programs are too boring to come with any embedded icons. So Windows 98 uses the same generic MS-DOS icon to represent all DOS programs.

Luckily, Windows 98 can jazz things up. You can assign any icon to any program, whether its ancestry is DOS or Windows 98.

A single icon comes packaged in a small file that ends in .ICO, such as BART.ICO or FLAVOR.ICO. A group of icons also can come packaged as a program — a file ending in .EXE. Some files ending in .DLL also contain icons. (Windows 98 usually hides extensions like EXE, ICO, DLL, and others, though, so you won't be able to see them.)

Windows 98 can mix and match any icon to any program — if you tickle the icon and program files in the right places.

Although wallpaper files and icon files both contain pictures, the two types of files aren't interchangeable. Their goods are stored in completely different formats.

Where to put icons

Although Windows 98 is picky about the location of its wallpaper and screen savers, icons can live anywhere on the hard drive. To stay organized, however, try to keep all the icon files in their own folder.

For example, create an Icons folder that's nestled in the Windows folder by following the instructions in Chapter 2. Then when you come across any new icons, copy their files into the new Icons folder for easy access. (Chapter 2 also contains instructions for copying files onto a hard disk.)

Finally, Windows 98 doesn't let you create your own icons; you need to find a program to do that. Also, Windows 98 won't let you change every icon on your desktop. You may have the best luck if you stick to fiddling with shortcut and program icons.

How to change an icon in Windows 98

To change the icon of a shortcut or program in Windows 98, follow these steps:

1. **Click on the program's icon with your right mouse button and choose Properties from the pop-up menu.**

   The program's Properties form appears.

2. **Click on the tab marked Shortcut or Program.**

   If you're changing the icon on a shortcut, click on the Shortcut tab; likewise, click on the Program tab if you're changing a program's icon.

3. **Click on the Change Icon button.**

   As shown in Figure 3-7, Windows 98 displays the icons available in the file currently displayed in the Properties or File name box.

   But here's the catch: The filename currently displayed in the File name box isn't always the name of the program that you're fiddling with. Yep — Windows 98 can reach inside other files and assign the icons from those other files to your current shortcut or program.

Figure 3-7:
Windows 98 displays the icons currently available to the file.

4. **Spot an icon you like? Double-click on that icon and choose OK.**

   Your newly chosen icon subsequently replaces your old icon. (Press F5 to refresh the screen if the new icon doesn't show up right away.) If you want to steal an icon from a different source, head for Step 5.

5. **Click on the Browse button, double-click on any of the icons you like in any of the folders, and click on the OK button.**

   Feel free to double-click on any of the folders throughout your hard drive. You can rob any icons you spot by simply double-clicking on them. Still don't find any icons you like? Head to Step 6.

   If you've copied a file full of icons into a folder on your hard drive — an Icons folder in your Windows folder, for example — move to that folder, and those icons appear in the window, ready for you to select.

6. **Type the name of an icon file in the <u>F</u>ile name box and click on the OK button.**

   Here are a few files full of icons that you find in Windows 98. Type any of these four names into the filename box, just as they appear here:

   ```
   Pifmgr.dll
   Moricons.dll
   Explorer.exe
   Shell32.dll
   ```

   After you click on the OK button, the screen clears, and you find some jazzy new icons to choose from.

How to get rid of dorky icons

After you start collecting icons, the little guys come on fast and furiously. Finding them packaged in groups of thousands is not uncommon.

When you find yourself with icons coming out of your ears, delete the yucky ones this way:

1. **Decide which icons to delete.**

   Figure out which icons you no longer need. (If you need help finding the files, see the instructions in the preceding section for finding excess wallpaper and screen saver files — you can use the Windows 98 file finder to search your hard drive for *.ICO files.)

2. **Drag the boring icons to the Recycle Bin.**

   Repeat these steps for each icon that you want to delete.

   • Yes, it's laborious. If all the icon files are in a single folder, however, Windows Explorer or My Computer can wipe out the entire folder at once.

   • Be careful when you delete files. To stay on high ground, just delete files that end in .ICO. If you delete a file that ends in .DLL, make sure that it's the file that contains the icons you want to get rid of. Many other programs use .DLL files — they don't all contain icons.

   • Dozens of shareware packages make creating icons, deleting icons, and assigning icons to programs easy. Check out CompuServe and computer bulletin boards, which I discuss in Chapter 7, for some icon programs.

What's the hard part?

You can't make your own Windows 98 icons. Paint can't handle it. And trying to rename your BART.BMP file to BART.ICO won't fool Windows 98, either.

The solution? Pick up an icon management program. Some of them enable you to create your own icons; you can use others to see the icons inside your icon files. And you can use still others to create animated icons that throw spitballs at each other and make splat sounds.

A Font of Font Wisdom

Different fonts project different images.

- ✔ People with large mahogany desks and antique clocks that play Winchester chimes like the traditional `Bookman Old Style` look.
- ✔ The arty types who like to buy clothes at thrift shops have probably experimented with the Impact look.
- ✔ People who like gothic novels can't resist **Garamond**.

The key here is the *font* — the shape and style of the letters. Windows 98 comes with a mere handful of fonts. Hundreds of additional fonts fill the store shelves, however, and you can find even more fonts on CompuServe and other online services.

Windows 98 uses several types of fonts, but the most popular by far is a breed of fonts called *TrueType*. TrueType is a fancy name for fonts that look the same on-screen as they do when you print them. Before TrueType fonts, fonts didn't look as good. In fact, a headline that looked smooth on-screen had jagged edges when you printed it out.

Fonts versus typeface

Traditional printers wipe the black off their fingers with thick towels and mutter, "The shape of the letters is called their *typeface,* not their *font.*"

Computer users retort, "So what? Language is changing, and desktop publishing is putting you guys out of business, anyway."

Technically speaking, and that's why this stuff is down here in the small print, a *font* refers to a collection of letters that are all of the same size and style.

A *typeface,* on the other hand, simply refers to the style of the letters.

Most computer users merely shrug and wipe their hands of the whole controversy.

What are font files?

The filenames for TrueType fonts end with the letters TTF. But who cares? Windows 98 comes with an installation program that handles all those loose ends, so you don't need to know what the filenames are called.

Where to put fonts

Just put the floppy disk in the disk drive. Windows 98 handles the rest.

How to install fonts

Windows 98 controls the font installation process through its Control Panel. Just follow these steps to font nirvana:

1. **From within the Start menu, choose Settings and click on the Control Panel.**

   The Control Panel hops to the screen.

2. **Double-click on the Control Panel's Fonts folder to see your computer's collection of fonts, shown in Figure 3-8.**

   The Fonts box appears, as shown in Figure 3-8, and shows your current selection of fonts. Double-click on a font's name to see what it looks like; a window opens, revealing its contents. (Click on the Done button to close the window; click on the Print button to see what the font looks like on your printer.)

Figure 3-8: Double-click on the Control Panel's Fonts folder to begin changing your system's fonts.

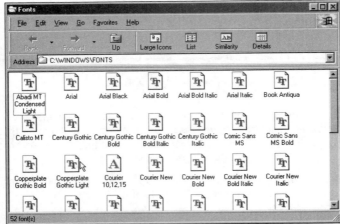

3. Choose File and then choose Install New Font.

The Add Fonts box shown in Figure 3-9 appears, eager to bring new fonts into the fold. But where are they? You need to tell Windows 98 where those fonts lurk, so move to Step 4.

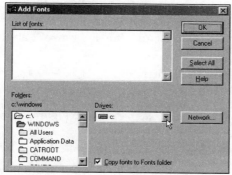

Figure 3-9:
The Add
Fonts box
enables you
to add
new fonts
to your
computer.

4. Click on the letter of the drive or folder that contains the new fonts you want to install.

Are the fonts on a disk? Then click on the little arrow by the Drives box and choose the disk drive where you placed the disk. (First make sure that you put the disk in the correct drive and close the little latch.)

Or if the fonts are already on the hard disk, click on the appropriate folder in the Folders box.

After you click on the folder or drive where the new fonts live, their names appear in the List of fonts box.

If a check mark isn't in the Copy fonts to Fonts folder box, click in the box. You *want* Windows 98 to copy the new fonts to its own folder.

Windows 98 chooses to copy incoming new fonts to the Fonts folder in your Windows folder, but discussing that setup earns strange looks in hotel lobbies.

5. Select the fonts you want.

You probably want to install all the fonts on the disk, so just click on the Select All button. Or if you're in a picky mood, click on the names of the individual fonts you're after.

6. Click on the OK button.

A moment after you click on the OK button, Windows 98 adds the new fonts to the list, one by one.

That's it! The next time you open the word processor, the new fonts will be on the list, waiting to be used.

How to get rid of fonts

The fonts that came with Windows 98 should stay with Windows 98. Only delete fonts that you *know* you've added. Many programs need Windows 98 fonts to survive. In fact, Windows 98 uses some of those fonts for its menus.

Getting rid of fonts is even easier than installing them:

1. **From within the Start button's menu, choose Control Panel from the Settings option.**

   The Control Panel hops to the screen.

2. **Double-click on the Control Panel's Fonts folder.**

   The Fonts box pops to the screen, seen earlier in Figure 3-8, showing the fonts currently installed on your computer.

3. **Click on the name of the font you're sick of.**

   If you're not absolutely sure which font you're sick of, double-click on the font's icon — the font appears on the screen so you can make sure that you've chosen the one you want to delete.

4. **Choose Delete from the File menu.**

   Windows 98 asks whether you're sure you want to delete the font, as shown in Figure 3-10. If you're *really* sure, click on the Yes button. If you want to remove more fonts, back up to Step 3. Otherwise, move to Step 5.

5. **Close the Fonts box.**

   That's it. You're back at the Control Panel, and the font has been erased from the hard drive.

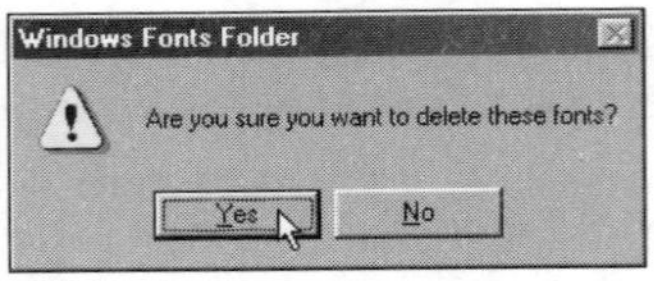

Figure 3-10:
Click on Yes
if you're
sure that
you want
to delete
the font.

Windows Fonts Folder

Are you sure you want to delete these fonts?

Yes   No

What's the hard part?

The hardest part of fonts comes from the language. Table 3-1 explains some of the weirdness.

✔ If you're not using a program called *Adobe Type Manager,* choose TrueType fonts whenever they're offered in Windows 98. They're much more hassle free and usually look better than the other fonts.

✔ In fact, you should almost always use TrueType fonts — except for use in professional-level desktop publishing, where PostScript fonts are more popular.

Table 3-1	Types of Fonts
These Fonts . . .	*. . . Do This*
Screen fonts	Windows 98 uses these fonts to display letters on your screen.
Printer fonts	Your printer uses these fonts to create letters and stick them on the printed page. (Some say the word *Plotter.*) Any printer fonts in a menu have a little picture of a printer next to them.
TrueType fonts	These fonts were introduced with Windows 3.1. Screen fonts and printer fonts are combined in one package to make fonts look the same on-screen as they do on the printed page. A little pair of *T*s appear next to any TrueType fonts that are listed in a menu.
PostScript fonts	An older type of font that is popular with professional-level desktop publishers. To use PostScript fonts in Windows, you need to have Adobe Type Manager (ATM).

Adding or Changing Sounds

For years, the howls of anguished computer users provided the only sounds at the computer desktop. Today, however, Windows 98 can wail with the best of them.

But one big problem exists. Windows 98 can't make any sounds until you attach a sound card and some speakers. Medium-range sound cards usually cost about $50 to $200.

What are sound files?

Windows 98 can play two popular types of sound files. The first type of files, known as *Wave* files, contain real sounds — a duck quacking or the sound of a tree falling in a forest (if somebody was there to record it). Windows 98 comes with several of these recorded sounds: chord, chimes, growling lions, "normal" beeping, and splashing oceans.

MIDI files are the second type of sound files. They aren't actual recordings. Rather, they're instructions for a synthesizer to play certain musical tones. Whereas Wave files usually contain short recorded sounds, MIDI files usually contain complete songs. In fact, Windows 98 comes with a MIDI file named Canyon. It's a pleasant jingle, the kind you hear while put on hold by a computerized answering machine.

Because Wave files contain actual recorded sounds, they can be huge. A ten-second sound can fill a floppy disk. MIDI files, in contrast, contain synthesizer instructions — not the sounds — so their size is smaller.

Some MIDI programs save MIDI files in different formats that end with different extensions than MIDI. Windows 98, however, prefers the MIDI format that ends in MIDI. Similarly, some sound cards come with sounds that are stored in an SND format. Windows 98 can't play those files, but your sound card or Internet browser may include a sound-playing program that can play them.

You can find plenty more help with sound files in the multimedia chapter, Chapter 10.

The MOD Squad

Okay, Windows 98 can play a third type of sound file — a MOD file. A mixture of Wave and MIDI, MOD files contain actual sounds, plus instructions to play them in sequence. They sound sort of like MIDI files, but with real instruments.

The problem? To keep space to a minimum, most of the sounds are repeats — the same drumbeat, the same guitar riff, the same hand clap, ad nauseam. Most MOD files sound rather robotic. But, hey, add a few strobe lights and tap while you type.

Windows 98 doesn't come with a MOD player or MOD files, but wherever you find MOD files, a MOD player shouldn't be far behind.

Where to put sound files

MIDI files can live anywhere on the hard drive. Chances are, the software included with your sound card contains a few MIDI files. Feel free to toss a few more MIDI files in the same directories.

Wave files can live anywhere on the hard drive, too. If you want to assign sounds to events — hear a duck quack whenever you start Windows 98, for example — then copy those particular sounds to the Windows folder (the same place where you keep wallpaper, as described previously in this chapter).

Chapter 2 explains how to create a folder on a hard drive and copy files to it from a floppy disk.

How to listen to sounds

After you hook up the sound card and install the driver (described in the section "Adding or Changing Drivers," later in this chapter), listening to sounds is a snap.

- ✔ From My Computer or Windows Explorer, double-click on the file's name.

- ✔ If you double-click on a MIDI file, the Windows 98 Media Player leaps to the screen and begins playing it. Simple.

- ✔ If you double-click on a Wave file, ActiveMovie leaps to the screen and begins playing it.

- ✔ Here's a quick way to listen to sounds: Load the Windows 98 Media Player; then place the Windows Explorer or My Computer program next to it. To hear a sound, drag a Wave or MIDI file from the Explorer or My Computer window and drop it onto the Media Player window. The sound plays immediately. (Never dragged and dropped? Chapter 1 has a refresher course.)

How to assign sounds to events

Windows 98 can let loose with different sounds at different times. Better yet, Windows 98 enables *you* to decide what sound it should play and when.

To assign different sounds to different events, follow these steps:

1. **From within the Start button menu, choose the Control Panel from the Settings area.**

   The Control Panel hops to the screen.

2. **Double-click on the Control Panel's Sounds icon.**

   The Sounds Properties box, shown in Figure 3-11, appears on-screen. It lists the sounds that are currently assigned to Windows 98 events.

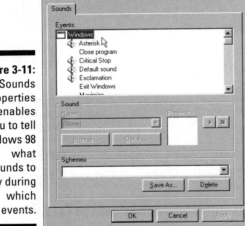

Figure 3-11: The Sounds Properties box enables you to tell Windows 98 what sounds to play during which events.

If you haven't set up and installed a sound card, you can't play with the settings. The sounds look *grayed out* — dimmer than the rest of the text — and you can't click on them.

3. **Click on an event and then click on the sound that you want Windows 98 to play when that event occurs.**

   Windows 98 is rather vague about what words in the Events box are supposed to mean. An event is usually a box that pops up on-screen. For example, the message in Figure 3-12 occasionally pops up on-screen. See the exclamation point in the left side of the box? Windows 98 considers that box an "Exclamation" event.

   Now look at the sound files listed in the Events box shown earlier in Figure 3-11. When you click on Exclamation, the Chord sound is highlighted to indicate that Windows 98 plays the Chord sound whenever the box with the Exclamation point pops up.

Figure 3-12:
The
exclamation
point in this
box means
Windows 98
considers
this to be an
"Exclamation"
event.

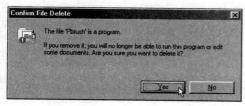

Table 3-2 explains the events that you can assign sounds to.

The Sounds Properties Name box lists all the sounds in the Windows folder. To see sounds in other folders, click on the Browse button.

4. Click on the Preview button.

Windows 98 dutifully trumpets the sound you selected. If you like it, click on the OK button, and you're done. If you don't like it, however, head back to Step 3 and click on a different sound.

Don't like any of the sounds? Then record your own! Head to Chapter 10 for the details.

Table 3-2	Windows 98 Sound Events and Their Causes
This Event or Picture . . .	*. . . Plays a Sound Because of This*
Asterisk/Information	A box has appeared on-screen, offering more information about your current situation.
Critical Stop	An urgent box warns of dire consequences if you proceed — but lets you click on the OK button to keep going, anyway.
Default Beep	The most common event; this means you clicked outside a dialog box or did something equally harmless.
Exclamation	This box urges caution, to a slightly less degree than the Critical Stop warning.
Exit Windows	This event plays when you shut down Windows 98.
Question	A box is asking you to choose among a variety of choices.
Start Windows	This event plays when you load Windows 98.

How to get rid of sounds

MIDI files don't take up too much room in the hard disk closet, but Wave files are clunkier than a cast-iron Hoover vacuum cleaner.

To get rid of sound files, head for the Start button's file finder program.

1. **Click on Find from the Start button menu and choose Files or Folders.**

2. **Type *.WAV into the Named box and click on the Find Now button.**

   Although sound files can be scattered throughout your hard drive, the ones assigned to your events usually live in the Media folder, which is tucked inside your Windows folder.

3. **Double-click on the name of the dorky sound file.**

   Windows 98 plays the file, so keep your ears ready. Is that *really* the dorky one? Then move to Step 4. Otherwise, keep double-clicking on the names of the listed sound files until you find the boring one.

4. **Drag the dorky sound file to the Recycle Bin.**

   That gets rid of the sound file.

What's the hard part?

The hard part of using sound in Windows 98 comes from the computer's sound card. If the sound card is installed correctly, with the right drivers, everything should work pretty smoothly. But until that sound card is set up right, things can be pretty ugly.

You're better off sticking with name-brand sound cards, like the ones made by Creative Labs or Turtle Beach. Some of the really cheap ones can cause awful headaches.

Adding or Changing Drivers

Even after you wrestle with the tiny screws on the back of the computer's case, slide in the new sound card, extract the tiny screws from the shag carpet, and reattach the computer's case, you're not through.

After you install a new gadget in the computer, you need to tell Windows 98 how to use it. Those instructions come in the form of a *driver* — a piece of software that teaches Windows 98 how to make that new gadget work.

Most gadgets — things like sound cards, video cards, and CD-ROM players — come with a driver on a floppy disk. Some gadgets can use the drivers that came with Windows 98. In fact, Windows 98 uses a concept called *plug and play:* After you install the new computer part, Windows 98 automatically sniffs it out, installs the correct driver, and makes everything work right.

But if your gadget is not working right under Windows 98, chances are it needs a new driver.

What are driver files?

Driver files end in DRV, but you can promptly forget that bit of information. The Control Panel handles all the driver installation chores, sparing you the trouble of searching for individual files, moving them around, or trying to delete them.

In fact, Windows 98 comes with a program called Windows Update that handles driver-file-upgrade tasks automatically through the Internet. Just choose Windows Update from the Start menu, and the Wizard leads you through logging onto the Internet and filling out the appropriate computing forms. Microsoft's computer subsequently diagnoses your computer and, hopefully, fixes what's wrong by copying the new driver onto your hard drive. You need a modem for this technowizardry, however, so pull out your computer's receipt if you're not sure parts lurk inside your machine.

Where to put drivers

When mailed from the manufacturer, drivers come on floppy disks. The Control Panel handles the installation chores, so merely put the disk in the disk drive and close the latch. If you downloaded the file from the Internet, be sure to keep track of the folder into which you downloaded the file.

How to install drivers

Don't try to add a driver until you install the new mouse, keyboard, video card, or whatever else you have. (If you've added a monitor, however, skip ahead to the tip at the end of this section.) Next, add the driver by following these steps:

1. **Shut down all your programs, leaving Windows 98 bare on the screen.**

   If something goes wrong, you don't want any programs running in the background.

2. **Click on the Control Panel from the Start button's Settings area.**

   The Control Panel appears on-screen.

3. **Double-click on the Add New Hardware icon.**

   A box appears, as shown in Figure 3-13, announcing the New Hardware Wizard's helpful arrival.

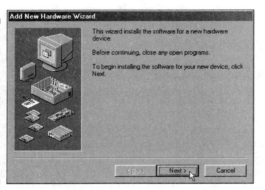

Figure 3-13:
Windows 98 can auto-matically set up most pieces of hardware you add to your system.

4. **Click on the Next button.**

   Windows 98 says that it will search for any new parts that it recognizes — Plug and Play parts — and return with a report. It also warns that the screen could go blank in the process, but that's normal.

5. **Click on the Next button and let the Wizard search your computer for new parts.**

   After warning you that the search may take a few minutes, Windows 98 begins rummaging through your hard drive, looking for the new part. After huffing and puffing, it reveals what it found in Step 6.

6. **If Windows 98 says that it didn't find your new part, you have to click on the Next button and pick it out of a list.**

   • If Windows 98 says that it found your part, it asks whether the new part came with a disk. If so, insert the disk into the drive and you're off; if not, Windows 98 uses one of its drivers. Either way, your new part should be up and running.

   • Windows 98 can't detect monitors, so they're not installed this way. Instead, click on a blank part of your desktop with your right mouse button and choose Properties from the menu. Click on the Settings tab and choose Advanced from the bottom of the box. Click on the Monitor tab from the screen's top, click on the

Change button, and let the Wizard take over. If you're at a loss as to what to choose, choose the closest one you find (usually Standard VGA or one of the SuperVGA types).

- Sometimes Windows 98 says that it already has a driver for a gadget. Then it asks whether it should use the current driver (the one already installed) or the new one (the one on your floppy disk). Choose the new one.

How to get rid of drivers

You need to get rid of drivers under only two circumstances:

- ✔ You're installing a new driver, and you want to get rid of the old driver first.
- ✔ You've sold your gadget or you've stopped using it for some other reason, and you don't want the driver installed anymore.

In either case, follow the bouncing ball to delete your driver:

1. **Load the Control Panel from the Start button's Settings area.**

   The Control Panel hops to the screen.

2. **Double-click on the System icon and click on the Device Manager tab.**

   As shown in Figure 3-14, the Device Manager box lists the currently installed gadgets and drivers on your system.

Figure 3-14:
The Device
Manager
box lists
the current
gadgets
and drivers
installed
on your
computer.

3. **Double-click on the name of the gadget that you no longer have installed on your computer and click on the Remove button.**

    Windows 98 asks whether you're sure that you want to get rid of that driver. If you are sure, click on the OK button, and Windows 98 sweeps it from the hard drive.

    You're through!

Make sure that you really don't need a driver before you remove it, however; its gadget can't work without it.

What's the hard part?

The hardest part of working with drivers is getting them set up right in the first place. But once drivers are up and running, they usually work well. Always keep your eye out for an updated driver, though. Manufacturers usually release new versions every few months to fix the problems found in the old ones.

Always keep a copy of your old driver as a backup before installing a new version of that driver. You never can tell when a new driver may cause more problems than the old one.

Ugly IRQs

Sometimes new computer gadgets — sound cards, for example — upset other parts of the computer. They argue over things such as *interrupts,* which are also known as *IRQs.* When you set up the card so that it works right, remember its settings. For example, if the sound card says that it uses *IRQ 7* and *Port* *220,* write down that information — no matter how technodork it sounds. Windows 98 may eventually ask you for the same numbers.

If the gadget doesn't work right, check out the book *Upgrading & Fixing PCs For Dummies,* 4th Edition. It may be able to give you a hand.

Chapter 4

Uh, Which Version of Windows Does What?

*P*C users used to line up into two distinct rows. One group loved Windows. Everybody else stuck with plain ol' DOS. And unless the two groups tried to compute while they were in the same room, nobody hurled food at anybody else.

It's not that simple anymore, though. That single row of Windows users now has several distinct split ends.

Which version of Windows does what? Which one is best? Which version do you have? And are you using the right one?

This chapter looks at the most common versions of Windows enveloping the world's computers. Chances are, yours will be right here.

Which Version of Windows Do You Have?

Don't know which version of Windows you use? Check the front of the Windows box; that's the easiest clue. No box? Then check the labels on the Windows floppy disks or compact disc.

If all that stuff fell off the pickup truck during the last move, try this: Click on the My Computer icon with your right mouse button and choose Properties. In Windows 98, you should see a box like Figure 4-1.

Figure 4-1: Click on the My Computer icon with your right mouse button and choose Properties to see which version of Windows you use.

No My Computer icon? Then load the Help menu of Program Manager: Click on <u>H</u>elp from the menu bar and then click on <u>A</u>bout when the little menu drops down.

A box like the one shown in Figure 4-2 lists the version number.

✔ Hopefully, you're using Windows 98. Plenty of people still use its predecessor, Windows 95, however. And more than a few holdouts still use Windows 3.1. Several scattered groups of people who don't like to change things are still hanging onto Windows for Workgroups, also known as Windows 3.11.

✔ If you use Windows 98, you can still run almost all your old Windows programs. But if you still use Windows 3.1 or anything earlier, you won't be able to run any Windows 98 or Windows 95 programs.

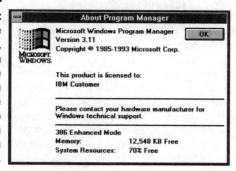

Figure 4-2:
In some programs, you can click on the <u>H</u>elp menu and choose <u>A</u>bout to see which version you use.

✔ If you still use Version 1.0 or 2.0 of Windows, your computer probably won't run *any* of the Windows programs on the market today.

✔ To see what sneaky little cartoons Microsoft sneaked into that innocent-looking About Program Manager box, sneak ahead to Chapter 21.

✔ The rest of this chapter describes all the versions of Windows that you may come across at the computer store, bundled with a PC, or on the shelf at the Salvation Army. Most important, it says what you can do with them and whether you should upgrade.

Windows Versions 1.0 and 2.0

Era: Announced in 1983, Windows 1.0 finally hit the shelves in November 1985. Windows 2.0 followed in December 1987.

Required hardware: Windows 1.0 required 256K of memory and two floppy drives. Anybody who wanted to do more than watch the mouse pointer turn into a perpetual hourglass needed a hard drive and at least 1MB of RAM.

Reason for living: Microsoft was trying to get rid of the computer's "type-writer" look. With DOS, people typed letters and numbers into the computer. The computer listened and then typed letters and numbers back at them.

It worked well — after people struggled through all the manuals. But it was, well, boring. A lot more boring than that "fun" Macintosh. Programmers designed DOS for other programmers, who thrived on elusive strings of techno-gibberish.

So to camouflage DOS's shortcomings, Microsoft released Windows 1.0. Windows enabled people to boss around their computers much more pleasantly. They'd slide a mouse around on the desk, pointing at buttons on the screen and clicking a button on the mouse.

Major features: Everybody hated Windows 1.0. The colors were awful. They looked as if they'd been chosen by a snooty interior decorator who was trying to make a *statement.* Windows wanted every window to be the same awkward size, and they couldn't overlap. To fine-tune the concept and attract new users, Windows 2.01 added *Dynamic Data Exchange (DDE),* a dramatic marketing term for a simple concept — letting programs share information.

For example, the golf scores in the spreadsheet could be "hot-wired" to the club newsletter in the word processor. When somebody typed the latest golf scores into the spreadsheet, the spreadsheet automatically updated the golf scores in the newsletter.

For the first time, club members actually volunteered to serve as the newsletter editor.

Verdict: Like the first microwave oven, Windows offered something dramatically new — and dramatically frightening. Most people simply ignored it. The final straw? Windows required an expensive, powerhouse computer, and back then, tiny little XT computers ruled the desktops.

Interest in Windows 2.0 picked up a little, mainly because of IBM's new AT computer. The AT's rocking 286 chip could open and shut windows much faster than the XT.

✔ Windows 1.0 and 2.0 are brittle antiques. Ninety-nine percent of today's software can't run on any version of Windows older than Windows 3.0. Hang on to those old versions only as appreciating collectibles, like the Marvel Comics *X-Men* series.

✔ Even as Windows 1.0 and 2.0 sat on the shelves, Microsoft's programmers toiled in the background, cranking out a few other special versions of Windows. They released Windows 286 for the new AT computers and Windows 386 for those super-new 386 computers. Yawn.

Windows 386 could finally run a DOS program in a little on-screen window instead of forcing it to hog the whole screen. These in-between versions were practice efforts for the upcoming Windows 3.0 version; neither can run most of the Windows software that is sold today.

Windows 3.0

Era: Born in May 1990.

Required hardware: Although the box said that Windows 3.0 worked on XTs, ATs, and 386s, it crawled on anything but a 386.

Reason for living: Windows finally grew up with this release. The powerful computers of the day could finally handle it, and Microsoft had sanded off the rough edges that plagued earlier versions.

Major features: Compared to the earlier Windows versions, Windows 3.0 took off like a cat stepping on a hot waffle iron. Cosmetically, Windows 3.0 *looked* better than earlier versions; plus, users could maneuver on-screen windows much more easily. Finally, it did a much better job of insulating users from ugly DOS mechanics; people could point and click their way through boring file-management tasks.

Windows 3.0 could handle networks for the first time (see the section "Windows for Workgroups," later in this chapter), and it did everything a lot faster.

Verdict: Most Windows software still runs under Windows 3.0. In fact, a few people still use Windows 3.0 — although they're always muttering under their breath about upgrading "real soon now."

What mode are you?

Windows 3.0 brought three new Windows *modes* along with it:

✔ **Real:** By loading Windows 3.0 in Real mode, users could still run some of the older Windows software that was written for Windows 2.0. Unfortunately, Real mode meant that Windows worked *Real slow*. But it was the only mode that XT computers could handle.

✔ **Standard:** In Standard mode, Windows programs could run at their quickest, but DOS programs suffered. DOS programs couldn't run in little on-screen windows; they had to fill the whole screen. And although several DOS programs could run at the same time, only the currently running DOS program could show up on-screen. The rest had to lurk in the background, frozen as icons.

✔ **386-Enhanced:** Designed specifically for the 386 chip (as well as any 286 chips), this mode let several DOS programs run simultaneously in their own on-screen windows. it also let Windows grab a chunk of the hard disk and pretend that it was memory, swapping information back and forth when *real* memory was too full to handle any more. (More swap file facts live in Chapter 5.)

Windows 3.1 dumped Real mode, but it still runs in the other two modes.

Windows 3.1

Era: Born in April 1992.

Required hardware: A 386SX or faster computer, at least 2MB of RAM, and at least 10MB of space on the hard drive. For best results, however, look for at least 4MB of RAM and at least an 80MB hard drive.

Reason for living: Ninety percent of Windows 3.1 is the same as Windows 3.0. That new 10 percent, however, makes quite a difference. Windows 3.1 got rid of those ugly jagged fonts and added sound support so that people can play with multimedia programs. It carries on the evolution toward making computers easier to use, as well as more fun.

Major features: Windows 3.1 continues the success of Windows 3.0. It adds a revamped, more efficient File Manager, easy-to-use TrueType fonts, more drag-and-drop features, and sound.

Verdict: Because more than 100 million people have been using Windows 3.1, it may have a few more years to come, especially on older computers that can't handle the faster stuff.

Windows 3.11 (Windows for Workgroups)

Era: Born in 1992.

Required hardware: Same as Windows 3.1, but toss in an extra megabyte or two of RAM.

Reason for living: For years, Steve printed out the spreadsheet and handed it to Jackie. Today, though, Jackie wants to read Steve's spreadsheet from her own computer. She needs a *network* — a way to link all the computers in the office so that everybody can share the same information.

Major features: In addition to linking all the computers, this version of Windows has a special mail and scheduling system. Without leaving their desks, workers can decide where to meet for lunch *twice* as quickly as people without a network.

Verdict: Windows 3.11 moved right onto the desktops like Windows 3.1. It's still out there. People still use it. Some people just don't like Windows 95 and 98.

Software Development Kits

A Windows Software Development Kit (dubbed SDK by highly paid marketing workers) helps programmers make little windows and menus pop onto the screen at the touch of a button.

An SDK, therefore, contains a bunch of weird code words to help programmers write Windows programs. Normal people find the SDK pretty useless.

You're not missing much, though; SDKs can cost about five times as much as Windows.

Windows for Workgroups looks pretty much like plain old Windows. But Windows for Workgroups has all the networking stuff built into it. It comes with an enhanced version of Windows software, long cables, and special cards that plug into a computer's guts. Stringing cables from computer to computer enables everybody to share spreadsheets and Solitaire scores — and to send their party fliers to the same printer as well.

Windows NT

Era: Born in 1993.

Required hardware: Back then, you needed a fast (at least 25 MHz) 386 computer or a 486. You also needed at least 12MB of RAM and about 75MB of free hard drive space.

Reason for living: Windows 3.1 didn't replace DOS; it rides on top of it, like a shiny new camper shell on a rusty old pickup truck. And DOS, designed for computers that were created more than ten years ago, simply couldn't take advantage of powerful computers. So Microsoft stuck its programmers in the closet for two years and came up with Windows NT.

Major features: The first versions of Windows NT looked like plain old Windows 3.1, but they were designed specifically for speedy computers. They could run bunches of programs at the same time without falling down and dropping everything. Big corporations liked it.

Verdict: Although Windows 98 currently rules, Windows NT may be coming around the bend. However, it's expensive and requires an expensive machine. Windows NT seems to work best when it's at the heart of a big network and is pumping files up and down cables into other computers. It's a little too fat for today's average desktop PC.

NT comes in two flavors. Windows NT Workstation is the cheap version for all the computers on a network. Windows NT Server is the expensive version that runs the computer in charge of pushing information back and forth between the workstations.

Windows 95

Era: Born on August 24, 1995.

Required hardware: At least a 386DX, with 8MB of memory.

Reason for living: Microsoft's Windows NT is too chunky for most people's desktops, and Windows 3.11 was getting too old. So Microsoft spruced up Windows again and released Windows 95.

Major features: Windows 95 finally combined DOS and Windows into one operating system. Plus, it finally lets you use filenames that are more than eight characters long — and you only had to wait 15 years!

Verdict: Here's a little secret: Lots of people ignored Windows 95, and it wasn't the overwhelming sales success that Microsoft expected. Corporations never snapped it up, either. But Bill Gates didn't care, and here's why: Gates forced all programmers to make their "Official" Windows 95 programs compatible with the new version of Windows NT.

When people begin upgrading to Windows NT to take advantage of their more powerful computers, they'll want to take their familiar program along with them. And they migrate painlessly from one Microsoft operating system to another. There won't be any room for a competing operating system to muscle in, and Windows NT programs will be everywhere! Sneaky, eh?

Windows CE

Era: Born in November 1996.

Required hardware: Windows CE looks like Windows 98, but it runs exclusively on those little "palmtop" computers, like the Sharp Mobilon or Casio Cassiopeia. Instead of using a mouse to control the on-screen action, you push the icons and buttons directly on the palmtop's screen with a little plastic pen. Windows CE swaps files and information with your desktop computer, but the palmtops can run only Windows CE-specific software — your desktop's Windows programs are useless.

Reason for living: After years of technical research, programmers discovered that laps disappear when a person stands up. A few nerds experimented by wearing their laptops on trays like those worn by cigarette sales girls in casinos, but others turned to palmtop computers. Mobile users can now poke Windows' on-screen buttons with a plastic pen rather than a mouse. Because using a palmtop computer is like writing on a notepad or punching a calculator, inventory crews can count cases of canned asparagus without sitting down and struggling with a laptop.

Major features: Windows CE works just like Windows 98, with a little plastic pen instead of a mouse. The problem with the concept lies in the palmtop: The batteries die quickly, especially when you try to be savvy by catching your e-mail at an airport's payphone. Still, if you need a tiny computer for grabbing e-mail or whipping up notes while on the road, a Windows CE palmtop may do the trick.

Verdict: Those little guys are somewhat pricey for what they do; in a few years, though, they'll be standard equipment on every car's dashboard so that thirsty drivers can find out how far ahead their next Slurpee lies. Windows CE software is currently on its second version, but the masses are clamoring for yet another version.

Windows 98

Era: Born in the middle of 1998.

Required hardware: If your computer handles Windows 95 well, it can handle Windows 98 well, too. You want more hard drive space and more memory, though, for better performance.

Reason for living: If you bothered to keep your copy of Windows 95 up-to-date — painstakingly downloading and installing two years' worth of new drivers, programs, and patches — from Microsoft's Web site, then you may have escaped any need to upgrade to Windows 98. That's because Windows 98 is pretty much a completely upgraded version of Windows 95. But it sure is convenient, isn't it?

Major features: Bill Gates is placing his bets on escalating Internet action, so Windows 98 completely wraps itself around the Web. It includes Internet Explorer 4.0 for Web browsing, FrontPage Express for publishing your own Web page, and Outlook Express for sending and receiving e-mail. It can embed Web pages onto your desktop as wallpaper, too.

Verdict: If you love the Internet, you'll love the way Windows 98 tackles every aspect of it. If you don't care about the Internet, you'll still enjoy how Windows 98 can handle today's hardware better. And if you like Windows 98's stability but the look of Windows 95, you can put a check mark in the <u>C</u>lassic style box to make Windows 98 look and act like Windows 95.

So Which Windows Is for What?

In a nutshell, Microsoft is doing three things:

- ✓ Trying to install Windows 98 onto as many computers as possible.
- ✓ Trying to make as many computer users as possible upgrade to Windows 98.
- ✓ Trying gently to steer people to buy Windows NT so that everybody can run all their Windows programs a little bit more efficiently on networks.

If you're happy with your current version of Windows, stick with it. No one says that you have to buy the latest version.

To Microsoft, however, you and your older versions of Windows are just tiny fish in the huge Windows sea. Those older versions are a dying breed, as is plain old DOS. You don't find as many new programs written for these older operating systems, nor is it easy to find technical support for them.

Part II
Entering the Internet with Windows 98

The 5th Wave By Rich Tennant

"I TELL YA I'M STILL GETTING INTERFERENCE—
— COOKIE, RAGS? RAGS WANNA COOKIE? —
THERE IT GOES AGAIN."

In this part . . .

By now, you probably have figured out the Windows 98 basics: Click here to make something appear; drag and drop something to move it around the page. Ho hum.

To keep things moving, this part of the book is packed with information on how to use Windows 98 to harness the Internet.

For beginners, the book explores Internet Explorer, the Windows 98 freebie program for browsing the Internet. Not signed up to the Internet yet? A section leads you through the process.

To send e-mail to all your friends, telling them that you've finally broken down and gotten a computer, use Outlook Express to send them electronic mail. Although the program's a freebie, like Internet Explorer, it's tough: Business users will enjoy the sections about automatically sorting the incoming stream of e-mail, moving important letters into one folder, and deleting junk mail.

Another chapter introduces the Active Desktop — a way to direct the flow of the Internet into constantly updating windows for the desktop.

After living the Web lifestyle for a few months, your e-mail address won't be enough: You'll want your own Web page. Windows 98 FrontPage Express — the Web-building program included with Windows 98 — and this part of the book can help build your own virtual villa on the Web wasteland. Enjoy!

Chapter 5

The Internet and Outright Exhaustion

Microsoft grabbed the operating system market years ago and never let go. Today, Microsoft CEO Bill Gates is the richest man in the United States of America. What's he doing with all that cash? He's trying to predict the future so that he can become the richest man in the galaxy.

Gates has his eyes set on the *Internet* — a collection of computers strung together throughout the world. Some people use the Internet to swap electronic mail (e-mail). Others prefer to create or browse *Web pages* — picturesque electronic bulletin boards displaying everything from battery replacement charts to live-action Hawaiian surf videos.

This chapter shows how to connect to the Internet, as well as fine-tune *Internet Explorer*, Windows 98's built-in program for flipping through the world's Web pages. Windows 98 tosses in several other Internet-related programs, also described here.

But be forewarned: Internet connections are some of the most difficult things to figure out in Windows 98. Some computers take hours to set up and some refuse to cooperate at all, despite the lure of fancy finger foods.

Those unfortunate souls with meatier problems should flip through *Windows 98 SECRETS,* by Brian Livingston and Davis Straub (published by IDG Books Worldwide, Inc.).

Flicking Windows 98's "Internet On" Switch

You need a computer, a modem, and a phone number to connect to the Internet. And after you arrive on the Internet's shores, you need software to begin traveling.

Luckily, you already have two of the four requirements: You have the computer, for example, and Windows 98 comes with built-in software for browsing the Internet — Internet Explorer.

That means Internet access is only two steps away: You need the phone number of an *Internet service provider* (ISP) for accessing the Internet, and a *modem* to call that number. The two are often related, as the upcoming sections show. (Some ISPs require special types of modems; others use the common "telephone-line" variety of modem sold in most computer stores.)

Step 1: Choosing a modem

Modems — mechanical gadgets that let computers talk to each other — come in a range of sizes, shapes, and even colors. But *speed* and *price* are the most crucial criteria.

Table 5-1 ranks popular modem speeds by listing the number of *Kbps* (kilobits of data per second, a common modem-measuring stick) that they can sling around. (Actually, the slick cable modem goes so fast that it's measured in *Mbps* — megabits of data per second, which is 1,000 times faster than Kbps.)

The first column shows how quickly the modems download a 10MB file from the Internet to your computer; the adjacent column shows the modem's required type of Internet connection.

Different modems meet different needs, but here's the scoop: The faster the modem, the more it costs. And the ultra-fast, expensive modems like ISDN and cable modems are the best deals for heavy Internet addicts, but there's a catch — those modems are only offered in special areas.

Compare current modem prices with their performance. Then see which modems are offered by the ISPs available in your area.

Table 5-1	Modem Speeds and Types of Connections	
This Modem . . .	*Downloads a 10MB File This Quickly . . .*	*And Needs This to Connect*
Regular, 33.6 Kbps modem	30 minutes	Regular phone line
56 Kbps modem	20 minutes	Regular phone line, but your ISP must support your particular type of 56 Kbps modem (two types are fighting each other for market share)
ISDN modem (128 Kbps)	10 minutes	Special, digital ISDN phone line
Cable modem (4 to 10 Mbps)	15 seconds	An option offered in some areas with existing cable-TV service

Step 2: Finding an Internet service provider (ISP)

While choosing a modem, check out the *Internet service providers,* or *ISPs,* in your area. The ISP gives you a phone number for the modem to dial into and mails you a bill each month. The best ISPs charge the cheapest rates, give the fewest busy signals, and route you through the Internet the most quickly.

As you saw in Table 5-1, choosing an ISDN or cable modem often alleviates your search for an ISP — your Internet bill comes tacked onto your monthly cable-TV or phone bill, although many large ISPs offer ISDN connections, if you choose that route.

Other companies, like CompuServe, America Online, and Prodigy Internet, run their own online services with special, subscriber-only content on top of the Internet stuff that everyone else sees. Because they offer Internet access, they still count as ISPs. As you see later in this chapter, Microsoft's MSN service, tossed in with Windows 98, falls under this two-headed, online-service-and-Internet-provider category.

Many people choose to go with an independent, Internet-only service. Like polliwogs after spring rains, the Internet boom has spawned thousands of independent ISPs. A glance at your newspaper's business section can reveal Internet offers through local ISPs, national ISPs, and even your local Bell telephone company.

Don't want to bother with finding an ISP? Windows 98 enables you to connect to the Internet without leaving your desk to grab a phone book. Just grab your wallet, and move ahead to Step 3.

Step 3: Dialing the Internet

After finding an on-ramp to the Internet, you need *software* to begin exploring. When you type a password, the software begins billing your account (arrangements differ — some ISPs bill for unlimited usage; others charge by the hour), and you begin sending and retrieving e-mail or visiting haunts like the Potato-of-the-Month Club Web site.

The best software works quickly and easily, and can handle the most advanced sound and graphics, displaying the Club's Yukon Golds and Dark Red Norlanders with delectable reality.

✔ Windows 98 comes with Microsoft's Internet Explorer software, an efficient and comfortable vehicle for connecting to your ISP and entering the Internet's World Wide Web: a huge network of computers offering information on nearly any subject.

✔ Still don't have an ISP? You don't need one to get started, because Windows 98 comes with one in the box. Microsoft's own ISP — The Microsoft Network (MSN) — walks you through signing up with Microsoft as your ISP. MSN's icon lives right on your desktop.

✔ Microsoft herded icons for all the competing online services into a separate desktop folder called Online Services. Open this for access to America Online, AT&T WorldNet, CompuServe, and Prodigy Internet. A Notepad document lists the other company's technical support phone numbers and other handy information.

✔ Finally, if you bypass Microsoft and sign up with a different ISP — your local cable company or a company that you learned about through a coworker or a newspaper ad — ask the ISP to give you the proper Internet browsing software and instructions on how to set it up.

✔ Which method is *really* the best? Right now, an awful lot of people prefer using software called *Netscape Communicator* for connecting to the Internet and exploring the World Wide Web. If you're serious about Web-surfing, you may want to download a copy; it's available for free on the Internet.

✔ Learning to use an Internet browser is like driving a car; after you find out how to use one browser, you can use them all — you just have to adjust the seat belts and side mirrors. After learning Windows 98's Internet Explorer, you can pick up Netscape Communicator with only a few adjustments, and vice versa.

Using Windows 98 to Connect to the Internet

Forget about all the complicated stuff. Microsoft enables you to connect to the Internet two ways: Microsoft's way and everybody else's way. (Guess which method Microsoft made the easiest?)

Microsoft prefers that you use The Microsoft Network as your Internet service provider (you have to pay Microsoft a monthly fee); it also makes you use Microsoft's Internet Explorer software to explore the Internet's World Wide Web.

The easy, Microsoft way of connecting to the Internet

Microsoft eases you onto the Internet when you follow this method. It's quick, it's easy, and it puts the most money in Microsoft's pocket. Just dance through the steps below, clicking on the <u>N</u>ext button after you make your choice.

1. **Buy and install a copy of Windows 98.**

   After upgrading your computer to Windows 98, Microsoft leaves an icon labeled MSN — The Microsoft Network — on your desktop. (Windows 98 comes with several other Internet utilities, too, all described later in this section.)

2. **Open the Set Up The Microsoft Network icon on the Windows Desktop, read the cheery words on the window, and click on the Next button.**

   The Welcome to MSN Setup window, shown in Figure 5-1, predicts that MSN will take between 2 and 15 minutes to install itself automatically. Raise a wary eyebrow and click on the Next button.

3. **Close all your currently running programs and click on the Next button.**

   Hoggy Windows 98 insists on having the entire computer to itself while installing The Microsoft Network. Windows 98 displays a list of the currently running programs, as shown in Figure 5-2. Minimize the window, close down all the programs, return to the installation window, and click on Next.

Figure 5-1:
Microsoft's
built-in
MSN Setup
program
offers you
Internet
access
in 2 to 15
minutes,
depending
on your
computer's
crankiness
level.

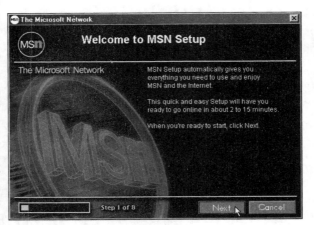

Figure 5-2:
Close any
currently
open
programs
before
installing
The
Microsoft
Network.

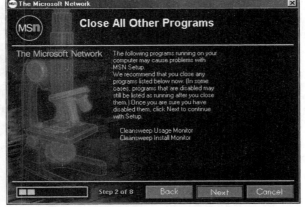

4. **Select your country of origin and click on Next.**

   This is easy enough.

5. **Read the licensing agreement and click on the I Agree button.**

   (Most people start nodding off *way* before it hits page 25. . . .)

6. **Click on Next to start the MSN software installation.**

   The screen reminds you that MSN's software consumes almost 3MB of hard disk space. If you're short on space, it's wise to stop the installation, make room on your hard drive, and start again later.

Evil Internet hackers can mess with your computer if it's hooked up wrong. To avoid this, Windows may start asking scary questions about "file and printer sharing" and people who might "access your files." To play it safe, follow Windows' instructions, letting it disable access in certain areas.

Your computer rumbles as it copies the program to the hard drive. Should Windows grow inquisitive about your current modem settings, press Ctrl+Esc (or just click on your Start button) and choose Control Panel from the Settings menu. Double-click on the Modems icon to see your current brand and setup.

Finally, the program leaves you at a You're Almost Finished window, as shown in Figure 5-3.

Figure 5-3:
Choose Yes
to access
The
Microsoft
Network
using
MSN's
network.

7. **Choose Yes, sign me up! I want a new MSN account, and click on Next.**

   As Figure 5-3 shows, MSN presents two options. Because this chapter explains the quickest, easiest way onto the Internet, you want a new MSN account on MSN's network.

   Choose the No option if you're setting up this software to access an existing MSN account.

   Click on the Next button, and the program dials MSN's accounting department.

8. **Fill out your name, choose your pricing scheme, read the MSN Membership rules, choose your user name and password, and click on Sign Me Up!**

   The MSN Signup Wizard sequence tosses several screens at you; answer the questions and click on the Next button between each step.

Remember, the *User Name* you choose is important. This is the "e-mail address" that everyone will ask for at cocktail parties — so don't pick anything too cutesy. For example, "jsmith" has a better ring to it than "Dangermouse."

Windows may tell you that it needs to write some information to your hard disk "in order to provide a more personal Web browsing experience." Go ahead and click on Yes or be subjected to endless messages begging you to do so.

9. **The sign-up part is finally done; reboot Windows 98, if the program asks. Then click on the desktop's MSN icon and type your name and password in the form that appears.**

   Or click on the new icon that now lives in the corner of Windows 98's toolbar, shown in Figure 5-4.

Figure 5-4:
MSN makes
itself
'handy'
on the
Windows
toolbar.

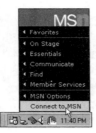

10. **Click on the Settings button, followed by the Phone Book button. Then scroll down to find your city and a phone number nearest you. After making your choices, click on OK.**

    Figure 5-5 shows you how it's done. MSN gives you the chance to select a backup phone number to dial in case your first choice is busy.

Figure 5-5:
MSN
provides
several
phone
numbers
for each
region.

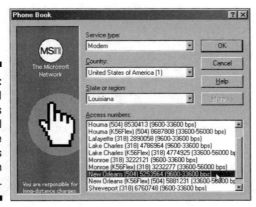

11. Click on the Connect button and then stamp your family's appropriateness level on the Internet.

Although the wild and woolly Internet is largely unrestricted, filling out these questions can help filter out varying degrees of sex, nudity, raw language, and violence from your computer. Basically, this feature requires users to type in a password before seeing anything you define for the computer as "naughty." Don't worry if you err on the side of caution when setting this up; MSN lets you change it later.

At long last, MSN stops asking questions and tosses out something interesting. Follow the menus on-screen to head wherever your interests lead you.

For example, MSN's MSNBC news guide offers extensive local coverage, as you can see in Figure 5-6.

MSN also serves as an "Internet Organizer," providing a handy starting point and guide for your Internet surfing.

Most of the information found on MSN is available free to *everybody* on the Internet. Your monthly MSN account fees basically pay for your e-mail and Internet access. Even non-MSN members can access MSN's city guides and MSNBC news partnership.

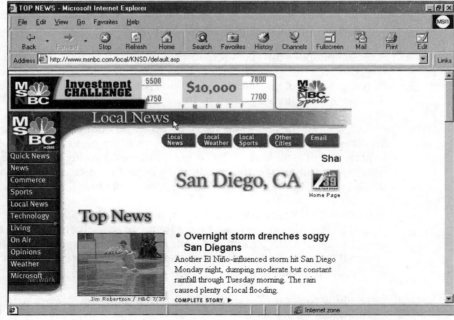

Figure 5-6: MSN allows easy access to Microsoft's wealth of Web sites and information.

What does my computer need to run MSN?

The bashful MSN says that it needs the hardware in this list. For best performance, however, you may want to double the requirements for modem speed, memory, and hard disk space.

✓ A computer with a 486/66 or higher processor

✓ 14.4 Kbps or higher modem

✓ 16MB memory

✓ 50MB additional hard disk space

✓ CD-ROM drive (if installing from disc)

✓ VGA or higher resolution graphics card (256 colors or higher)

✓ Sound card (recommended)

✓ Mouse or compatible pointing device

✓ Internet Explorer or Netscape Communicator

The more difficult, non-Microsoft way of connecting to the Internet

Although Microsoft may offer the quickest and easiest way to access the Internet, it's not necessarily the best, most extensive, or quickest. For example, it can't be accessed by cable modems yet, meaning you're probably stuck with a modem and a phone line. (MSN offers ISDN access, but that doesn't help cable modem subscribers.)

So some people skip The Microsoft Network and sign on to the World Wide Web through their own Internet service provider, like CompuServe, America Online, or a "dedicated Internet service provider" that provides access to the Internet exclusively.

In fact, a lot of these people also use Netscape Communicator — a competing, non-Microsoft Web browser that's a lot more popular than Internet Explorer. Microsoft knows that it can't force everybody to use The Microsoft Network for jumping into the Internet's seas, but Microsoft still wants you to use Internet Explorer as your Web surfboard of choice.

You can set up Windows 98 to use a non-Microsoft brand of Internet service provider, but the process can take a lot more time than Microsoft's method described earlier. Depending on your computer's setup, you may find yourself treading into some awfully unfamiliar territory filled with weird words and numbers.

Here's how to set up Windows 98's Internet Explorer to work with your current, non-Microsoft ISP:

1. **Buy and install a copy of Windows 98.**

   An icon for the Internet Explorer automatically appears on your desktop.

2. **Double-click on the Internet Explorer icon.**

   If you're clicking on it for the first time, a window for the Internet Connection Wizard appears, as shown in Figure 5-7.

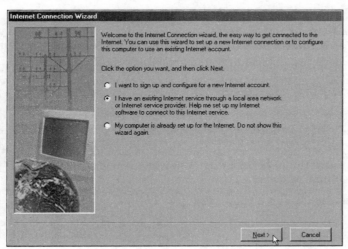

Figure 5-7: The Internet Connection Wizard tells Windows 98 about your existing Internet account.

3. **Choose the middle of the three options so the Wizard knows that you want to set up your existing Internet account, then click on Next.**

   The first option is for people who want Microsoft to handle all the work of choosing an ISP.

   Confused and want a way out? Click on the third option, saying that your computer is already set up for the Internet. The Wizard disappears, ready to reappear only when you ask for another visit.

4. **Choose the option that best describes how you plan to connect to the Internet, and then click on the Next button.**

   The Wizard then asks whether you plan to connect to the Internet over telephone lines, like most people, or over a local area network (LAN) of computers.

   Most people choose the Connect using my phone line option; that enables them to dial the Internet with an ordinary modem and phone line.

If you work in an office that shares a modem over a LAN, a network guru (officially called a network administrator) can probably set this one up for you. To run the Internet on a LAN, you may need something called "proxy numbers;" network gurus like to memorize those things.

5. **Choose the Create a new dial-up connection option; then click on Next.**

    To introduce Windows 98 to your Internet connection, you need to plug in a whole new set of numbers. That requires a whole new dial-up connection (and some patience).

6. **Find out what telephone number connects your modem to your ISP; type it and fill out the rest of the form. Click on the Next button.**

    Whether you use CompuServe, America Online, or some other variety of ISP, type in the phone number your modem dials to reach that provider.

7. **Fill in the User Name and Password that you chose when you signed up with your Internet service provider; and click on the Next button.**

    Don't remember your user name or password? You may need to shuffle through the papers that arrived when you first signed up for your ISP or online service.

8. **Choose No and click on the Next button.**

    A curiously unfriendly window asks if you need to change the mysterious Advanced Settings. Just say No, unless your ISP says to do otherwise.

    At last check, CompuServe users needed to dig into the Advanced Settings, turn to the Logon Procedure window, and type this information into the Browse box:

    ```
    C:\Program Files\Accessories\Cis.scp
    ```

9. **Create a name for your new connection, type it into the Connection name box, and click on the Next button.**

    The name you type in this box isn't as important as the number that goes into the next two boxes. After all, your mail still gets to your house if your name is spelled wrong — it's the *address* — the number on the street — that makes the difference.

10. **Click on the Yes button to set up your Internet Mail Account, and click on the Next button.**

11. **Choose the Create a new Internet mail account, and click on the Next button.**

12. **Type in your first and last name and click on the Next button.**

13. **Type in your e-mail address and click on the Next button.**

    Use the same e-mail address that you've used previously, usually
    something like dragonbreath@fire.com. Your ISP can help you figure
    out your e-mail address if you're confused.

14. **Fill in the E-mail Server Names form and click on the Next button.**

    Here's where Microsoft makes things a little sticky. First, it tosses out
    language like *POP3* and *IMAP*. Actually, POP3 is a format supported by
    almost all the main service providers, so don't let the weird words
    worry you. Just ask your ISP what to type in the form, and click on Next
    when you're done.

15. **Fill in the Internet Mail Logon form and click on the Next button.**

    With most ISPs, your e-mail logon is the same thing as your e-mail
    address. Check with your ISP to make sure. This form also asks for your
    password — the one your ISP gave you at sign-up time.

16. **At Microsoft's urging, choose a "friendly" name for your new ac-
    count. Type it into the box and click on the Next button.**

    Nothing secret here; just type in the name of your ISP.

17. **Choose Yes to set up for the Internet discussion forums called
    newsgroups, and click on the Next button.**

18. **Choose Create a new Internet news account and click on the Next
    button.**

19. **Type your first and last name and click on the Next button.**

20. **Type the e-mail address that your ISP assigned to you and click on
    the Next button.**

    Yawn. You did this way back in Step 13, too.

21. **Type the name of the Internet news server that your ISP gave you
    and click on the Next button.**

    The name of the news server computer is another one of those details
    that only your ISP can give you.

    When in doubt as to your official news server's name, just type in the
    word *news,* all by itself. That's the name that most servers use, anyway.

22. **Think up another "friendly name," this time for your news setup.
    Type it in and then click on the Next button.**

    Just type the word *news,* all by itself.

23. **Choose No for setting up the Internet Directory Service and click on
    the Next button.**

    This is one of those "extras" that you can set up later if necessary.

24. **Click on the Finish button.**

Now you can test the thing and hope that it works. If you have a dedicated Internet service provider, Internet Explorer may be able to log on without problems. If you have an online service, Internet Explorer probably won't work on the first try.

The Wizard reminds you that you can tweak your hard-won setup anytime you want. Just click on the Windows 98 Start button and place the cursor on <u>P</u>rograms and then on Internet Explorer. Finally, click on Connection Wizard.

25. **Return to the Windows 98 desktop and double-click on the Internet Explorer icon to test everything.**

You should now head onto the Internet without much more ado — but get a little rest, eh? Bypassing Windows' built-in machinery to install your own Internet parts is like bringing your own bottle of wine to a fancy restaurant: You know that the owners don't like it, but they put up with you in the hopes that you may become a steady customer.

Similarly, Microsoft hopes Internet Explorer's ease of installation, constant presence, and strong barrage of features can keep you from bringing any competing brands of wine close to your keyboard.

Making Internet Explorer Behave Properly

Microsoft blurs the boundaries between its Internet software — Internet Explorer — and Windows. Buttons beckon from every crevice, begging to send Internet Explorer scurrying off to the Internet to ferret out information.

Vice versa, Internet Explorer can run any of your Windows 98 programs just as easily. If you're in the mood, you can decorate the Windows toolbar with customized Internet on-ramps.

The following tips and tricks for Internet Explorer make sense of the shuffle and let you get some actual work done.

Creating shortcuts to favorite Internet sites

Under Windows 98, Internet Explorer makes it almost too easy to head to the Web for information or entertainment. Now you can create shortcuts to your favorite Internet sites — storing them right on your desktop or inside any folder that you prefer.

1. **Start Internet Explorer and head to your favorite Internet site.**

2. **Right-click on an empty area on your chosen Web page.**

   A menu rises from the depths.

3. **Choose the Create Shortcut option and click on the OK button on the following page.**

   Internet Explorer announces that it will create a shortcut to that Web page; click on the OK button, and the shortcut icon appears on your desktop, like the one in Figure 5-8.

sandiego.sid...

Figure 5-8:
Collect shortcuts to favorite Internet sites right on your desktop.

When your desktop starts showing too much of a good thing, simply drag the Web page shortcuts into any folder that seems to be a good fit.

If the pop-up menu features a <u>S</u>ave Picture As option instead of Create Shor<u>t</u>cut, you need to right-click on a different spot, away from the page's graphics or pictures. Move to a relatively blank area and try again.

Using AutoSearch to find something fast

The Internet Explorer Address bar — that box along the window's top where you type in your destination — normally whisks you off to another computer. Type **www.usatoday.com** into the Address bar, for example, and press Enter; Internet Explorer whisks you to the *USA Today* Web site and starts flipping the pages.

But the Address bar wears other hats, too. In fact, the Address bar is one of the most convenient ways to rip a quick piece of information from the Internet's vast drawers — even when you don't know exactly which Web page you need.

When you need answers — *fast* — put Internet Explorer's timesaving AutoSearch tool to work at filtering through the Internet's vast amounts of computerized information.

1. **Start Internet Explorer.**

2. **Think of words that describe your subject.**

   Don't get elaborate here; in fact, the fewer words, the better.

3. **Click in the Address bar and type** go, **a space, and your search term.**

   After wiping the paint from his hands, Paul Cézanne types **go watercolor supplies** into the Address bar and presses Enter. Internet Explorer automatically chooses an appropriate search engine and digs up whatever information it can.

   Typing **go watercolor supplies** in the Address bar yielded the results in Figure 5-9.

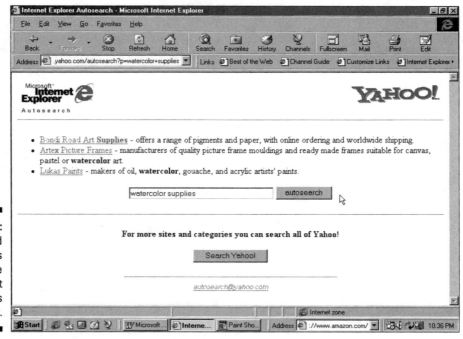

Figure 5-9:
Harried
searches
are the
Internet
Explorer's
specialty.

Downloading a file

The Internet has never been more packed with free programs and files. If you trust a Web site and the programs or files it offers — some sites *do* have evil viruses, you know — feel free to copy 'em onto your computer.

1. **Start Internet Explorer and head to the Web page.**

2. **Right-click on the desired program's name or icon, known as its *link* in Web parlance.**

   Internet Explorer tosses out a window similar to the one in Figure 5-10, asking whether to run that program or file immediately or save it to your computer's hard disk.

Figure 5-10: Download new files onto your computer's hard drive and scan them for viruses before running them.

3. **Choose the S̲ave this program to disk option and click on OK.**

   Always save a new file to your hard disk instead of running it right away. Doing so gives you a chance to scan the download for *viruses* — malicious programs that can destroy your computer's data. Virus checkers are described in Chapter 15.

4. **When Internet Explorer asks where to store the newcomer, create a customized folder that's easy to identify later, store the file inside the new folder, and click on S̲ave.**

   Just as with Windows 95, a click on the little exploding folder icon in the Save As window's upper-right corner creates a new folder in your current window. Give it a name that describes its upcoming contents and click on S̲ave.

   The file begins to copy onto your computer. Always helpful, Internet Explorer gauges the file's progress in a window similar to the one in Figure 5-11, showing you how much of the file remains to be downloaded, as well as how long it should take.

Figure 5-11:
This
antivirus
program
shouldn't
take too
much
longer to
download.

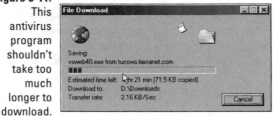

5. Click on OK after the program finishes downloading.

After the program arrives on your hard drive, check it for viruses. You probably have to use WinZip (described in Chapter 12) to decompress the file, too.

Importing Netscape or another browser's bookmarks into Internet Explorer

The new, improved Internet Explorer just might break your romance with an old Internet browser, like Netscape Communicator. But packing up your Internet lifestyle and moving it to another browser can cause big problems.

First and foremost, how can you save the locations of all those treasured Web sites listed in your Netscape program? What happens to those Netscape bookmarks?

A *bookmark* is the Netscape browser's name for "saved" Web sites; it's the same as an Internet Explorer "Favorite" — a quick way to return to a site of special value to you.

Alas, no simple "Import Bookmarks" command exists. You have only three ways to import your old bookmarks: an easy but time-consuming way, a more complex but faster way, and a cheating method that doesn't import the bookmarks at all but makes them easily accessible.

First, here's the easy-but-slow method:

1. Start Internet Explorer.

2. Click on File, choose Open, and then click on the Browse button.

3. **Find your Netscape folder, open the Users folder, and open a file called bookmark.**

   If several people use your computer, you may need to open another folder — one with your name on it — before reaching the coveted bookmark file.

   A list of your old bookmarks should appear in Internet Explorer.

   Second, here's the quick cheating method of transferring bookmarks: While the list of your old bookmarks appears on-screen in Step 4, click on Favorites, choose Add to Favorites, and name the spot as your Old Bookmarks. That leaves you with a handy, clickable reference of your former Netscape addresses. It's so handy, in fact, that you may not want to bother reading the rest of this section.

4. **Right-click on a bookmark in the Internet Explorer window, and then click on Add to Favorites.**

5. **Lather, rinse, and repeat Step 4 for each of your old bookmarks.**

The third and fastest method, recommended by Jay Tsukamoto, Honolulu Web Guru, involves Microsoft's free Bookmarks Converter program that converts all your Netscape bookmarks to Internet Explorer Favorites. Type **support.microsoft.com/download/support/mslfiles/Winbm2fv.exe** into Internet Explorer's Address bar and press Enter to download the program. Double-click on the 150K file when it arrives, and it begins converting bookmarks to Favorites.

Weaseling out of tricky Internet situations

Some Windows 98 setups involve uncomfortably special situations. These additional nudges can help get that Internet connection going.

Can I share a single fast modem among my computer network?

Face it: A network can be expensive to set up. Each computer needs a special network card and cable to connect to the network. Wouldn't it be nice to save some cash by letting all the computers on your network share a single fast Internet connection? Why buy a fast modem and phone connection for each computer on the network?

The prospect of a single connection probably sounds even more enchanting to cable modem users, who want all their network's computers to benefit from the ultra-fast download times.

If this describes your situation, check out WinGate — software that enables a network of computers to share a single Internet connection.

To share a modem under WinGate, the computers must be equipped with network cards and configured in a LAN (local area network), as described in Chapter 17.

Install WinGate on the computer with the Internet connection and configure the Internet Connection Wizard to work under a LAN setup. Finally, tell Internet Explorer and Outlook Express (covered in Chapter 6) to run under a *proxy server*.

WinGate's detailed Help file gives the full scoop on proxy servers and other bits of network hogwash, but don't try installing WinGate the day before your report's due. This sort of networking can take a few tweaks before everything's comfortable with each other.

WinGate charges by the number of computers that you plan to connect with it. Connecting two computers is freeware — you don't have to pay to use the program — and the price rises from there. For more information, visit the WinGate site at www.wingate.net and nose around.

I need to reach a computer that isn't on the Internet!

Windows 98 comes with a program called HyperTerminal that can dial up any computer fitted with a modem — even if it's not a Web site. The equivalent of today's slide rule, HyperTerminal remains a remnant of earlier days when everybody dialed computers directly — they didn't go through the Internet's vast network of computers.

Chances are, you may never need to use HyperTerminal. That's because it's meant for text, not pictures. You may find colors and colored text, but certainly none of the flashy stuff seen on the Internet.

But if you do need a bare-bones telecommunications program, HyperTerminal's icon hides in the Start menu's Communications menu area (which lurks in the Accessories menu of the Programs menu).

- ✔ HyperTerminal keeps a few icons in its folder. Open the CompuServe icon to visit CompuServe's text-based forums, or check your e-mail on AT&T Mail or MCI Mail.

- ✔ To download goodies, first tell the computer that you've dialed to start sending the files; then click on <u>R</u>eceive File from HyperTerminal's <u>T</u>ransfer menu and choose Zmodem with Crash Recovery as your receiving protocol.

Internet Explorer toys

Windows 98 stashes a host of Internet-related programs under the Start button. Click on Start, then Programs, and finally Internet Explorer to see them.

Unfortunately, this program lineup isn't as exciting as it first appears. Table 5-2 gives you the scoop.

Table 5-2	Internet Explorer's Army of Free Programs
This Program . . .	*Does This Stuff*
Address Book	Windows 98 stores e-mail addresses and gobs of other contact information here; it's covered in Chapter 6.
Connection Wizard	This program helps connect Windows 98 to the Internet. Return here anytime to reconfigure any option.
FrontPage Express	FrontPage Express is Microsoft's pared-down Web page builder, covered in Chapter 8.
Internet Explorer	Ignore this one. It's yet *another* place to load Internet Explorer, if you can't find the Taskbar, desktop icon, or appropriate corner of just about any folder.
Microsoft Chat	This program enables you to type casual conversation to other Microsoft Network users sitting at their keyboards around the world. Genuine chat fans yak for hours, discussing topics from taxes to taxidermy.
Microsoft NetMeeting	Like Microsoft Chat, NetMeeting enables businesspeople to carry out their conversations over their keyboards instead of over the boardroom table. Add a speaker, microphone, camera, and video capture card, and everybody can see and hear everybody else. Additional options include a whiteboard for sharing drawings or text.
NetShow Player	Microsoft developed NetShow Player to work with multimedia files like audio and video. Simply click on a NetShow icon and Player should reveal its contents. Although designed specifically to work with NetMeeting (see above), NetShow Player can play any compatible content — and you're seeing an increasing amount of it on the Internet.
Outlook Express	This new and improved e-mail program is covered in Chapter 6.
Personal Web Server	Another program tailored to those who create their own Web pages; see Chapter 8.
Web Publishing Wizard	You guessed it: This one's also covered in Chapter 8.

Chapter 6

Outlook Express: The E-Mail Lasso

....

....

*O*utlook Express, Windows 98's nifty new e-mail program, does a lot more than let you swap mail over computer screens. By flipping some switches, you can make it filter out junk mail — in advance — and organize the messages that you *do* want to read.

Forget about black letters on a computer's white background; Outlook Express offers themed stationery, fancy fonts, and even colors to create customized messages.

This chapter shows you how to put Microsoft's Outlook Express to work at sending, receiving, and organizing your electronic mail.

Configuring Outlook Express

Chances are, you already set up Windows 98 to work with your Internet service provider (ISP); if not, that stuff's covered in Chapter 5. After you introduce Windows 98 to your ISP, Outlook Express should be armed with the picky details that it needs for sending and retrieving e-mail. Rev up Outlook Express by double-clicking on its icon on your desktop, and you're off.

If you haven't formally introduced Windows 98 to your Internet account, however, the Internet Connection Wizard bullies its way onto the screen. Flip back to Chapter 5's section, "The more difficult, non-Microsoft way of connecting to the Internet" for a blow-by-blow description of your upcoming fight with the Internet connectors. (Aw, it might not be *that* bad. . . .)

Moved? Changed your ISP or e-mail account settings? Then tell Outlook Express by clicking on Tools and choosing Accounts. From there, click on the appropriate tab to change your settings.

I've moved! Can I import old e-mail addresses into Outlook Express?

Most people consider e-mail to be the Internet's most valuable aspect. That's why changing e-mail programs can be as frightening as moving the Steinway to a new apartment: Switching to Outlook Express means moving all the old program's e-mail addresses to the new program. How?

Fortunately, Outlook Express extends a welcoming hand almost immediately.

1. **Click on the program's Inbox icon.**

2. **Click on File from the main menu.**

3. **Follow that with Import and then Address Book.**

4. **When a list of competing e-mail programs pops up in a window, select your old program's name from the list and click on the Import button.**

   Your addresses copy themselves into their new mailbox, as shown in Figure 6-1.

5. **Click on the Close button to finish.**

Figure 6-1: Eager to upgrade, Outlook Express handily extracts e-mail addresses from other programs' address books and places them into its address book.

Address Book Import Tool

Address book import has completed successfully.

Eudora Pro or Light Address Book (through v3.0)
LDIF - LDAP Data Interchange Format
Microsoft Exchange Personal Address Book
Microsoft Internet Mail for Windows 3.1 Address Book
Netscape Address Book (v2 or v3)
Netscape Communicator Address Book (v4)
Text File (Comma Separated Values)

Import

Close

If Outlook Express can't locate your old address book, it invites you to search yourself. Click on <u>Y</u>es for a chance to rummage through the lists of files, folders, and disk drives in the window that appears.

When you find the program's address book, double-click on its filename; Outlook Express takes over from there.

Outlook Express can also salvage old messages from the e-mail program that you're now tossing by the wayside. Click on <u>F</u>ile from the Outlook Express main menu, and then click on <u>I</u>mport and choose the <u>M</u>essages option. Choose your old e-mail program's name from the list, just as you did with the address book, and the converter does its work. Saved messages can be crucial to tracking and carrying out projects, so import your old messages immediately after importing your old address book.

Getting Familiar with Outlook Express

The overeager Outlook Express constantly fills the screen with windows, bars, buttons, and other embarrassing frivolity. Once you pass its initial barrage of visual confetti, however, the program works surprisingly well.

Easy-to-find buttons enable you to write mail, send and receive messages, and look up e-mail addresses of your friends.

Everything's neatly organized in two (or more) on-screen columns. The Outlook bar lives on the left, where its clicked-upon icons spill their contents onto the folder list in the middle; a batch of messages or icons appear in the right-most column.

For example, see how the Outlook bar's Outlook Express folder is highlighted in Figure 6-2? That folder's contents appear on the right: amazingly realistic buttons resembling envelopes, a message pad, address book, and other goodies. Click on any of those buttons to activate the program. Click on the address book to search for a friend's e-mail information, for example.

To nudge some of these menu bars aside and make more elbow room for composing and reading actual e-mail, strip down Outlook Express to a more utilitarian layout. For example, dump the left-most Outlook bar (a flashy but useless duplicate of the information in its neighboring Folder list), head to the menu bar, click on <u>V</u>iew, and then click on <u>L</u>ayout. Click next to the <u>O</u>utlook Bar option until the check mark disappears. (Head back here to turn off the program's Tip of the Day, too.)

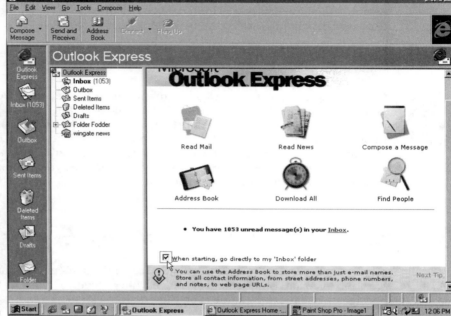

Figure 6-2:
Outlook
Express
houses
buttons for
reading and
composing
e-mail, as
well as
working
with
newsgroup
messages.

Viewing a message in Outlook Express

Click on the Inbox or Read Mail icon to start reading messages that have landed in your electronic mailbox. The Outlook Express window splits in half; the top displays a list of message subjects, with one header highlighted. The window's bottom half displays the contents of the highlighted message.

Click once on a message's header to see a quick view of its contents — the message spills its guts in the bottom half of the main Outlook Express window, called the *preview pane,* as shown in Figure 6-3.

Prefer seeing a message in its own window? Double-click on a message header, and the message's contents leap to the forefront inside their own new window.

You can set up Outlook Express to display your Inbox — the holding tank for all new e-mail — automatically whenever you launch the program. Head to the main Outlook Express page — the top-most page with all the slick envelope and memo icons — and click in the bottom-most box next to the option <u>W</u>hen starting, go directly to my 'Inbox' folder. (You can change this setting back to normal if the pressure of all that unanswered e-mail gets to be too much.)

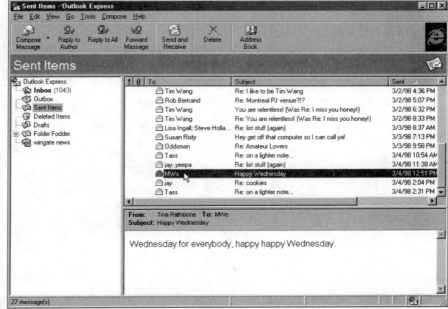

Figure 6-3:
Click on a
message
header,
and that
message's
contents
appear
below.

Reading your e-mail

Even if nobody knows your e-mail address yet, chances are that at least one
e-mail message is waiting in your Inbox folder: Friendly ol' Microsoft automatically welcomes everybody to Outlook Express.

To read your greeting, click on the Inbox folder. Double-click on your
message's little envelope icon — the one addressed from Microsoft. The
Message Window appears, containing the text of your message. From here,
you can click on any of the message window's toolbar icons to Save, Print,
Copy, Delete, Reply to, or Forward your message.

A right-click on any message header in Outlook Express brings a large menu,
as shown in Figure 6-4. Choose your option, and Outlook Express carries out
your command.

Replying to your e-mail

You should thank Microsoft for sending you your first Outlook Express
message, and for several reasons:

 ✔ First, responding to e-mail is good practice for beginners.

 ✔ Second, it's a good way to make sure that your oft-complicated e-mail
 system is finally set up and working.

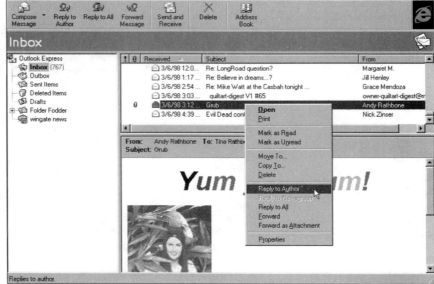

Figure 6-4:
Right-click
on any
message's
subject line
for quick
access to
frequently
used
commands.

> ✔ Finally, you can be sure that nobody will laugh at you if something goes
> wrong with your message: All of Microsoft's welcoming e-mail is pro-
> cessed by robots.

Follow these steps to reply to a message:

1. **Click on the Inbox folder from the Folder list.**

2. **Double-click on Microsoft's "Welcome" or "Security Features" message from the message list.**

   A window appears, displaying Microsoft's message.

3. **Click on the single person icon — the button where a single arrow
   points to a guy's chin.**

   Figure 6-5 shows which button to push (the arrow's pointing at it in the
   figure). If you prefer using the menu bar, choose Reply to Author from
   the Compose menu.

4. **Type your message in the window.**

   Two cool things happen. The person you're replying to appears in the
   To field, while the subject line of the original message shows up in the
   Subject field, preceded by Re: (for Regarding).

   Also, the entire text of the original message shows up in your reply.
   Outlook Express automatically quotes the sender's message to make
   sure that everybody remembers what they're talking about.

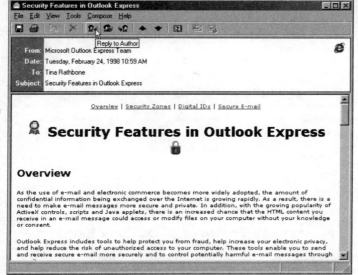

Figure 6-5: Click on the first of the three "person" icons to reply to the author of the message.

Don't see the text of the message you're replying to in the message body window? Choose <u>T</u>ools from the Outlook Express program's menu bar and click on <u>O</u>ptions. Finally, click on the Send tab, and click until a check mark appears in the In<u>c</u>lude message in reply box.

Be sure to delete all but the most pertinent parts of the original message quote — retaining just enough text to remind your correspondent what your conversation's about. Use the mouse to highlight the extraneous text, and then press the Delete key.

People may look at you as a woefully inept newbie if you thoughtlessly quote an entire message body in your reply. It's particularly embarrassing when the quote is much longer than your reply.

5. **Click on the Send button along the message toolbar, as Figure 6-6 shows.**

   A copy of your reply automatically appears in your Sent Items folder.

If you don't see copies of sent messages in your Sent Items folder, head to the Menu bar and choose <u>T</u>ools➪<u>O</u>ptions. Click on the Send tab, and click until a check mark appears next to the Sa<u>v</u>e copy of sent messages in the Sent Items folder option box.

Can't see any messages in your Sent Items folder? Do the other folders in which you store old messages look empty, too? Don't panic; you've probably told Outlook Express to display only *unread* messages. To view all your messages — read and unread — head to the menu bar and choose <u>V</u>iew➪ Current <u>V</u>iew, and click on the <u>A</u>ll Messages option.

Figure 6-6:
Click on the
Send button
after you
finish your
reply.

Composing a message on a brand-new topic

After the whole e-mail thing becomes routine, you may find that most of your e-mail correspondence involves replying to others' messages. When you want to send a message on a brand-new topic, follow these steps.

1. From the menu bar, click on Compose and then click on New Message.

A window similar to the one in Figure 6-7 appears, with the cursor blinking in the To field.

2. Type your correspondent's name or e-mail address in the To field.

If the name already exists in your Address Book, the sly Outlook Express immediately commandeers the keyboard and fills in the remainder of the name for you.

To browse your Address Book for the recipient's e-mail address, click on the little index card icon to the left of the blank To field.

Figure 6-7:
Composing
a message
in Outlook
Express.

3. **Click to the right of the Subject field and type a brief summary of your message's topic.**

4. **Click in the large message body window and type your message.**

5. **Check your spelling, if you wish.**

   Although it's entirely up to you, checking for any particularly embarasing mispeled words before sending off that message is a good idea. Click on Tools on the menu bar, and then click on Spelling. Outlook Express highlights the questionable words it finds and displays the Spelling dialog box, where you can correct the word by typing over it or adding it to the built-in dictionary.

6. **Click on the Send button on the Outlook Express toolbar.**

   Your message travels to your Internet service provider's mail computer and on to your recipients.

   Of course, no law says that you have to send the message immediately. Choose Send Later from the File menu to save your handiwork in your Outbox until you're ready to send it. Or if your message is a work in progress, save your message as a draft by choosing Save from the File menu. When you're ready to work on it some more, head to the Folder list, click on the Drafts folder, and locate and double-click on your message.

Doing More with Outlook Express

The following tips and tricks enable you to get even more out of working with Outlook Express. You may not send and receive lots of e-mail, but you can waste a lot of time on fun, frilly stuff, like using pretty colors and automatically organizing your incoming mail into its own folders.

Making lavish e-mail with swirling backgrounds, fancy fonts, and pretty colors

If your recipient uses Outlook Express or some other e-mail program that can handle special formatting, you don't have to rely on words alone to get your message across. Outlook Express can gussy up your messages with fancy fonts, colors, numbered lists (like the upcoming one), links to Web sites, pictures, and other enhancements.

Because most e-mail programs can handle *HTML code* — a special formatting language — follow these steps to add more pizzazz to your e-mail messages. But if your buddies say that your incoming e-mail looks weird or is hard to read through their e-mail readers, ignore this section; stay away from the HTML options described in this section and use plain ol' text.

1. **Choose Compose Message from the menu to start a new message.**

2. **From the message window's menu bar, choose Rich Text (HTML) from the Format menu, and start typing your message into the window.**

   A black dot appears next to the Rich Text (HTML) option. Remember, if you're sending mail to somebody whose older computer chokes on fancy formatting, choose the Plain Text option instead.

3. **In your message window, click where you want the special formatting to appear.**

   If you want to add a numbered list to your message, for example, click where you want the list to start.

   Or if you want to change your text to, say, bright green, highlight the text to change, as you would in your normal word-processing program.

4. **On the formatting toolbar, that new clump of tools that appeared in Step 2, click on the effect that strikes your fancy.**

   Figure 6-8 shows the word *Red* after being tinted red with a click on the formatting toolbar's palette tool. As the figure shows, you can easily go wild and choose dozens of other formatting options as well.

   Now you can click on the Send button or decorate your message further.

Neighbourhood Watch

The following information has been received from the Police

Spate of burglaries in Ferry Brow and Netherton areas.

Increased vigilance particularly at night time. There will be additional Police officers in the area. Dial 999 if needed.

Neighbourhood Watch

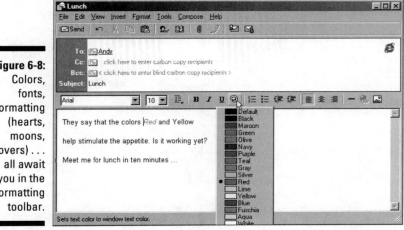

Figure 6-8:
Colors,
fonts,
formatting
(hearts,
moons,
clovers) . . .
all await
you in the
formatting
toolbar.

 Use restraint when you're tempted to get fancy with formatting — or your recipients may consider you dorky. That's especially true when sending messages to a *mailing list* or *newsgroup* where you can't be sure that everyone's e-mail program enjoys the same HTML capabilities.

Using stationery

If somehow the formatting tools in Outlook Express seem boring, you can type your message in one of dozens of predesigned stationery forms by following these steps:

1. **Click on Compose from the menu, click on New Message using option, and click on one of the stationery styles that pops up.**

   Don't like those styles? Click on More Stationery to bring up a list of other styles.

2. **Double-click on a name that sounds interesting.**

   Outlook Express gives you peek at it.

3. **Choose the stationery that you like, type your message, and click on Send as usual.**

   In Figure 6-9, for example, More Stationery uncovered this great Chicken Soup form.

Checking automatically for e-mail

If you stay online for long periods, you may enjoy the ability to tell Outlook Express to check for e-mail automatically and let you know when something's waiting in the mailbox.

Figure 6-9:
You can
choose one
of the
stationery
forms for
added fun.

1. **Choose Options from the Tools menu and click on the General tab.**

2. **Click in the box next to the Check for New Messages Every 10 Minutes.**

   When the check mark appears in the box, Outlook Express checks for new messages every 10 minutes.

On a cable modem, a network, or another service that's constantly connected to the Internet? Feel free to change the 10 minutes to 1 minute. That's the quickest way to know about newly arriving e-mail.

Organizing your e-mail

Outlook Express works like a giant filing cabinet and comes with its own set of folders — logical places to receive, store, organize, and retrieve your e-mail.

- ✔ The Inbox folder holds your new e-mail; messages remain here even after you read them until you move them into other folders.

- ✔ The Outbox folder holds messages you compose if you click on the File menu's Send Later instead of Send Message. This folder empties after you click on the Send and Receive button, when your messages shuttle over the Internet to your recipients.

✔ The Sent Items folder stores every message you've ever sent to anyone — a great record-keeping system.

✔ The Drafts folder stores messages that you still want to work on a little
more before sending — but only if you click on File and then click on
Save instead of clicking on Send Message.

Automatically sorting your e-mail

After living the e-mail lifestyle for a few months, the deluge begins: Junk
mail — often called *spam* in the computer community — begins to infiltrate
your electronic mailbox. Luckily, the ever-helpful Outlook Express offers a
way to keep the trash from reaching your mailbox.

Plus, it organizes and prioritizes the incoming letters so that you can read
the good stuff before plowing through the boring stuff. The key is the Inbox
Assistant, called into service from the Tools menu.

Click on the Inbox Assistant's Add button and begin customizing your setup,
as shown in Figure 6-10.

Figure 6-10:
Create a
customized
page
describing
each of
your special
searches,
and Inbox
Assistant
filters that
incoming
information
into special
folders
for easy
access.

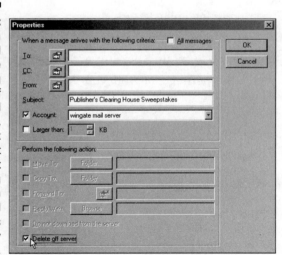

For example, following these steps stops all the "You're Invited to Visit"
messages from reaching your mailbox.

1. Choose Inbox Assistant from the Tools menu.

2. **Click on the Inbox Assistant's Add button.**

   You need to click on this Add button for each special filter that you want to set up.

3. **Type the subject that you want filtered in the Subject box.**

   For example, if you want to filter out all mail that arrives in your mailbox with the word *sex* in the subject line, type the word **sex** into the Subject box.

   Or if you particularly enjoy mail from a particular person, type that person's last name in the From box. Step 5 shows you how to make Outlook Express automatically save that mail in a special place.

4. **Click in the Account box and choose your Internet account from the list.**

   You probably have just one to choose from.

5. **Click on the action you want taken with those filtered messages.**

   In this case, you want any message with the word *sex* in its subject box to be deleted from the server, so put a check mark in the Delete off server box.

   Or if you want to move your favorite friend's e-mail to a special folder, click in the Move to box, click on the Folder button, and choose a folder for stashing your friend's incoming letters.

6. **Click on the OK button to save those criteria.**

7. **Repeat Steps 2 through 6 to set up filters for any other information.**

   The filter works great for putting mail from your favorite people into a special folder. Feel free to filter any "adult" message junk mail from your mailbox before you even see it. (After using the Internet for a few months, you'll become aware of the message headers used by most "adult" messages.)

   Although these filters are a great start for organizing your incoming e-mail and filtering it automatically, they're not always completely dependable. If the hospital sends you e-mail with the subject saying, "Sex of Your Baby is Boy," your filter will mistake it for trash and delete it automatically. Be careful.

Creating a folder of your own

It's easy to forget to answer an important e-mail message because it gets lost in the pile. To make sure that you remember, create a new folder called Answer this, and then file urgent messages there as you read them in your Inbox.

To create the new folder, right-click on any folder in the Folder list and choose New Folder. A window similar to the one in Figure 6-11 appears. Click on the folder where you want the new folder to appear, and type **Answer this** into the box, as shown in Figure 6-11.

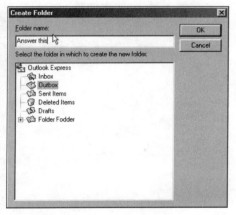

Figure 6-11: Outlook Express makes a folder where you can stash e-mail that requires your immediate response.

When traveling or checking your e-mail on somebody else's computer, tell Outlook Express to save your messages on your Internet service provider's mail server. Normally, Outlook Express deletes read messages. But because you want to have the messages waiting for you at home, follow these steps:

1. **Choose Tools from the menu bar and click on Accounts.**

2. **Click the Mail tab and make sure that your mail account name is highlighted.**

3. **Click on the Properties button and then on the Advanced tab.**

4. **Under the Delivery option, click until a check mark appears next to Leave a copy of messages on server.**

Chapter 7

Taming the Active Desktop

· ·

· ·

*W*indows 98's Active Desktops don't vibrate, unless you whack the side of your monitor. No, an Active Desktop is just another way Microsoft intends to blend Windows 98 and the Internet into a single product.

If you don't give a gnat's navel about the Internet, don't bother with this chapter; it's for Internet users looking for a simple new way to tap into the Web's flow of information.

However, you really don't have to care about the Internet to enjoy Active Desktop. There's nothing complicated about cranking up your PC's speakers, connecting to the Active Desktop Jukebox, and enjoying hearing the latest releases from major labels.

Toss in constantly updating sports scores or news headlines, and Active Desktop starts making sense to anybody. Active Desktop users don't need to bother calling the Internet; the computer automatically dials their ISP and connects to their favorite Web sites and uses the information as intelligent wallpaper. Want a perpetually scrolling stock ticker or a weather map that constantly stays up-to-date? Active Desktop's click-n-go gallery of programs may be right up your alley.

Turning On the Active Desktop

Turning on the Active Desktop is a simple, two-click process: Right-click on any blank part of the desktop, point at <u>A</u>ctive Desktop from the pop-up menu, and click on View As <u>W</u>eb Page, as shown in Figure 7-1.

Figure 7-1:
Right-click on a blank area of your desktop, and choose View As Web Page to turn on your Active Desktop's features.

As the Active Desktop springs to life, it brings along its channel bar — a computerized remote control for transporting you to nearly a dozen on-screen *channels*. Channels are tickets to the promotional lobbies of Disney, Warner Bros., America Online, and a handful of others, but forget about the channels for now; rumor has it that Microsoft's going to drop them soon.

Instead, check out the real goods: Active Desktop's gallery of goodies for embedding in your desktop. Table 7-1 describes some of the Active Desktop fun; the next section shows you how to place any of these items on your desktop.

Table 7-1	Active Desktop Items
What It Is	*What It Does*
Channel Bar	Jumps quickly to a variety of potential Active Desktop locations.
Microsoft Investor Ticker	A customizable ticker of Wall Street quotes, constantly spewing prices and business news.
CNET	Flashing computer-news headlines.
Women's Wire	A publication dealing with women's issues.
Fortune Stock Chart	A cool chart showing exactly how much money you're currently making (or losing) on the stock market.
Desktop ScoreCenter — CBS SportsLine	Want to know who's beating whom? Put this little scorekeeper in the screen's corner to keep constant track.

What It Is	What It Does
ESPN SportsZone	Same scores, different provider.
AudioNet Jukebox	Got a sound card and some speakers hooked up to the computer? Listen to cuts from CDs. (And hook up that computer to the stereo, too, eh?)
eDrive: Entertainment Drive: Movie News	Linda Fiorentino tells all!
Paramount Entertainment News	Howard Stern tells all!
Sony Desktop Item	A commercial for Sony music.
Trip: World Pictures	A revolving collage of postcards from exotic places.
Expedia Maps: Address Finder	Way cool, if you live in the USA. Enter any two street addresses in the USA, and Expedia spits out a map detailing the route between the two points.
MSNBC Weather Map	Big and boring, it tacks a few temperature numbers on a few states and calls it a day.
MSN Custom Page	The "Control Panel" of the Active Desktop, this lets you customize the news, sports scores, and other information that floats through the Internet and onto your desktop.
3D Java Clock	A spiraling digital clock.
Site Builder Network	Basically a magazine for Web programmers.
Search the ZDNet Archives	More computer news headlines, as well as an electronic librarian for searching back issues of Ziff Davis computer magazines like PC Week.
Microsoft Search Component	Type your subject in the box and click on Go to search the Web.
Companies Online	A peek at a company's stock updates, as well as the last business week's worth of updates.
Comic Clock	Bored? Click here to see a new comic strip. Or just wait; the strip updates itself at certain intervals.
J-Track Satellite Tracking	A fantastic map of the world with moving pictures showing the current locations of satellites. It's fun, especially when you turn the weather stuff on!

 ✔ Active Desktops work best for people who have constant, fast connections to the Internet, like those supplied by many networks and cable modems. You need that constant connection to have a constant update on your desktop.

 ✔ Active Desktop makes up for slower, intermittent connections in other ways, however. For example, it can dial your Internet provider at midnight, download your favorite Web site's entire sum of information, and leave it on your hard drive for perusal the next day. Or if 24-hour grabs aren't quick enough, Active Desktop can dial up for hourly updates.

 ✔ Setting up an Active Desktop is easy; fine-tuning one can be time-consuming, especially getting everything arranged artfully on a desktop smaller than 1024 x 768.

 ✔ With more Channels appearing daily — each with a custom set of options — an Active Desktop can be a fantastic procrastination tool.

Putting an Active Desktop item on your desktop

Although you can transform any favorite Web site into a constantly monitored Active Desktop item, start with something quick and easy. Visit Microsoft's gallery and try one of the prepackaged items.

1. **Right-click on any blank part of the desktop and point at <u>A</u>ctive Desktop from the pop-up menu.**

2. **Click on View As <u>W</u>eb Page.**

   You saw that stuff in Figure 7-1; the channel bar appears, as shown in Figure 7-2. Now it's time to start adding the fun stuff.

   Note: Clicking on View As <u>W</u>eb Page in Step 2 toggles the Web page view on and off. Click until the option has a check mark next to it on the menu.

3. **Right-click on a blank part of the desktop, choose P<u>r</u>operties, and click on the Web tab.**

   The Active Desktop window appears, as shown in Figure 7-3.

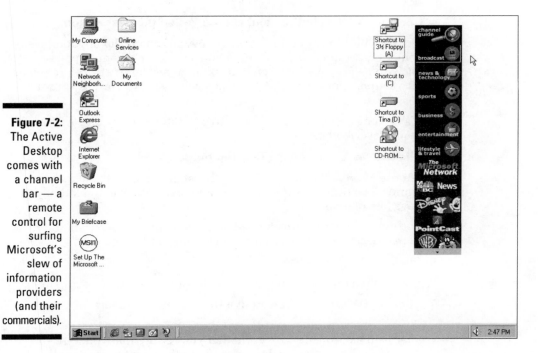

Figure 7-2:
The Active
Desktop
comes with
a channel
bar — a
remote
control for
surfing
Microsoft's
slew of
information
providers
(and their
commercials).

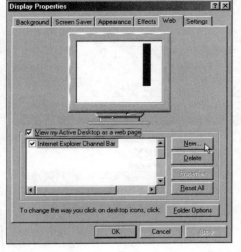

Figure 7-3:
The Web
tab displays
the channel
bar's
placement
on your
monitor and
lets you
choose new
Desktop
items.

4. Click on the New button, and choose Yes on the next button.

The New button says that you want new, automatically updating Web content on your desktop. The Yes button says you want to peruse Microsoft's prepackaged Active Desktop items. Internet Explorer leaps into action, connecting to Microsoft's gallery of goodies, as shown in Figure 7-4.

A sparkling carnival of activity, Active Desktop Gallery displays the items described in Table 7-1.

5. Click on an Add to Active Desktop button.

Choose Microsoft Investor Ticker's constant stream of Wall Street figures: The little Ticker looks cool, and onlookers will think that you have lots of money.

The mouse pointer turns into a hand when hovering over an Add to Active Desktop button, as shown in the bottom of Figure 7-4.

6. Click on the Yes button.

Yes, you're sure that you want to check out the Active Desktop item.

7. Click on OK, and the new Active Desktop item appears on your desktop.

Microsoft asks one last time whether you're sure that you want to download that Active Desktop item, but offers a bit more than that. Click on the Customize Subscription button to choose how often your system looks for updated content on the Internet.

Figure 7-4: Microsoft's Active Desktop Gallery comes with a variety of prepackaged items for spiffing up your desktop.

At the click of the OK button, Windows connects to the Internet, grabs the content of your Active Desktop item, and places it on the desktop, as shown in Figure 7-5.

Drag the new items around the desk until they fit in with everything else. Desktop items cover up your wallpaper, but they remain beneath your desktop icons for programs, folders, and other common fare.

To turn Desktop items on and off quickly and easily, right-click on your desktop, choose Properties, and click on the Web tab. The little monitor shows the locations of your Desktop items, which are listed in a box below. Clicking on the boxes next to the Desktop items turns them on and off.

Using an Active Desktop item

A newly energized Active Desktop constantly flashes enticing news headlines across the screen. How do you grab a newscast from the past?

Just click on the item — be it a window or little box — and Windows leaps into action, immediately connecting to the Internet and bringing up a Web page with the information pertaining to that item.

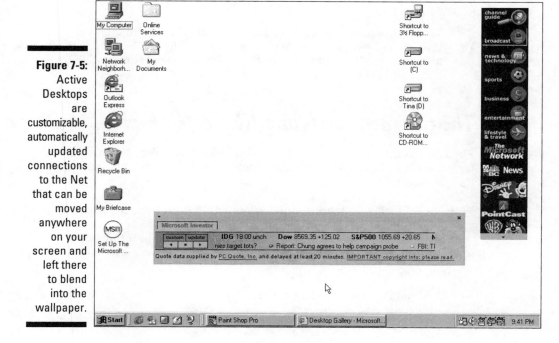

Figure 7-5: Active Desktops are customizable, automatically updated connections to the Net that can be moved anywhere on your screen and left there to blend into the wallpaper.

A click on the word *IBM* as it rolls by on Microsoft's Investor Ticker, for example, brings up Microsoft Investor — Microsoft's Web site for portfolio and investment tracking, business news, company profiles, and other financial information. From there, follow the menus to find out why IBM's name just flashed onto the screen.

If you prefer the Internet's style of mouse etiquette — single-clicking to activate items — open Explorer or any folder, click on the <u>V</u>iew menu, and choose Folder <u>O</u>ptions. Click on the General tab, choose <u>W</u>eb style, and Windows starts to work like the Web. Now you point at an item to select it, and click on it to activate it. Best yet, the mouse operates like that for all your non-Internet programs, too.

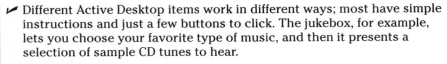

✔ Different Active Desktop items work in different ways; most have simple instructions and just a few buttons to click. The jukebox, for example, lets you choose your favorite type of music, and then it presents a selection of sample CD tunes to hear.

✔ Feel free to add your own favorite Web page as an Active Desktop item. Windows checks in and updates it, just like any other Active Desktop item. To add your own favorite sites, follow Steps 1 through 4 in the preceding section, but click on <u>N</u>o instead of <u>Y</u>es in Step 4. A box lets you type in your favorite URL: Anything with a name like www.usatoday.com or tabloid.net will do. (Click on <u>B</u>rowse and search through the Links folder to see your current list of favorite Web sites.)

✔ To quickly update your Active Desktop's displays, right-click on the desktop, choose <u>A</u>ctive Desktop, and choose <u>U</u>pdate Now from the pop-up menu. Windows connects to the Web and makes sure that all its information is up-to-date.

That computer looks like a Web site!

The computer and folders in Figure 7-6 sure look like Web sites, don't they? That's because Windows 98 is running in Web mode and dressed in its Web finery.

With the following directions, putting Web clothes on the emperor is simple:

1. **Right-click on any blank part of the desktop and point at <u>A</u>ctive Desktop from the pop-up menu.**

2. **Click on View As <u>W</u>eb Page.**

   That puts a check mark next to the option.

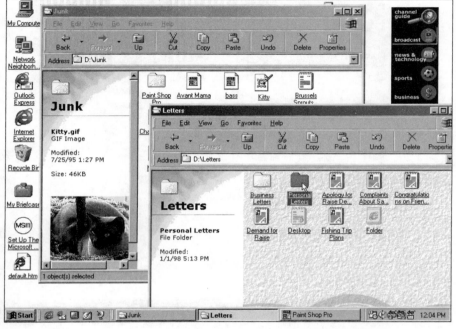

Figure 7-6:
When
running in
Web mode,
Windows 98
looks like
and acts
like a Web
page.

3. **Open My Explorer, choose View, and choose Folder Options. Then click on the General tab, and choose the Web style option.**

   As in Step 2, that puts a check mark next to the option to turn it on.

4. **Click on the adjacent View tab and click on the Like Current Folder button at the window's top.**

   Your computer immediately starts becoming more useful. For example, look at the My Computer page, shown in Figure 7-7.

   In fact, Windows 98's Web view can also show a thumbnail preview of the files inside a folder.

5. **Right-click on a folder, choose Properties from the pop-up box, and click on the Enable thumbnail view option.**

   Now hover the mouse pointer over various icons in the folder, and watch details about those objects appear along the folder's left edge. Figure 7-8, for example, shows the little arrow resting over the Cathy file, and what appears but a picture of Cathy, the comic-strip character.

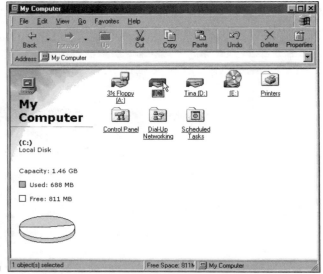

Figure 7-7:
When
tacked onto
the folders,
Web mode
sometimes
makes
Windows 98
easier
to use.

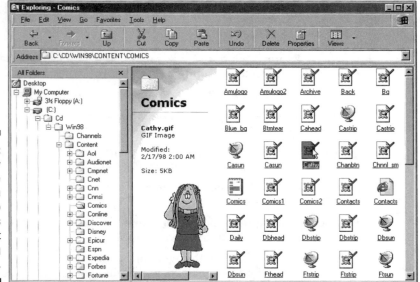

Figure 7-8:
The handy
Web mode
lets you
peek into
graphics
files without
opening
them.

✔ By turning on Windows 98's Web view and enabling the thumbnail view on your folders, Windows 98 quickly and easily displays a file's name, size, and type, as well as the size and amount of free space on your disk drives. In addition, it displays views of many graphic files on your desks — bitmap, jpg, and gif files.

✔ Don't like all this Web stuff but like the thumbnail views? Then follow Step 4 and open the folder. At first glance, nothing has changed. Choose View from the folder's menu bar, however, and choose the newly installed Thumbnail view option. The icons change their views to reveal more about their contents, as shown in Figure 7-9.

✔ Thumbnail views can be dragged around the desktop just like normal icons; feel free to right-click on them, or even to drag those unnecessary files to the Recycle Bin for disposal.

Figure 7-9:
You don't need a Web connection or any Web options activated to enjoy the thumbnail views.

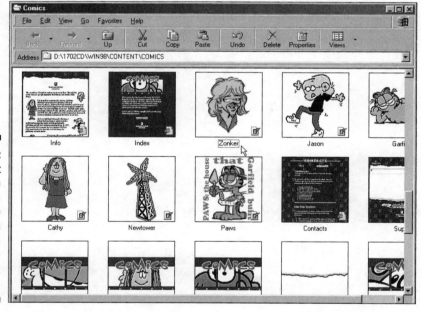

Chapter 8

Rolling Your Own Web Page

- -

In This Chapter

▶ Building your own Web page

▶ Publishing your page on the Web

▶ Spiffing it up with pictures, sounds, and graphics

- -

*W*indows 98 has a tight hold on the Internet. Internet Explorer, the built-in Web browser, moves information around seamlessly. But Microsoft wants you to experience the Net in other, more intimate ways.

So Microsoft tossed in another Internet freebie — a Web publishing program called FrontPage Express — to create your own cyber-scrapbooks.

This chapter explains how to create your own Web page by using FrontPage Express. You sprinkle in pictures, fancy backgrounds, and colors between your menus. Then you send the package of files to your Internet service provider's computer, where they're viewed as your Web page by any onlookers who drop by.

Building Your Own Web Page through Your Internet Provider

To build a Web site, you create the page on your own computer by using Windows 98's free FrontPage Express program; that's described in the very next section. Then you upload the newly created files to a special spot supplied by your Internet provider — the company mailing you the monthly bill for Internet access.

That's it! However, different Internet providers vary in the way they dish out Web site areas to their customers. If you haven't yet landed an Internet provider, ask the following questions when shopping around:

✔ **How much space do I get on the Web server?** Three to five megabytes is par . . . and more than enough to start, considering that the average Web page takes up only about 30 kilobytes until you start adding fancy photos.

✔ **How much information can visitors request from your site each month?** Your provider may call this the *bandwidth limit*. My Cox@Home service bandwidth limit is 300MB per month — more than enough for most users.

✔ **Are any Web page enhancements prohibited?** It's fun to add mini-programs called Java applets, JavaScript, CGI scripts, and ActiveX applets to jazz up your Web pages, so be sure to read the fine print. (In fact, ask your own provider whether these enhancements are allowed on your system; if not, you may want to do some shopping of your own.)

Introducing FrontPage Express

The first time you run it, FrontPage Express looks much like your garden-variety word-processing program, as shown in Figure 8-1.

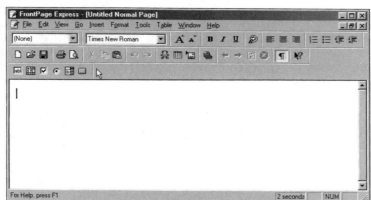

Figure 8-1:
Bold,
Center,
Fonts, and
Tables . . .
FrontPage
Express has
lots of
commands
in common
with your
word
processor.

A word processor? Yep. And here's a secret: A Web page is really just a collection of instructions on how your computer should display some files.

When you visit a Web site, hidden instructions from the site tell your Web browser how to display the site's information; your computer then re-creates the site's information and images in the way the author arranged them. (That explains why some Web pages — the ones made by really arty composers — take forever to load in your Web browser.)

FrontPage Express works as a buffer between you and HTML — the language that programmers use to create elaborate Web pages with pictures, sounds, and graphics of little spinning creatures. With FrontPage Express, you don't have to be a programmer to have a Web page. Indeed, if you can use a word processor, then you can create a Web page.

After word gets out that you know how to create Web pages, be prepared to field requests for Web pages from church groups, local pubs, and other groups in your social circle.

Discovering the Personal Home Page Wizard

As you'd suspect, working with HTML is just a *little* trickier than simply typing a letter in your word processor. To cut some of the needless complexity, FrontPage Express comes with several helper programs called Web Page Wizards, which help ease the daunting task of creating your first Web page.

This chapter tells you how to use the Personal Home Page Wizard to create your first Web page. Other FrontPage Express Web Wizards, like the Survey Form and the Confirmation Form, are slightly more complicated, requiring you to store your Web page by using Internet Information Server, Microsoft's Web server program. That process is way too complicated to discuss in these pages, but if you want your Web visitors to fill out forms and surveys, head to those Wizards for help with those more advanced features.

Building a Web page with Personal Home Page Wizard

A *home page* is your Web site's first page, and the Windows Personal Home Page Wizard helps creates the first page visitors see when they open your Internet door. Chomping at the bit to create your first Web page? Start with page one, and follow these steps to put the Personal Home Page Wizard to work.

Personal Home Page Wizard lives along Windows 98's other Internet attendants in the Internet Explorer area of the Start menu. To find them, click on the Start button, choose <u>P</u>rograms, and click on Internet Explorer.

1. **Open FrontPage Express, click on <u>F</u>ile from the menu bar, and click on <u>N</u>ew.**

   The program comes with freebie templates that help set up Web pages for different needs. I'll use the Personal Home Page Wizard for this example.

2. Click on Personal Home Page Wizard, and then click on the OK button.

The Wizard window appears, as you can see in Figure 8-2, suggesting items to include on your site. Place check marks next to things you may want to include on your new Web page.

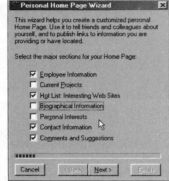

Figure 8-2:
The Page Wizard suggests stuff to include on your page, but adding or deleting any of the options is easy.

3. Click on additional sections that you want to appear on your page, click on any checked options that you don't want, and then click on the Next button.

A new window asks what URL to give this page; that's how people can find your page. It also asks for a page title.

4. Replace home1.htm **with** index.html **in the top box; then click in the blank under Page Title and type a name for your home page.**

After thinking long and hard, my wife and I chose Rathbones' Home Page for our family Web page.

Your Web page name in the Page Title text box is important if you want people to find you. Text placed there guides the various Internet search engines. If you want people to be able to find your page by typing your last name, use it in your page title. If your page focuses on pollywogs, of course, you should opt for *pollywogs* instead.

Hip Web gurus say that the term *index.html* works better than Microsoft's suggested *home1.htm* because it's used more often.

5. Click on Next.

Follow along and fill in dialog boxes as the Wizard tosses them to you, as you see me doing in Figure 8-3. (*Remember:* The pages you fill out will vary, depending on what options you click in Step 3.) Continue to click on formatting options and fill in blanks; click on the Next button after completing each page.

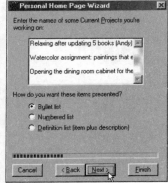

Figure 8-3:
Creating the
contents
of the
Wizard's
Current
Projects
section.

Did you include the Comments and Suggestions section as part of your page? If so, choose the third option in the Wizard's form, "Use link, send e-mail to this address;" then fill in the blank with your e-mail address. That way, you'll receive any feedback on your Web site as regular e-mail messages.

The Wizard shows you a list of your home page sections and asks you to reorganize them in the order you'd like them to appear on your page.

6. **Click on a section and then click on the Up or Down button to change the section's order on your page.**

7. **Click on the Next button when you're done; then click on the Finish button on the next page that appears.**

Doing so pokes the Wizard to start constructing your home page; when it's done, the page jumps to your screen, as mine did in Figure 8-4.

To see all the blechhy HTML coding that the Wizard helps you circumvent, head to the menu bar and click on View and then on HTML. Your page appears, riddled with brackets and HTML codes, in a ghastly window that looks something like the one in Figure 8-5. Quickly click on the Cancel button!

Saving your first Web page

You've already come pretty far with your first Web page, thanks to the Personal Home Page Wizard. But you probably want to make a few changes before publishing your creation on the Web (like finding something to replace that dreary background, perhaps).

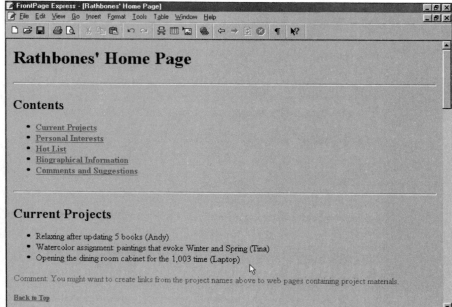

Figure 8-4:
Despite the icky gray background, this could be the start of a wonderful home page.

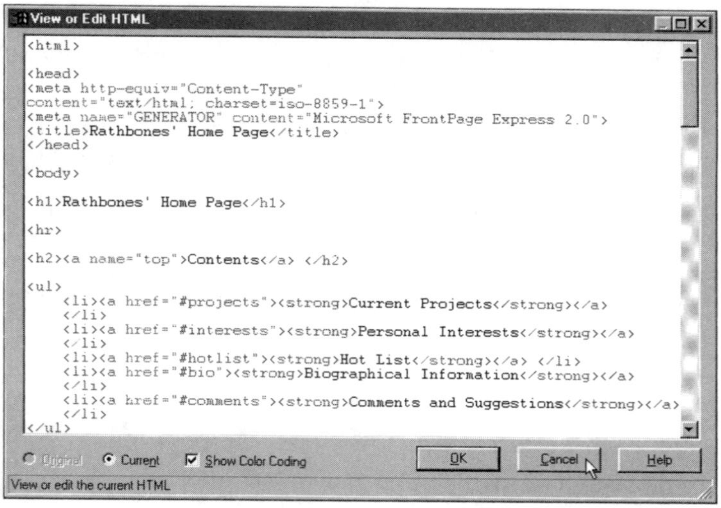

Figure 8-5:
However simple and unassuming it appears, the Personal Home Page Wizard saves much programming labor.

Fortunately, it's easy to save your home page to a file that you can open and work on later. Follow these steps:

1. From the menu bar, click on File and then on Save As.

A Save As dialog box appears, as shown in Figure 8-6.

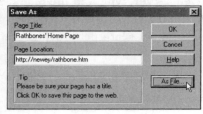

Figure 8-6:
Save your
temporary
Web page
before
touching
it up.

2. **Click on the button marked As File and browse your folders until you decide where you want to store your new home page.**

   My Documents may be a good choice. The best solution is to devote a folder to your Web page; the next section explains why.

3. **Click on the Save button.**

Don't neglect to back up your Web pages each time you change them. Your Internet provider does not keep a spare copy and probably won't be able to help you if a computer glitch wipes you out.

Publishing your page on the Internet

Now you have the page. But how can you publish it on the Net, in front of the eyes of the world?

If you've set up a chunk of Web space with your Internet provider, as discussed earlier in this chapter, Windows 98 can handle the rest. Yet another Windows 98 freebie, Microsoft's Web Publishing Wizard, can work in tandem with FrontPage Express to put your Web page on the Net in a hurry. Here's what you do:

1. **Click on the Start button, choose Programs, open Internet Explorer, and choose Web Publishing Wizard.**

   The Wizard reminds you that you need to ask your Internet provider to set up a Web space for you, and it gives you one piece of information: the URL to your Web space.

2. **Click on the Next button in the window that appears.**

3. **Locate your Web page file, type its path name in the blank, and click on the Next button.**

   Or click on Browse Folders or Browse Files and rummage through your hard disk for the file.

4. **Think up a name for your Web server, type it in the blank, and click on the Next button.**

   You can type anything here . . . try your Internet provider name and the words *Web Server.*

5. **In the top box, type the URL that points to your Web space on your Internet provider's computer.**

   This is the piece of information that you confirmed with your Internet provider back in Step 1 — it's the URL (like `http://myinternetsite.com`) that people will type in their Web browser to reach your page.

6. **In the bottom box, type the path name to the directory on your computer where you store files related to this Web site, and then click on the Next button.**

   Doing so gives you a single directory for storing all the Web-page-related files you want to work with: your FrontPage Express pages, plus sounds, images, and the like. When it's time to publish a page, the Wizard knows where to look.

7. **Type in your Internet account user name and password and then click on OK.**

8. **Click on Next when the Wizard displays the Specify a Service Provider window.**

9. **Click on the down arrow. If you see your Internet provider's name in the list, lucky you! Highlight it and click on Next. Don't see your provider's name? Select FTP from the list. Now click on Next.**

   Don't worry if you end up choosing FTP: Most people do, since Microsoft can't foresee the names of all the world's Internet providers.

10. **In the top box, fill in the name of the provider's FTP server. In the bottom box, fill in the name of your Internet provider's folder that contains your Web page. Click on the Next button when you're done.**

    The Wizard is asking for information that your Internet provider gave to you when you signed up for a Web space.

11. **If all goes well, the Wizard tosses up a window and informs you that it's ready to publish your files. Click on Finish.**

    You'll have to sit and twiddle your thumbs until the Wizard reaches your Internet provider's Web server and transfers your files there.

    Does the Wizard balk at locating your server? Call your Internet provider and double-check your URL, user name, and account info. Then repeat Steps 1 through 11.

12. **Test everything by loading Internet Explorer, clicking on File and then on Open, and typing in your new Web address — the same thing that you typed in Step 5.**

    Or you can click on the Browse button and head to the Web folder that you created to store your Web page. Figure 8-7 shows mine. Click on the filename (make sure that it has the *htm* on the end of its name), click on Open, and then click on OK. Your page should leap to the screen.

Figure 8-7:
Open your
Web page
from your
hard disk.

Slapping Together Your Cyber-Scrapbook

The bare-bones Web page that you created earlier in this chapter needs some work — there's no doubt about it.

Don't despair if your page doesn't look quite like CNN's or MTV's . . . yet. Peruse this section's gaggle of tips and tricks to polish your page to a bright gleam. It shows you how to do all your editing work, in case you're paying long-distance or hourly charges. It shows you how to add headlines, colors, and pictures. Finally, it shows you how to stick the best thing into a Web page: a hyperlink that "bounces" a viewer off to another Web site upon a click.

Sprucing up Web page text while offline

Whether or not you've published your Web page on the Internet, you can easily tweak and improve that page anytime you want.

Offline, you can open the page by starting FrontPage Express, heading to the menu bar, and clicking on File. The last four pages you've opened show up at the bottom of the File menu, so your fledgling Web page should be among those listed. Click on your Web page's filename, and it loads into FrontPage Express.

Not listed in the last few opened pages? From the File menu, click on Open. Click next to the From File option, and then click on the Browse button to locate your page's file in your Web stuff folder.

After you open your Web page, editing is simply a matter of placing your cursor on the page and typing.

- ✔ Select words and add emphasis by using bold or italic type; changing the letters' size works well, too. All these tools are available from the Format toolbar. (Click on View and then on Format Toolbar to make sure that it's visible.)

- ✔ Fonts go far to change the mood of a paragraph or even a single word. To try some out, select some text, choose Font from the Format menu, and click on a cool-sounding font name in the scrolling box. In the bottom-left corner of the Font window, a sample of text in that font appears. You can even make text blink: Click on the Font window's Special Styles tab and choose Blink. Fun!

- ✔ Your visitors won't be wowed by your fancy type unless they have that font installed on their computers, too. They can still read your page, but it shows up in their browser's default font. Many Web authors make free fonts available for downloading — if so, you can use it and offer it to your visitors to download, too.

- ✔ Web pages, like all formatted documents, adhere to the classic maxim *less is more.* Computer veterans can tell war stories about the first days of desktop publishing, with newbies adding several fonts and effects to a single page. Many Web pages bear similar battle scars. Strive for a balance between boring and bad taste when touching up your Web pages.

Changing a Web page's text while online

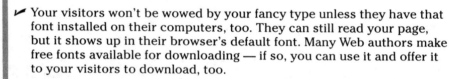

You can make a quick change to your Web page while you're online. Follow these steps to change your page even as you surf!

1. **Start Internet Explorer and head to your page.**

2. **Click on Internet Explorer's menu bar, choose Edit, and click on Page.**

3. **Click on your page title and type a descriptive word to personalize it.**

   Aw, c'mon — you can always edit it out later. I'll add *Family* to make it Rathbones' Family Page.

4. **Click on Save to save the edited page on your Web page. If you'd rather save it as a file on your hard disk and publish the altered page later, click on Save As and then choose the As File button.**

Editing the new text on your page, whether it's changing the page's title or adding a quick essay about Francoise Guizot's political treatises, is as easy as that.

Just editing your file and saving it on your local computer is not enough: You must publish it on the Web site (overwriting the old file's name — in this case, index.htm) before visitors can see the new changes. Always test your page after making changes: Simply visit it yourself with Internet Explorer and see what it looks like. (Call your friends and ask them to look at it, too.)

Adding cool backgrounds and stuff

You've seen those eye-popping pages on the Web, with cool colors, textures, and themed graphics serving as a canvas for the text. An interesting background goes far to perk up your page, too, and achieving a cool effect isn't all that hard.

Nothing guarantees repeat visitors more than a warm welcome. To rescue your page from the dull "sea of text" feeling, put the power of FrontPage Express to work. Add some fun things, as described in the next few sections.

But most important, be sure to keep updating and freshening your Web page with timely information, or it will be as useful as a magazine that died after publishing only a single issue.

Adding a background graphic

Before you can add a background graphic, you need a background graphic file, which is really only a tiny image in either .gif or .jpg file format. Use Windows 98's Find program, found on the Start menu, to search your hard drive for these files. (***Hint:*** The Windows 98 CD contains dozens of them.)

After you choose a background graphic, call up FrontPage Express and follow these steps.

1. **Click on the Format menu and then on Background.**

   The Page Properties dialog box appears.

2. **Click on Background Image, click on the Browse button, click on From File, click on Browse, and locate the background file in your Web folder or wherever you stashed it.**

3. **Click on Open and then on the OK button.**

   Your page looks much better now. Whew!

   Be sure to save your FrontPage Express file each time you make a change, both by saving it to a file on your hard disk (choosing Save As from the File menu) and, when you're ready, publishing it on your Web space (choosing Save from the File menu).

✔ Download new graphics from almost any Web-building-related site by firing up your favorite Web search engine and typing **background graphics** in the box.

✔ The following Web site points to other sites that give away thousands, possibly millions, of free background graphics and textures:

```
http://www.cyberia.co.th/corp/cyberia/resources/
        backgrounds.html
```

✔ Spot a cool graphic while on the Web? Right-click on the image and then choose Save Picture <u>A</u>s from the pop-up menu. A menu option next door lets you turn the image into instant wallpaper, too.

The Point 'n' Pluck lifestyle of the Internet has some folks concerned, especially the creators of the art that's being snatched. If you grab an image and use it on your personal computer without trying to make any money off it, you're doing nothing wrong. Enjoy it. But the best way to make sure that you're not doing anything wrong is to send an e-mail to the page's creator and ask for permission.

Using color for background

Although background files add color, they also add texture — something you may not always want. For a more minimalist treatment, use the FrontPage Express background feature to pour color onto your pages:

1. **Click on F<u>o</u>rmat and then on Bac<u>k</u>ground, as in the preceding example.**

2. **Click on the box next to Background <u>I</u>mage so that no check mark appears.**

3. **Click on the down arrow next to the Ba<u>c</u>kground option, scroll down to click on Custom, and start playing with the ultra-cool color window, shown in Figure 8-8.**

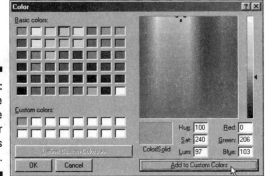

Figure 8-8:
Color alone can set the mood for your page's message.

4. **Click on any of the boxes under the Basic Colors section.**

   Notice how a "target" marker in the large window moves with each new hue selected. You can also click in the large window, or click on any of the gradations shown on the very right. You can even save a favorite color by clicking on Add to Custom Colors and clicking on OK, and then clicking on OK again.

Voilà! You can perform similar colorizing feats with the links and other text on your page — but just make sure that everything's still legible.

Image is everything

The best Web sites bustle with pictures, animations, buttons, and other doodads. Here's how FrontPage Express helps you add these "not-so-extras" to your page.

Adding a picture

Pictures work their magic to set the mood of your Web page and, as they say, are worth many, many words.

Recent advances in graphic file formats mean that you don't have to worry as much as the early Web pioneers did about pictures adding frustrating downtime for visitors waiting to download a Web page.

Follow these steps to add an image to your page:

1. **Load FrontPage Express.**

2. **Place the cursor where you want to place your image.**

   You may have to press the Enter key a few times to make some room.

3. **From the menu bar, choose Insert and then click on Image.**

4. **Use Browse to locate your graphic file, highlight its filename, and click on Open.**

   Your graphic should appear, as in Figure 8-9.

5. **If you prefer, you can center your graphic and page title as I did in the figure; simply select them with your mouse and then click on the center-text icon on the formatting bar.**

Some people opt to browse with graphics capabilities turned off. Tell them what they're missing by adding a small text description to your image. Right-click on the image, choose Image Properties, type something descriptive in the General tab's Text box (found in the Alternative Representations section), and click on OK, as in Figure 8-10.

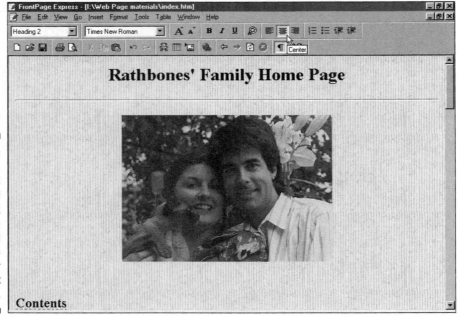

Figure 8-9:
Good
graphics
are small
for quick
downloading
but colorful
enough to
get their
point
across.

Figure 8-10:
Take care
to label
each image
with a text
description
for visitors
who are
browsing
with the
graphics
option
disabled.

Adding a hyperlink

The best Web pages use lots of *hyperlinks.* A hyperlink, or *link,* is just like a button — a way for visitors to jump around to the best spots within a single site and/or jump to other Web sites.

Do you recall visiting a Web page that seemed to scroll on forever like an unfurling tablet? That page needed links to take visitors quickly to new pages on the site. The best-linked pages contain a Back hyperlink so that visitors can quickly return from unpleasant trips and resume exploring in a different direction.

Follow these steps to create a hyperlink to a second page on your Web site:

1. **While examining your Web page in FrontPage Express, highlight the word, image, or area of it that you want to connect with a hyperlink.**

2. **From the menu bar, click on Insert and then on Hyperlink.**

   The Edit Hyperlink window appears. (To link to an existing page created by someone else, click on the World Wide Web tab and follow the instructions.)

   Because you're linking to part of your own page, however, click on the tab marked New Page to point to a second Web page that you'll create and store on your Web space. Your Web site is already expanding!

3. **Click in the box beside Page URL and type the URL of the second — the target — page on your Web site. Click on OK.**

   A URL, or *Uniform Resource Locator,* is an identifying mechanism used for tracking information as it travels from site to site on the Internet.

   The URL is exactly the same URL as your index.html page, except the filename changes from index.html to a new filename. FrontPage Express dubbed my new page banana.html, taking the cue from the word I selected as the hyperlink. Figure 8-11 shows the New Page tab of the Edit Hyperlink dialog box. Click on OK to see the New Page window.

Figure 8-11:
FrontPage
Express
asks you
to type
the exact
name and
location of
your new
page.

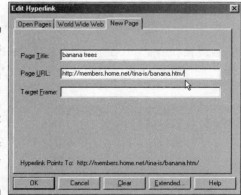

Even though the URL you're asked to make up is false for now because you haven't actually published the page to that location yet, go ahead and type it in as if it's already there.

4. In the New Page window that appears, select Normal Page and click on OK.

A blank page appears. This is what it's like to build a Web page without using the Wizard. Luckily, you can pretty much dump your information here and save it.

5. Edit the new page with whatever graphic or text you want to link to.

Here's the easy way: Copy your sought-after graphic or text to the Clipboard, and then paste it into FrontPage Express. After you bring the image into the program, you can manipulate it with the array of tools along the program's top.

When you're through, save the image; FrontPage Express uses the URL chosen in Step 4.

Figure 8-12 shows what happens when visitors click on the word *banana* on the Web page; it takes them to this cool new banana.html page. It has just a tiled background, a tool available in the Background area of the Format menu. A single picture rests above the background of tiled images.

6. Before saving any page, add a way for visitors to return quickly to your "top" page by typing this line at the bottom of your page:

```
</A><A HREF="main.html">Return to Top<BR>
```

You can substitute your own words for the terse "Return to Top," as shown in Figure 8-12.

7. Save your page on your hard disk and publish it on your Web site.

Don't forget to fire up Internet Explorer to test that hyperlink!

Feel free to explore with different pictures and colors, as shown in Figure 8-13. After you grow familiar with the program's menus, you'll begin to add tables and sounds to your creations.

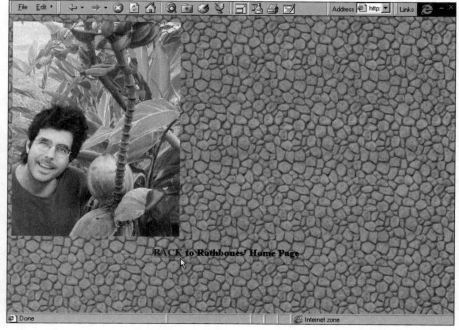

Figure 8-12: Combine graphics, a background, and some text for a nice second page on your Web site.

Figure 8-13: FrontPage Express can add sound and tables to create successful Web pages.

Part III
Getting More Out of Windows 98

The 5th Wave   By Rich Tennant

YES, MASTER?

In this part . . .

A little lube in the tracks can make a window much easier to open and close. The same holds true for the windows on your computer. But forget this metaphor stuff. Where are the tracks? Where's the lube?

This part of the book explains how to make Windows 98 work a little bit faster, a little bit easier, and without crashing as much.

Chapter 9

Stuffing Windows onto a Laptop

- -

In This Chapter

▶ Installing Windows on a laptop

▶ Stuffing the Briefcase

▶ Making Windows easier to see

▶ Working with a mouse or trackball

▶ Making batteries last longer

▶ Traveling tips with Windows

▶ Making Windows run better on a laptop

- -

*F*or years, nobody bothered trying to run Windows on a laptop. Windows was simply too big and too clumsy, and the laptops of the day were too small to digest it.

Windows 98 is bigger than ever. But today's laptops are much more powerful than before: Most of 'em can digest Windows 98 without even chewing. This chapter shows the *right* way to feed Windows 98 to a laptop, as well as some things to try if the laptop tries to burp Windows back up.

Installing Windows 98 on a Laptop

A laptop is a completely different organism than a desktop computer, so stuffing Windows 98 onto a laptop takes a few extra tricks. To make sure that Windows knows that it's heading for a laptop's hard drive, you have to push a few different buttons while installing Windows.

In fact, if you *already* have installed Windows on your laptop, head for the chapter's later sections. There, you can find information about Briefcase, a program that simplifies the chore of moving files between your laptop and desktop. You also find tips on ways to make laptopping less awkward.

If you're getting ready to install Windows 98 on your laptop right now, however, keep a wary eye on the next few sections.

Reinstall Windows 98; don't LapLink it over

A program by Traveling Software called LapLink can be a lifesaver. By installing LapLink on both your laptop and your desktop computer — and then stringing a cable between the serial or parallel ports of the two computers — you can quickly copy or move files back and forth between the two computers.

In fact, Windows 98 comes with a Direct Cable Connection that lets you perform many of the same tasks. (Direct Cable Connection is covered later in this chapter.) However, *don't* use either LapLink or Direct Cable Connection to copy Windows 98 from your desktop computer to your laptop. It won't work.

- ✔ Sure, that may be a quick and tempting way to install Windows 98. But even though Windows 98 files would be located on your laptop, the Windows 98 program would still think that it was living on your desktop. It wouldn't be able to find its favorite files, and you may not be able to see it on your laptop's temperamental screen.

- ✔ Although it takes more time, install Windows 98 onto your laptop the old-fashioned way: by inserting the disks into the floppy drive, one at a time. (Or if your laptop has a CD-ROM drive, you suave sophisticate, install Windows 98 from the CD.)

- ✔ When laptopping in a hot-air balloon, don't bother wearing a heavy jacket. All that hot air overhead keeps you surprisingly warm in that little dangling basket.

Choose the Portable option when installing Windows 98

When installing Windows 98 on a laptop, choose the Portable option, not the Typical option. By choosing Portable, you tell Windows 98 to include files that come in handy for laptop users.

Specifically, you get the following laptop-based goodies:

- ✔ A program called Briefcase, described later in this chapter, makes it easier to keep track of which files are the most up-to-date when you start moving files between your laptop and desktop computer.

- ✔ A Direct Cable Connection program lets you squirt files back and forth between your laptop and desktop computer through a serial or parallel cable.

✔ Microsoft Exchange, described in Chapter 6, lets you keep in touch with your e-mail while on the road. Plus, a fax program enables you to send and receive faxes — if your laptop's modem can handle faxes, that is.

✔ Windows 98 adds support for PC Cards, formerly known as PCMCIA cards. The size of a tiny stack of business cards, these take the form of modems, network connectors, and even memory cards for digital cameras and palmtops.

✔ Advanced Power Management enables you to customize your laptop's battery usage and suspend levels to save the most power.

If you didn't select these options when installing Windows on your laptop, check out the Windows Setup tab of the Control Panel's Add/Remove Programs icon.

Stuffing the Briefcase

Have you already installed Briefcase onto your computer? If the little Briefcase icon doesn't sit on your desktop, try clicking on a blank part of your desktop with your right mouse button and looking for Briefcase under the New menu. If the word Briefcase *isn't* listed, head for the Windows Setup tab under the Control Panel's Add/Remove Programs icon.

After you install Briefcase, here's how to make it work. These steps show you how to grab your desktop computer's Briefcase, stuff it onto your laptop for some work at the pier, and dump the Briefcase's updated contents at the end of the day.

1. **Click on a blank part of the desktop with your right mouse button and choose Briefcase from the New menu.**

   A little briefcase icon appears on your desktop.

2. **Decide which files you want to work on while waiting for the fish to bite.**

   For example, decide which letters, spreadsheets, reports, or other files you need to complete.

   Briefcase moves only the data files, not the programs required to edit those data files. When copying files to your Briefcase, make sure that your other computer has the appropriate programs available to open and edit your files. To be specific: You need a copy of Microsoft Word for Windows on both your laptop *and* your desktop computer in order to edit the Word files in your Briefcase.

3. **Drag and drop those files to your Briefcase icon.**

   Windows 98 creates shortcuts to those documents in the Briefcase folder, keeping track of where the original files are located on your hard drive, as well as the file's current time and date.

   In fact, you see that information, shown in Figure 9-1, if you double-click on the Briefcase icon.

4. **Close the Briefcase window.**

   The Briefcase latches itself shut with its new contents.

5. **Drag and drop the Briefcase to its new home on the laptop.**

   The happiest Briefcase users quickly drag and drop the Briefcase icon onto their laptop by using a network or cable connection. The unhappiest Briefcase users drag and drop the desktop computer's Briefcase to a floppy disk and reinsert the floppy disks into their laptops. Either way, always keep track of the folder where your Briefcase lives, because you'll need to fish it out later.

   If you're copying the Briefcase to a floppy disk, make sure that all the files fit onto a single floppy. If you try to copy too many files, you have to use more than one disk, and Briefcase won't be able to keep track of which files belong where. (Network and Direct Cable Connection worshippers don't have this worry.)

6. **Double-click on the Briefcase icon from within the laptop.**

   The Briefcase opens up, showing you the files you placed inside it from your desktop computer.

7. **Edit your files.**

   Do that "work on the road stuff" work, pretending that the guy next to you on the plane isn't watching everything you type. (But you know that he is because he has nothing else to do, and somebody else has already done the in-flight magazine's crossword puzzle.)

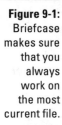

Figure 9-1:
Briefcase
makes sure
that you
always
work on
the most
current file.

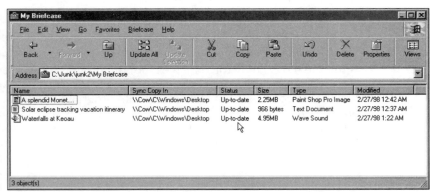

8. **Upon your return to the home or office, connect the laptop and desktop computers through the network or cable. Not using a network or cable? Put your floppy with Briefcase into your desktop computer's floppy drive.**

   At this point, Briefcase hasn't done anything but serve as a glorified folder with an icon that looks like a briefcase. But the next few steps show you its magic.

9. **Choose Update All from the Briefcase menu.**

   Briefcase compares its file collection with the ones on your desktop, decides which ones are most up-to-date, and shows you a cool chart to make sure that it's copying the right files to the right places, as shown in Figure 9-2.

Figure 9-2: Briefcase tells you which files are out-of-date and asks permission to update them.

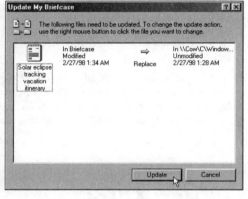

10. **Click on the Update button.**

    Briefcase copies the appropriate files back into your Briefcase.

11. **Close the Briefcase and put the floppy disk into your desktop computer.**

12. **Open the Briefcase on your floppy disk.**

    See how the Briefcase lists the files that need to be updated in Figure 9-3?

13. **Choose Update All from the Briefcase menu.**

    Once again, Briefcase shows you the cool chart and asks permission to copy the updated files to your hard drive, effectively replacing the older ones you started with in Step 1.

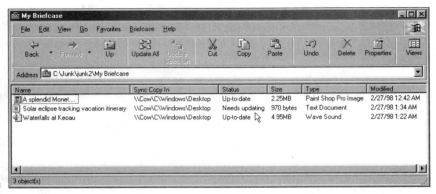

Figure 9-3: Briefcase lists the files that need to be updated.

✔ When using Briefcase, you can edit the files either from within their hard drive folders or directly from inside Briefcase. Because Briefcase contains only shortcuts, the two icons actually point to the same file. Just remember to leave the Briefcase on the floppy disk — it can't be moved around like the files can.

✔ When deciding which is the more up-to-date of two files, Briefcase looks at the time and date that you last edited the file. So be sure to keep your computer's clock set to the correct time, or Briefcase won't know which file is really the most recent. Don't let a dead battery wipe out an hour's worth of work.

Transferring Files with a Direct Cable Connection

You can transfer files between your laptop and your desktop computer the old-fashioned way: by copying the files onto floppy disks and moving them from one drive to another.

Or you can go the high-speed route of connecting the computers with a cable. This route is called *Direct Cable Connection,* and it works like this:

✔ Buy a special *null modem* serial or parallel cable. (Or if you already have a spare cable lying around that's *normal,* buy a *null modem* adapter to convert it to a null modem serial or parallel cable.) A plain old serial cable won't work, unfortunately.

✔ If you installed Windows 98 with the Portable option, you already have the Direct Cable Connection software installed on your computer. (It's listed in the Communications menu, found in the Accessories area of your Start menu's <u>P</u>rograms area.) Not listed? Then install it through the Control Panel's Add/Remove Programs icon: Double-click on that icon, click on the Windows Setup tab, and you find the cable stuff listed under Communications. Whew.

After you install the cable program, here's how to set it up.

1. **Connect a port from your desktop computer to a port of your laptop computer.**

   Use a null modem serial or parallel cable. Then make sure that you connect the same type of ports on both computers. (You can't connect a null modem serial to a parallel port. You can connect your null modem serial cable to COM1 on one computer and COM2 on the other, however.)

2. **On your desktop computer, load Direct Cable Connection from the Accessories area of the Start menu's <u>P</u>rograms area.**

   The configuration screen appears, as shown in Figure 9-4.

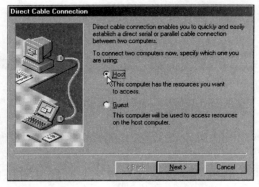

Figure 9-4:
Set up one
of your
computers
as host and
the other
as Guest.

3. **Choose <u>H</u>ost and click on <u>N</u>ext.**

   Because you're grabbing files off your desktop computer and putting them onto your laptop, your desktop computer is Host.

4. **Click on the <u>F</u>ile and Print Sharing button.**

   Because you want the computers to share files, you need to create a sort of *mini-network.* So the Network page appears, as shown in Figure 9-5.

5. **Click on the Identification tab and make sure that a name is typed in for your computer.**

   Type in an individual name for your computer; each computer must have its own name. Both of the linked computers need to have the same name listed under Workgroup, though.

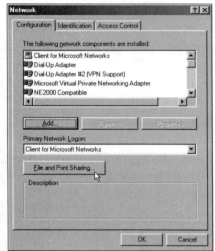

Figure 9-5:
Click on the
File and
Print
Sharing
button.

6. **Click on the Configuration tab and then click on the File and Print Sharing button.**

   Yep, this is the second time you've clicked on a File and Print Sharing button.

7. **Click on the I want to be able to give others access to my files box and then click on OK.**

   Feel free to click in the box that lets people access your printer, too, if you want the laptop to be able to print through this mini-network.

8. **Click on the OK button.**

9. **Click on the OK button to let Windows restart the computer.**

   Be sure to close down any open files. When the computer comes back up, your mini-network should be in place.

10. **Load Direct Cable Connection from the Accessories area, just as you did in Step 2, and then select Host and click on Next.**

11. **Select the port you want to use and click on Next.**

    Choose the port you plugged your cable into, as shown in Figure 9-6. (The ports are often marked on the back of your computer, luckily.)

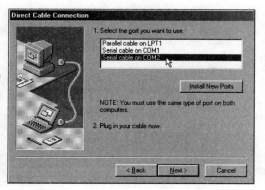

Figure 9-6:
Select the
port into
which you
plugged
your cable.

12. **On your desktop computer's screen, use your right mouse button to click on the folders that you want the laptop to be able to grab.**

13. **Choose the Sharing option from the pop-up menu.**

14. **Click on the Shared As button and click on OK.**

15. **Click on the Next button in the Direct Cable Connection box.**

16. **Set up your laptop computer as Guest, using the proper port, and click on the Finish button of the Host computer.**

    Choose Guest from the Direct Cable Connection box and then choose the port you connected your cable to on your laptop computer.

    The laptop computer tries to connect to your desktop computer. If nothing went wrong, you should be able to access the folder that you set up as shared on your desktop computer.

    ✔ If something does go wrong, however, click on a blank part of your desktop, press F1, click on the Contents tab, and double-click on the Troubleshooting option. Choose Windows 98 Troubleshooters, double-click on Direct Cable Connection, and Windows 98 takes you through a step-by-step list of things to check.

    ✔ For a quicker solution, consider installing a network. Complete instructions await in Chapter 17.

    ✔ Those nifty cables from LapLink software don't work with the Direct Cable Connection software. Sniff. You can find the cables at most computer stores, however, as well as from Parallel Technologies at 800-789-4784.

Making Windows Easier to See

One of the biggest problems with running Windows 98 on a laptop, especially an older model, becomes apparent when you look at the screen: It's often hard to see what's going on. Some of the boxes have funny lines running up and down the screen, the mouse pointer often disappears at the worst possible moment, and your finger can get a workout adjusting the laptop's contrast or brightness knobs — especially if you're foolhardy enough to believe the ads where people laptop by the pool.

Unfortunately, no surefire cure exists. Unlike desktop computers, laptops find themselves under various lighting conditions. Working beneath a tree in an Amtrak station calls for a slightly different screen setup than working under the little swiveling overhead light on an airplane.

Here are some lighting weapons to keep in your armament bag; keep trying them until you find the one that works for your particular situation.

Wallpaper may look cool on a desktop computer, but take it easy on a laptop. Most wallpaper just gives the mouse pointer another place to hide.

Adjusting the contrast knobs

Your first line of defense comes from the little contrast knob found on nearly every laptop, either along one edge or near the screen.

Whenever the laptop's screen looks a little washed out, try giving the knob a quick turn to control the light source.

Changing to a better mouse pointer

Even when the laptop's screen is easy to read, your troubles aren't over. The mouse pointer on a laptop sometimes disappears when you move it — the screens simply can't update themselves quickly enough to reflect the movement on the screen. And because the mouse pointer is moving about 90 percent of the time, a disappearing mouse pointer can be a problem on older laptops.

Here's one way to make the pointer easier to spot:

1. **From the Start menu's Settings area, click on the Control Panel icon.**
2. **Double-click on the Mouse icon.**

   The Mouse Properties control box appears.
3. **Choose the Motion tab.**
4. **Click in the box next to Show pointer trails.**

   As soon as a check mark appears in the Show pointer trails box, your mouse begins leaving mouse droppings all over your screen (see Figure 9-7).

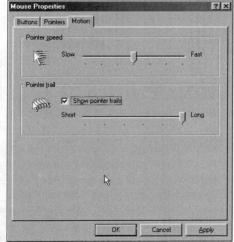

Figure 9-7:
Choose
Show
pointer
trails to
make your
mouse
easier to
see on a
laptop's
screen.

✔ Some mice or trackballs come with software that makes their pointers easier to spot. For example, Microsoft's clip-on trackball comes with a special Control Panel that makes the mouse pointer as big and black as a Happy Hour meatball.

✔ Several shareware and public domain programs also can make mouse pointers easier to spot. Turn to Chapter 5 for tips on downloading those programs.

The letters are all too small!

A laptop's screen is nearly always smaller than a desktop monitor. Text often looks smaller than the ingredients list on a package of Hostess Chocodiles. Luckily, fonts are easy to enlarge in both DOS and Windows programs.

Windows programs: When using Windows word processors, spreadsheets, or other Windows programs with text, tell the program to use larger fonts. Usually the program's Format menu contains a Font or Size option.

DOS programs: Windows can enlarge the fonts used by DOS programs, but only while the program runs in an on-screen window and doesn't use any fancy graphics. To enlarge the fonts, click on the little box in the DOS window's upper-left corner (or press Alt+spacebar) and choose Properties from the menu that drops down. Click on the Font tab and choose the 10 x 18 option to make the window larger and easier to see.

The DOS window's new larger size probably keeps it from fitting completely on-screen, but Windows automatically shifts your point of view, keeping the cursor in sight.

If the DOS program looks too small when run in an on-screen window, press Alt+Enter. The DOS program fills the screen, making it much easier to see. Press Alt+Enter again to return it to its own window.

Waiter, There's No Mouse on My Laptop

A mouse makes Windows easier to use on a desktop computer, but it often gets in the way on a laptop. Luckily, you have a few alternatives.

Trackballs: These little guys look like tiny upside-down mice that clip to the side of your laptop. Some laptops come with a trackball built in near the screen. Just give the ball a deft spin with your thumb, and the mouse pointer stumbles across the screen. Definitely give yourself a few days to get used to it.

Trackballs work on desktop computers as well as laptops. To get used to the trackball's different feel, clip it to your desktop computer's keyboard. After giving it a whirl for a few days, you'll feel more confident thumbing a trackball while you're on the road.

Touchpads: Slide your finger across a little pad below the spacebar, and the mouse pointer simultaneously moves across the screen. Touchpads are fun, easy, and awfully difficult to get the hang of. After you've slid your fingers around one for a while, however, you may wish that your desktop computer had one as well.

Keyboard: Some laptops let you move the mouse pointer by pressing a special function key and tapping the arrow keys. It's as awkward as it sounds, but arrow keys are better than the last alternative, described next.

Memorizing keystrokes: You can control Windows exclusively through the keyboard. See those underlined letters on the menus of just about any Windows program? Press and release Alt and then press one of those underlined letters, which activates the command. For example, press Alt, F while you're in WordPad, and the File menu drops down.

> ✔ Ever tried to change a window's size by using a trackball? Grabbing a window's border is like trying to pick up a toothpick with salad tongs. The border is just too skinny to get a grip on.
>
> To enlarge the border, head for Control Panel's Display icon, and then to the Appearance tab in the Display Properties box. Then under Item, change the Active Window Border to 5 and click on OK. If the border is still hard to grab, increase the number to 6 and try again.

✔ Don't have much space to move your mouse on the airplane's fold-down tray? Head for the Control Panel's Mouse icon, click on the Motion tab, and change the Pointer <u>s</u>peed to fast. A subtle push then sends the mouse flying across the screen. Keep fine-tuning until you have the speed adjusted to the way you like it.

Making Batteries Last Longer

Laptops drain batteries faster than children drain grape juice at Chuck E. Cheese. Plugging in the AC adapter recharges the batteries, but what do you do to maximize the time spent between AC outlets? Plus, even the fanciest (most expensive) laptop batteries start to lose their oomph after 500 or 600 rechargings. That's about one or two years for most users.

To keep your batteries breathing as long as possible, try some of these tricks:

✔ New batteries come uncharged and need to be broken in. Charge and immediately discharge your batteries a few times before relying on them. (Discharge portables by leaving them unplugged from the wall and turned on for a few hours — or even overnight.) In fact, keep up the habit of fully draining and recharging your batteries once a week.

✔ Clean the contacts on your rechargeable batteries and charger. A cotton swab and rubbing alcohol can do the trick.

✔ Head for the Control Panel, open the Power Management area, and make sure that Windows knows it's running on a laptop and needs to save as much power as possible. That way, it can shut off the hard drives when they aren't being used, for example, or turn off the screen.

✔ When not using something with your laptop, turn off its power. Remove PC cards, for example. You can leave your modem PC card inside, though, if you make sure that your modem program isn't configured to receive calls. Otherwise, the PC card stays on, draining power as it awaits a phone call that never arrives.

✔ Leaving a disc in your laptop's CD-ROM drive is actually beneficial; your computer peeks inside the drive at random intervals, and it takes less energy to *find* a disc than to *search* for one.

Today's popular NiCad rechargeable batteries come with a memory problem: They tend to remember the last time they were recharged, and they subsequently think that's the extent of their life span. For example, if a two-hour NiCad battery is consistently used for 30 minutes before being recharged, the confused battery's run time eventually shrinks to 30 minutes. To avoid this problem, drain your batteries completely before recharging them, and use *battery conditioners* from battery suppliers like 1-800-BATTERIES that completely drain your battery before recharging it. Also, newer technologies like lithium batteries forgo the memory problems but are costly and hard to find.

Recycling a dead rechargeable battery

Don't just toss that old rechargeable battery in the trash. According to the battery supplier 1-800-BATTERIES, the Environmental Protection Agency estimates that 200 tons of cadmium and 260,000 tons of lead enter the waste stream annually, contributing to polluted water and air. Forget the trash can; if you can't find a local recycler, send your dead rechargeable batteries to 1-800-BATTERIES for safe recycling: Attn: Recycling Department, 2301 Robb Drive, Reno, NV 89523.

In fact, 1-800-BATTERIES (found on the Internet at www.1800batteries.com) can be a great source for hard-to-find laptop batteries; they carry more than 6,000 varieties of batteries and battery supplies. (International callers can reach the company at 702-746-6140; people who don't like to translate letters into phone numbers can reach them at 1-800-228-8374.)

On the Road . . .

Laptops are made to travel — except when in Libya, Tunisia, Syria, and Ethiopia. Technology and current politics currently don't mesh well in those spots. Indeed, when traveling abroad anywhere, carry a photocopy of your laptop's receipt, as well as a letter from your boss on company letterhead, explaining why you're there.

Here are a few other tips for laptop luggers:

- ✔ The cigarette lighter socket on some small boats operates at 24 volts, not the 12 volts dished up by most cars. Although some cigarette lighter adapters can detect the difference and pour the right juice into your laptop, some adapters aren't as smart: They can fry your laptop without a second thought.

- ✔ While working, keep an eye on the airplane seat in front of you — if it reclines too quickly, the back of the seat can catch the top of your open laptop's screen, effectively sheering it off at the hinges. The worst part: Seats usually recline unexpectedly at the *beginning* of a long flight.

- ✔ Do you frequently change your laptop's time when traveling? Then double-click on the taskbar's little clock to bring up a menu for changing your time zones and the current time.

- ✔ Some people not only carry aboard laptops but also place small printers and printer cartridges in their luggage. Airplane pressure problems can cause printer cartridges to leak, however, so put the cartridges in a plastic bag before stuffing them into your suitcase with your socks and underwear.

✔ Always travel with a fully charged battery or two — even if you don't plan to work. You need to turn on your machine at every airport's security area, and AC-adapters are cumbersome to unpack. Keep the laptop and disks away from the metal detector and off the X-ray machine's conveyor belt — the magnetic fields of these machines can erase your data. Plus, these counters can be hectic, and you don't want your laptop falling onto the floor.

Chapter 10

Sound! Movies! TV! Multimedia Stuff!

· ·

In This Chapter

▶ Figuring out Media Player

▶ Figuring out Sound Recorder

▶ Figuring out CD Player

▶ Playing music (those MIDI files)

▶ Playing sounds

▶ Playing musical CDs

▶ Watching movies

▶ Recording sounds

▶ Watching TV on the computer

▶ Watching Internet multimedia with ActiveMovie

▶ Fixing sound and video problems

· ·

*A*ll the really *fun* computers — from that somber-voiced "working" computer on *Star Trek* to that flailing-armed "Danger! Danger!" robot on *Lost in Space* — have one important thing in common: They can make *noises*, for cryin' out loud.

For years, *real-life* computers could only cut loose with a rude beep, which they issued to harass confused users who pressed the wrong key. Windows 98, however, bursts onto the screen with a choir of sunshine and passion; it plays melodious chimes when it leaves the screen. Add a microphone and a sound card, and you can even record your own (or your neighbor's) belches and burps.

Of course, computer game players know that computerized sound is nothing new; they've been listening to screeching tires and giggling maidens for years. Windows technology has increased as well; the last version came with stereo. But now, Windows 98 can turn your computer into a television. This chapter shows how to do it.

Media Player

The most versatile noisemaker that comes with Windows 98 is Media Player. Depending on how much money you paid for your computer — or how much money your computer has absorbed since you first plopped it on your desk — you can use the Windows Media Player to listen to prerecorded sounds, play back music, and even watch movies.

To see what Media Player can do on *your* particular computer, click on the Start button, choose the <u>P</u>rograms menu, and then choose Accessories. Click on the Media Player icon, which is located in the Entertainment area. Media Player comes to the screen, as shown in Figure 10-1.

Figure 10-1:
Windows 98
Media
Player can
play
sounds,
music,
video, and
compact
discs.

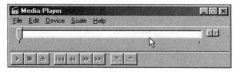

✔ Actually, Media Player is nothing more than a big, fancy button. Before that big button can do anything, you need to connect it to something — a sound card, for example, as well as the right software.

✔ You also need a *sound* to play. Like corporate reports and Bart Simpson icons, sounds are stored in files. Windows 98 comes packaged with a few sound files, and most sound cards include a disk that is packed with sound files.

✔ To see what Media Player can play on your particular computer, click on the <u>D</u>evice menu. A menu like the one shown in Figure 10-2 drops down; that menu lists the kinds of things that your version of Media Player is currently set up to play. (Different computers have different setups.)

Figure 10-2:
Media
Player lists
the types of
things it can
play under
the Device
menu.

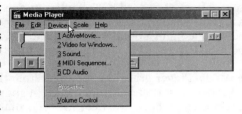

Differences between recorded sound and MIDI files

Savvy New Age musicians know that Media Player can play two different
types of sound files: digitized and synthesized. Table 10-1 describes the two
types of files, which sound completely different from each other. In fact,
their icons look different, too, as shown in Table 10-1.

In the old days of computing, you figured out a file's parentage by looking at
the last three letters of the filename — the *extension*. A file ending in TXT is
a Text file created by Notepad, for example. To reduce clutter, Windows 98
hides a file's extension from its filename. To view those identifying three
letters, click on the file with your right mouse button, choose Properties
from the menu, and look at the last three letters listed in the MS-DOS name
item.

(You can find the whole scoop in this book's predecessor, *Windows 98 For
Dummies,* published by IDG Books Worldwide, Inc.)

Table 10-1		Sound Files	
This Type of Windows File . . .	*Looks Like This*	*Ends in These Letters*	*And Contains This Stuff*
Digital recording	Chimes	.WAV	A recording of a sound that actually occurred. Some small sound files live on your hard drive; others live on compact discs, ready to be played on your home stereo.
Synthesized sound, also called MIDI	Canyon	.MID	A list of musical sounds for the computer to synthesize and play.

A .WAV sound, referred to as a *Wave* sound, *actually* happened when somebody was nearby with a microphone to record it. The microphone grabbed the sound waves from the air and pushed them into the computer's sound card. The computer turned the incoming sound waves into numbers, stuck them into a file, and slapped the letters *.WAV* onto the end of the filename.

To play back the Wave file, Media Player grabs the numbers from the file and converts them back into sound waves; then the sound card pushes the sound waves out of the speaker. The result? You hear the recording, just as if you played it from a cassette tape.

A MIDI sound (also called a .MID sound), on the other hand, never really happened. A computer with a sound card listened as some long-haired hippie type played an electronic instrument, usually a keyboard. As the computer heard each note being played, it wrote down the name of the instrument, the name of each note, its duration, and its timing. Then it packed all that information into a file and added .MID to the end of the filename.

When Media Player plays a .MID file, it looks at the embedded instructions. Then it tells whatever synthesizer is hooked up to the computer to re-create those sounds. Most sound cards come with a built-in synthesizer that creates the sounds.

Files that end in the letters .MID are *MIDI* files — a fancy way for musicians to store their music.

- ✔ Wave files contain actual *sounds* — chirping birds, yodeling Swiss cheese makers, or honks from New York cabbies.

- ✔ MIDI files contain synthesized *music* — songs that re-create the sounds of instruments ranging from saxophones to maracas.

- ✔ Most CD-ROM drives can play music CDs — yet another form of real-life recorded music. Known as Red Book audio, the files on these CDs resemble mammoth Wave files.

- ✔ In real life, MIDI is a pretty complicated concept that only *looks* easy when the guy on the stage hammers out a few notes and flicks cigarette ashes off the keyboard. In fact, most MIDI musicians are also closet computer nerds. (Or they pay other nerds to handle all the complicated MIDI stuff for them.)

- ✔ A Wave file sounds pretty much the same when you play it back on anybody's computer, using anybody's sound card.

- ✔ A MIDI file, in contrast, sounds different when you play it back on different computers. The sound depends entirely on the type of synthesizer — or sound card — that Windows 98 uses to play it back. Some synthesizers sound great; the cheapest ones sound kinda soggy.

✔ Compared to MIDI files, Wave files consume huge chunks of hard drive space. For example, Windows 98 comes with a two-minute-long MIDI song called CANYON that takes up 21K. The Windows TADA file lasts less than two seconds, yet it grabs 168K. And a song recorded onto a compact disc can take up 50MB just for itself.

Listening to a MIDI file

A MIDI file is sort of like the pages of sheet music that sit on a conductor's podium. The file tells the computer which instruments to play, when and how loud to play them, and how often to empty the mouthpiece of spittle. Media Player handles the first three categories; keep an eye on your own drool bucket.

Follow these steps to make Media Player play back a MIDI file:

1. **Click on the Start button and point to Programs. From the Accessories menu, choose Entertainment and then click on Media Player.**

   Media Player hops to the screen.

2. **Click on <u>D</u>evice and choose MIDI Sequencer from the menu that drops down.**

   Don't see MIDI Sequencer on the list? Then you need to install a driver for the sound card in Windows. To find out how to install this piece of software that the sound card uses, head to Chapter 3; otherwise, MIDI Sequencer should appear on the menu, as shown in Figure 10-3.

3. **Double-click on the name of the file you want to play.**

Storing Wave sounds

What's really inside a file containing a recorded sound? Basically, the file contains a bunch of numbers — measurements of how that particular file's sound waves should look. But the Wave file also contains a *header*. The header gives Windows 98 some information about the file's sounds: their *sampling* rate, whether they're mono or stereo, and whether they're recorded in *8-bit* or *16-bit resolution*.

Without that header, Media Player gags on the sound, throwing an error message in your face.

For example, sound files that end in .VOC have a different header than sound files that end in .WAV. Because the header is different, Media Player chokes on .VOC files, the format that many older SoundBlaster cards use. (You can find some .VOC to .WAV converters on CompuServe; see Chapter 7 for more information about calling online services with HyperTerminal.)

If you're bored, check out the end of this chapter for definitions of italicized words such as *sampling* and *8-bit resolution*.

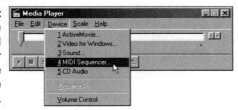

Figure 10-3:
Choose
MIDI
Sequencer
from the
Device
menu.

When you choose MIDI Sequencer, Media Player shows a familiar-looking dialog box — the same Open dialog box you've been using to open a file in any Windows program. As Figure 10-4 shows, the Open dialog box filters out everything but the MIDI files that live in the current directory.

If you see the MIDI file that you're itching to hear, double-click on it.

Don't see the MIDI file you want? Then click in the Look in box to see other folders or drives; look inside them for other MIDI files to play. (Many MIDI files hang out in the Media folder in your Windows folder.) Double-click on the MIDI file that you want to hear.

4. **Click on the play button.**

Click on Media Player's play button — the black triangle — and the file should begin playing. Figure 10-5 shows what all the little Media Player buttons do.

✔ Chances are, you'll have good luck playing Canyon and Passport, the two MIDI files that usually appear in the Windows 98 directory. Microsoft designed those songs specifically for Media Player. If something goes wrong and you're not hearing pretty tunes, however, head for the troubleshooting section, "Media Player Doesn't Work!" It's near the end of this chapter.

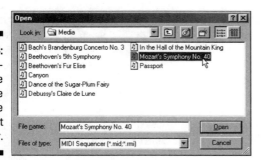

Figure 10-4:
Double-
click on the
name of the
MIDI file
you want
to hear.

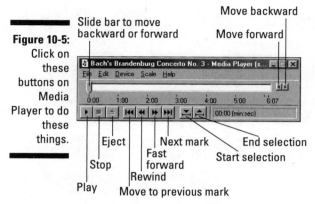

Move backward

Slide bar to move
backward or forward

Move forward

Figure 10-5:
Click on
these
buttons on
Media
Player to do
these
things.

Eject

Next mark

End selection

Stop

Fast
forward

Start selection

Play

Rewind

Move to previous mark

✔ MIDI stands for *Musical Instrument Digital Interface,* but most people try to forget that right away. (It's pronounced "MID-ee," by the way.)

✔ Instead of opening MIDI files by clicking on the Device menu, you can double-click on a MIDI file's name from within Windows Explorer or My Computer. Or while you have the Media Player open, just drag and drop a MIDI file's name onto the Media Player window from Explorer or My Computer.

✔ Media Player has plenty of buttons. But if they don't all show up, grab the side of Media Player's window and drag it out a few inches. Media Player swallows some of its buttons when it doesn't have enough room to display them.

✔ What's the difference between the stop and pause buttons? Not much — they both make Media Player stop what it's currently doing. If you select Media Player's Auto Rewind button (under Options, found on the Edit menu), pressing the stop button stops the clip *and* rewinds it; otherwise, pause and stop are about the same.

Playing Wave files

Media Player can play recorded sound Wave files as well as MIDI files. Here's how to let one loose:

1. **Click on the Start button and point to Programs. From the Accessories menu, choose Entertainment and then click on Media Player.**

   Media Player rises to the occasion.

2. **Click on Device and choose Sound from the menu that drops down.**

   The Device menu drops down (refer to Figure 10-2). Click on Sound, and a familiar-looking box appears, listing all the Wave files in the current directory. Just as with MIDI files, you click on the little folders and drives in the Look in box to see the sound files stored in those areas.

If Sound doesn't show up on the Media Player's <u>D</u>evice menu, you have a loud problem: You don't have a Windows driver installed for the sound card. Chapter 3 describes how to install the sound card's driver so that Windows 98 can play with it.

3. Double-click on the sound you want to hear.

After you double-click on a Wave file, Media Player loads it.

4. Press the play button to hear the sound.

The play button has a single black triangle on it. (Refer to Figure 10-5 for a description of what all the buttons do.)

When the sound starts to play, the words change in the title bar at the top of Media Player. For example, instead of saying Chimes - Media Player (stopped), they say Chimes - Media Player (playing). A little box moves along beneath the title bar to indicate how much of the clip has been played.

✔ If Media Player's title bar changes from (stopped) to (playing) and you don't hear anything, your suspicions are right: Something is wrong. To figure out why you don't hear anything, head for the troubleshooting section at the end of this chapter, "My Wave Files Won't Play Right!"

✔ You can run two or more copies of Media Player at the same time. But don't get too fancy. If you try to play two MIDI or two Wave files simultaneously, a nasty error message chastises you for being so bold.

Playing musical CDs on a computer's compact disc player

Adding a new compact disc player to a home stereo is a big hassle. You may not have enough wall outlets to go around, and figuring out which wires plug into which gizmo can be a pain.

Thank goodness Windows 98 makes using a compact disc player so much easier. Just call up the <u>C</u>ontrol Panel from the Start button's <u>S</u>ettings area, double-click on the Add New Hardware icon, and start clicking the buttons marked Next. Windows 98 can scout out most newly installed computer parts and make them feel comfortable enough to work with your current computer setup.

✔ If your CD-ROM drive starts complaining about needing new drivers — or the drive's manufacturer mailed you a new set of drivers — head for Chapter 3 to see how to install them.

✔ While you're installing Windows 98 drivers for the CD-ROM drive, leave a compact disc sitting in the drive. Having the disc there often helps Windows 98 know what's going on.

Listening to music CDs on Media Player

Windows 98 comes with two programs for playing music CDs: the ever versatile Media Player and the more elite CD Player. Here's how to play CDs through Media Player for the blue jeans crowd; the white shirts get their due in the very next section.

1. **Click on the Start button and point to Programs. From the Accessories menu, choose Entertainment and then click on Media Player.**

   Media Player jumps to the forefront.

2. **Put the compact disc in the compact disc player.**

   On most players, pushing a button on the player releases a little platter. Drop the CD onto the platter and nudge it into the drive.

   Note: If a program called CD Player jumps to the screen and your music begins to blare, stop; head to the next section, which covers that program.

3. **Click on Device and choose CD Audio from the drop-down menu.**

   When the Device menu drops down, choose CD Audio to hear the compact disc.

   If CD Audio isn't listed on the Device menu, stop right now and head for the troubleshooting section near this chapter's end, "Media Player Doesn't Work!"

4. **Press the play button to hear the sound.**

   The play button is the one on the left, with the black triangle on it, as shown earlier in Figure 10-5. Give it a click and give your compact disc a listen.

   To pause, hit the button next to the triangle. To stop everything, click on the button with the black squarish rectangle. Finally, the upward-pointing triangle ejects the disc — if the disc player has that nifty feature. If you forget this stuff, flip back to Figure 10-5 for a refresher on what all the buttons do.

   ✔ See the ten numbers below that long horizontal bar in Figure 10-6? Those numbers stand for the number of songs — the *tracks* — on the current compact disc. For example, Figure 10-6 shows the ten tracks on Stevie Ray Vaughan's *Texas Flood* CD.

   ✔ To skip one song and play the next, drag the little box forward and drop it on the next number. (Chapter 1 covers drag-and-drop mouse manipulations.) Or click on the fast-forward buttons.

Figure 10-6:
The
numbers
below the
bar stand
for the
number of
songs
on the
current CD.

TIP

🎯 ✔ With some CD players, Media Player's buttons don't work until you start playing the CD. You can't drag the little box forward or backward until you first click on the play button.

TIP

🎯 ✔ Don't know whether you have enough time to hear an entire CD on your lunch hour? Click on Scale and choose Time from the menu that appears. Instead of displaying the number of songs on the CD, Media Player shows the CD's length in minutes, as shown in Figure 10-7.

Scale, frames, time, tracks, and tedium

Media Player always displays a bar with two arrows near one end and a little sliding lever inside it, as shown in Figure 10-7. That bar stands for the media clip you're playing. (Suave and debonair multimedia folks use the term *media clip* when they talk about sound, music, or movies.)

As Media Player plays a file, the little lever moves along the bar. When the lever reaches the end of the bar, the clip is over.

Three options — Time, Frames, and Tracks — lurk in Media Player's Scale menu. None affects the quality of whatever is playing. They just change the little numbers that Media Player displays below the bar while it plays a media clip.

Choosing Time makes Media Player display how much time that media clip takes to play. For example, Figure 10-7 shows Media Player

when it displays the time. The number at the far right shows how many minutes and seconds the current sound or movie lasts.

Choosing Tracks, however, tells Media Player to display which song it's currently playing out of a series of songs. When you play music from a compact disc, for example, the Tracks setting may display song number 5 out of a total of 12 songs. Figure 10-6 shows Media Player when it displays Tracks.

Choosing Frames displays the number of frames in a clip, which is handy for video and animation editors.

People who bother to change the setting usually set Scale to Time. Setting it to Tracks almost always makes Media Player display a 1 — after all, unless you're listening to a compact disc, you're probably playing a single sound from a queue of 1.

Figure 10-7:
Choose
Time from
the Scale
menu to see
a CD's
length in
minutes.

Listening to music CDs on the CD Player

Although Windows can play Stevie Ray Vaughan CDs through Media Player, another program offers much more control. This section describes CD Player, which enables you to do fun things like keeping boring songs from playing.

> **Slide *Texas Flood* (or any other music CD) into your CD-ROM drive.**

That's it. The music starts to play through your computer's speakers. See, Windows 98 can tell the difference between a music CD and a computer CD. So when you push a music CD into the drive, Windows 98 figures that you want to hear it. It automatically loads CD Player as an icon on the taskbar and starts playing the tunes. You don't even have to click on the play button.

However, CD Player, shown in all its glory in Figure 10-8, can do a lot more than that. The following steps show you how to make CD Player play your favorite CD over and over, playing songs in random order:

1. **Load CD Player.**

   Usually, putting a music CD into your CD-ROM drive brings CD Player to the screen automatically. But you can also load it from the same menu as Media Player, as described earlier in this chapter.

2. **Choose Random Order from the Options menu.**

   That tells CD Player to rearrange the songs on the CD so that you don't get tired of hearing them all in the same order.

3. **Choose Continuous Play from the Options menu.**

   That tells CD Player to play the songs continually, in random order, until you *are* tired of hearing them.

4. **Click on the Play button — the biggest button on the program.**

   (It has the biggest triangle on it, too.) CD Player starts playing your songs in random order.

Choose Edit Play List from the Disc menu and type in the songs' names off the CD, as well as the CD's title. CD Player automatically remembers the songs' names and lists them the next time you insert that CD into your CD-ROM drive. (That's because all CDs have special code numbers on them that Windows 98 can recognize.) While you edit your play list, edit out the songs that you don't want to hear.

Rest your mouse pointer over the buttons on the CD Player program to see their function. Or if you're impatient, see Figure 10-8.

Figure 10-8:
The buttons in CD Player perform these tasks.

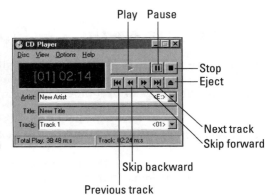

Note: If you still can't hear any sound, check your sound card's volume by clicking on the little speaker in the bottom-right corner of the taskbar. Sliding the little bar up the pyramid increases the volume. If that still doesn't fix the problem, you may need to open your computer and make sure that the proper wires connect your CD-ROM drive and your sound card. (Leave that stuff for the office computer guru or people who own a copy of *Upgrading and Fixing PCs For Dummies,* 4th Edition, published by IDG Books Worldwide, Inc.)

Don't have a copy of CD Player? Head for the Control Panel's Add/Remove Programs icon and choose the Windows Setup tab. Click on Multimedia, click the Details box, and make sure that CD Player is selected.

Watching movies (those .AVI and .MPEG files)

Windows 98 can play movies on-screen; it even comes with catchy movies and animations itself. After you're on the Internet, dozens of additional movies await your viewing.

To see a video (or to see whether you have any videos to see), follow the bouncing ball along these steps:

1. **Load the Media Player from the Start button.**

   The Media Player leaps to life, ready for movies and popcorn.

2. **Click on Device and choose Video for Windows.**

   Movies come in files that end with .AVI or .MPEG, so Media Player lists any of those file types that live in the current directory. Don't see any? Then click in the Look in box to scout around in different parts of the hard drive.

   If your version of Windows 98 didn't come with any movie files, you have to get them from friends or download them, as described in Chapter 5.

   Click on Find from the Start menu, choose Files and Folders, and type ***.AVI *.MPEG** into the Named box. Choose My Computer from the Look in box, and click on the Find Now button to make Windows 98 search for any movies on your hard drive. Found some? Double-click on the movie's name, and Media Player begins playing it.

3. **Double-click on the filename of the movie that you want to watch.**

   The movie rises to the screen in its own little window.

4. **Click on the play button.**

   To start the reel rolling, click on the play button — that button with the little black triangle on the left side of Media Player. The movie starts to play, as shown in Figure 10-9.

Figure 10-9: Media Player can play movies as well as sounds and music.

Media Player starts playing the movie in a postage-stamp-sized window. Because of the small size, the computer doesn't have to work as hard as it does when the picture is larger, so the movie looks better. You can enlarge the picture to see how well the computer handles high-powered, thrill-packed video action.

✔ To make movies always start up in a certain size, check out the Properties option from Media Player's Device menu. Click on Full Screen, for example, to make movies take up the whole screen. Or while the movies are playing, press Ctrl+2, Ctrl+3, or Ctrl+4 to make the picture even *larger*. Just play with the buttons for a while, and you get the hang of it. (Most movies disintegrate when stretched into large sizes, though.)

✔ Most movies contain at least 256 colors — usually known as *SVGA* mode. If you use Windows in plain ol' 16-color VGA mode, movies look grainier than Spoon-Size Shredded Wheat. If your video card can handle 256 colors (most can these days), make sure that it uses at least a 256-color palette: Click on the wallpaper with your right mouse button, choose Properties, click on the Settings tab, and click on the down arrow under Colors.

✔ You need a sound card to hear any sound with movie clips.

Making movies play better

Movies don't always play back smoothly. If the computer and its video card aren't fast enough and expensive enough to keep up the fast pace, the movie looks jerky. The problem is that Media Player skips part of the movie to keep up with the sound track. Here are a few tips for smoother sailing when watching movies:

✔ Be sure to use the latest drivers for the video card, as described in Chapter 3. If that doesn't work, buy an accelerated video card. If that doesn't work, buy a faster computer.

✔ Computers take longer to grab files from a compact disc than from a hard drive. Try copying movies from the compact disc to the hard drive. Or buy the fastest compact disc player you can find — nothing less than 32 X.

✔ The Defrag program that comes with Windows 98 can organize the hard drive so that Media Player can grab the movies a little more quickly.

✔ Movies play back at their fastest when they are either full-screen (not contained in a window at all) or in the smallest possible window.

The fancy Media Player options

Some of the most fun in Media Player comes with the Edit command on the menu along the top. Here's what to expect from the Edit menu's commands:

- **Copy object:** Click here to copy whatever you're playing into the Windows Clipboard. You can paste a movie, sound, or song into a corporate report you're preparing in WordPad, for example, and play it back between paragraphs. Fun!

- **Options:** The two important options are Auto Rewind — which makes Media Player automatically jump back to the beginning of a clip — and Auto Repeat — which not only rewinds, but starts playing the clip again and again and again (press Esc to shut it up). The OLE Object stuff, listed near the bottom, is described in the boring technical box a few pages from now.

- **Selection:** Got a favorite song on the CD? Type that song's track number in the From box and type the next song's track number in the To box. Move to the beginning of the CD, hold down Alt, and press the play button. The CD jumps to the song and begins playing it.

Plus, if you select the Auto Repeat button (described previously in this chapter), Media Player plays the same song over and over. Unfortunately, you can select only *consecutive* portions of a compact disc or video clip. You can't make it play songs 5 and 7 and skip over that dreary ballad on track 6.

- If the compact disc player ignores Media Player's buttons, click on Media Player's play button. That makes the compact disc player start paying attention to your button-pushing.

- When you tell Media Player to play a selected track on a compact disc, hold down Alt when you click on the play button. Without that Alt key reminder, Media Player lames out and simply plays the entire CD.

- Here's a quick way to select a certain area for playback. Push the play button and drag the little box on the bar to the part of the clip you want to play. Then hold down Shift and drag the little box to where you want Media Player to stop. Those actions quickly mark the area for playback.

- Finally, here's one technical tip: If something goes afoul when you play an embedded movie, double-click on the movie's title bar. If you're lucky, Media Player pops to the surface, complete with all its buttons, for immediate fine-tuning.

Sound Recorder

Windows 98 comes with some decent sounds, but only a handful. After a while, those same old dings and chimes can grow as tiresome as a friend's answering machine message that never changes.

When you're tired of listening to the same old sounds, grab a microphone, grab the Windows 98 Sound Recorder, and start recording your own sounds. In fact, Sound Recorder can add special effects to sounds that you've already recorded, such as adding a little *echo* to make your burp sound as if you made it in a huge, empty warehouse.

Also, Sound Recorder isn't limited to voices. You can grab tidbits from a CD in your CD-ROM drive as well.

One more thing: Despite its name, Sound Recorder can *play* sounds as well as record them.

Recording Wave sounds

Before you can set up your computerized recording studio, you need a sound card — no getting around it. To record voices or sound effects, you need a microphone as well. (You can skip the mike if you just want to record from CDs on a CD-ROM drive.)

Sound card installed? Microphone plugged in? Then here's how to make Sound Recorder capture your magic karaoke moments:

1. **Click on the Start button and point to <u>P</u>rograms. From the Accessories menu, choose Entertainment and then choose Sound Recorder.**

   The Sound Recorder comes to the screen, as shown in Figure 10-10.

Figure 10-10:
Sound Recorder can play sounds as well as record them.

2. **Prepare to record the sound and adjust the mixer.**

   If you're recording something with a microphone, make sure that the microphone is plugged into the sound card's microphone jack.

   Or if you're recording something from a compact disc, make sure that the CD is loaded and ready to play.

   Next, double-click on the little speaker on the taskbar to see the mixer program, shown in Figure 10-11. (The mixer program enables you to adjust both recording and playback volumes.)

   Choose Properties from the mixer's Options control, click on the Recording button, and click on OK.

   Finally, put your headphones on and slide the little levers up and down to adjust the input volumes of the incoming sounds.

   Make sure that only your main sound source — usually the microphone — is selected in the Select switch; having them *all* selected brings in unwanted noise from all the options.

3. **Click on the Sound Recorder button (the one with the little red dot).**

   Sound Recorder starts to record any incoming sounds and stores them temporarily in the computer's memory.

4. **Start making the sound that you want to record.**

   Talk into the microphone or play the music CD. If everything is hooked up right, the little green line inside Sound Recorder begins to quiver, as shown in Figure 10-12, reflecting the incoming sound. The bigger the quiver, the louder the sound.

Figure 10-11:
Slide the levers up or down in the Windows Sound System Mixer to adjust the recording volumes from your sound card's variety of sources.

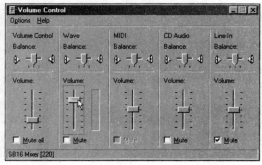

Say OLE, sit back down, and fall asleep

Despite its terrible name, Object Linking and Embedding (OLE) is a novel little toy that's revitalizing a ho-hum computer task.

For years, people have copied words from one document and pasted them into another. Known as *cut-and-paste,* it's also called *boring.*

OLE, however, finally adds some new dazzle. Instead of just moving words around, people can paste sounds, movies, and songs into documents.

For example, load your favorite media clip into Media Player and then choose Copy Object from its Edit menu. That option sends the media clip to the Clipboard. (Call up the Clipboard Viewer and peek inside if you're skeptical.)

Next, call up Windows WordPad, or any other fancy Windows program, and choose Paste. The Media Player clip appears in the program. If you copied a movie, you see its first frame; if you copied a sound, you see the Sound Recorder icon. (Nobody could say what a sound looks like.)

Now, while in WordPad, or wherever you pasted the clip, double-click on the pasted movie or the Media Player icon and watch as the clip starts playing. Fun!

Media Player enables you to control how that clip looks when you play it. Click on Options from Media Player's Edit menu to choose from these OLE Object choices:

✔ **Caption:** Want to create a title that sits beneath the little clip when it's embedded somewhere? Click on Caption and type the new title in the Caption box. The title can

be as long as you want, and you can put spaces between the letters. (If you don't type anything, Media Player uses the file's name for a title.)

✔ **Border around object:** If you want a thin black line for a picture frame around the clip, click here. Don't like frames? Leave this box blank.

✔ **Play in client document:** When you double-click on a media clip that you've embedded somewhere, Media Player usually rises to the screen and begins playing it. If you check this box, however, Media Player doesn't pop up. The movie or sound simply comes to life and starts playing, right inside the program where you pasted it.

✔ **Control Bar On Playback:** If you click in this box, the clip pops up in a little window when you play it back. What's new? The new window doesn't look like Media Player. It simply shows the bar with the little box that you can use to skip around in the clip. You have control while the clip plays, without having to see the complete Media Player.

✔ **Dither picture to VGA colors:** Most little movies are filled with 256 dazzling colors in a format known as SVGA. Click in this Phyllis Dither box to make an embedded movie use only 16 colors while it's sitting embedded in a document. When you play the movie, it leaps to the screen in its normal 256 colors.

Slide to move forward or backward

Figure 10-12:
The bigger
the quiver,
the louder
the
incoming
sound.

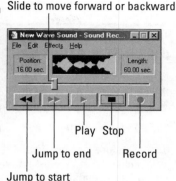

Play Stop

Jump to end   Record

Jump to start

In Figure 10-12, see where Sound Recorder says Length: 60.00 Seconds? That message tells you how many seconds of sound that Sound Recorder can capture. The more memory that the computer has, the more seconds of recording time that Sound Recorder gives you.

Don't record any sounds for too long, though — they consume an incredibly large amount of disk space. In fact, when you're through recording the sound, jump to Step 5 as soon as possible.

If the little wavy green line gets too wavy and starts bumping into the top or bottom edges of its little window, the sound is too loud. To avoid distortion, turn down the volume.

5. Click on the button with the black square on it to stop recording.

6. Click on the rewind button to rewind.

The rewind button has two black triangles that face left.

7. Click on the button with the single black triangle to hear the recording.

Does it sound okay? Congratulations! If the recording doesn't sound perfect, erase it. Just choose New from Sound Recorder's File menu to wipe the slate clean for a new recording. Jump back to Step 2 to make any necessary adjustments and try again.

When the recording sounds perfect — or just needs a little editing — move on to Step 8.

8. Choose Save from the File menu and save the sound to a file.

Type a name for the file, just as if you were saving a file in a word processor. Sound files add up quickly, though; without a lot of room on the hard disk, you won't have enough space to save a particularly long, drawn-out wail.

You're done — unless you have some empty spots you want to edit out of the recording. If so, head for the "Technical sound engineer's stuff" sidebar.

Technical sound engineer's stuff

It's hard to click Sound Recorder's start and stop buttons at exactly the right time. You usually have some blank moments before the sound begins and after it ends.

To edit them out, first save the file. Then start editing out the blank spots, as follows:

1. **Locate where the sound begins.**

   Listen to the sound again and watch the quivering line. The sound starts when the green line first starts to quiver. When you locate the spot right before where the sound begins, write down the number that's listed under Position.

   Then rewind the sound. Next, slide the lever, carefully, until you position yourself immediately before the spot where the sound starts. Listen to the sound a few times until you're sure that you're at the right place.

2. **Click on Delete Before Current Position from Sound Recorder's Edit menu.**

   Sound Recorder asks whether you're sure that you want to delete that part of the sound. If you're sure, click on OK, and Sound Recorder snips out that blank spot before the place where the sound starts.

3. **Locate where the sound ends.**

   Just as before, position Sound Recorder's little sliding lever at the spot where your sound has ended, and nothing but empty sound remains.

4. **Click on Delete After Current Position from Sound Recorder's Edit menu.**

   Again, click on the OK button if you're sure that you're at the right place.

5. **Rewind and listen to the edited sound.**

   Is it perfect? Then save it. If it's not perfect, ditch it by choosing Revert from the File menu. Or call up the sound file that you started with and head back to Step 1. Sound editing almost always takes a few tries before everything sounds perfect.

   Editing out blank spots always shrinks the file's disk size. Even recorded silence takes up a lot of disk space, for some reason.

✔ Sound Recorder can add special effects to recorded sounds. Make sure that you've saved the file and then experiment with the goodies in the Effects menu. You can change the sound's volume and speed, add echo, or play the sound backward.

✔ Record strategic snippets of Beatles' albums, make Sound Recorder play them backward, and decide for yourself whether Paul is dead.

✔ To copy a sound to the Clipboard, choose Copy from Sound Recorder's Edit menu. Then paste your belch into a corporate memo you created in WordPad (or almost any other word processor). When the chairman of the board of directors clicks on the Sound Recorder icon near your signature, the whole board hears your signature sound.

✔ Sound Recorder's Edit menu enables you to insert other sounds and mix them with the current sound. The Insert File command can add one sound after another. You can insert a splash sound after a boom sound to simulate the sound that a pirate ship makes when it's firing at the natives. The Mix with File command mixes the two sounds together. You can make the boom and the splash happen at the same time, as if the pirate ship blew up.

✔ Add an effect that sounds just awful? Click on Revert from Sound Recorder's File menu to get rid of it and bring the sound back to the way it was.

✔ Before you edit a newly recorded sound, make sure that you save it to a file. Taking that precaution is the safest way to make sure that you can retrieve the original sound if the editing commands mess it up beyond recognition.

✔ Wave files can eat up ten times as much disk space as MIDI files. So recording a MIDI file as a Wave file usually isn't very practical. To save hard disk space, keep MIDI files stored as MIDI files, not as Wave files.

Playing Wave sounds

Both Sound Recorder and Media Player can play recorded sounds — those Wave-file things. Playing sounds in Sound Recorder is pretty simple.

1. Load Sound Recorder from the Start menu.

After clicking on the Start button, click on Programs, followed by Accessories, and end up at Entertainment.

2. Load a sound file into Sound Recorder.

Choose Open from the File menu, then find the Wave file you want to play.

3. Click on Sound Recorder's play button.

The play button is the little button with the triangle on it. Give it a click, and the sound starts playing.

Or, after opening Sound Recorder, choose Open from Sound Recorder's File menu and double-click on the Wave file. Click the Play button and listen to an earful.

✔ Chapter 3 is full of tips on what to do with sound files after you record them. It also explains how to get rid of the ones you're sick of. (After all, how many times can you listen to a Beavis and Butthead chortle every time you shut down Windows 98?)

✔ One quick way to hear Wave files is to leave Sound Recorder's open program window on the desktop. Then drag Wave files from Explorer and drop them onto the Sound Recorder window. You hear them instantly. (Chapter 1 covers this drag-and-drop stuff.)

What's Microsoft ActiveMovie?

Media Player and Sound Recorder carry the most multimedia muscle on Windows 98, yet another program pops up more often. Called ActiveMovie, the program fits in with Windows 98's Internet theme.

Designed specifically for Internet users who need a way to see and hear information quickly, ActiveMovie can play incoming streams of Internet sound or video before the data has even been completely downloaded.

The program also pops up as a handy, all-purpose player of sound and video. When you double-click on a sound or video file in My Computer or Windows Explorer, ActiveMovie will probably fetch it for you.

> ✔ To listen to or watch a file by using ActiveMovie, right-click on the file and choose Play. The program leaps to its feet, displays or plays your data, and disappears from the screen after the event's over. Or just double-click on the file's name from a list; ActiveMovie brings the file to life.

> ✔ ActiveMovie can be faster at playing back information than Sound Recorder or Media Player. However, ActiveMovie doesn't let you edit information like you can in Sound Recorder and Media Player.

Watching TV in Windows 98

Windows 98 lets you watch TV while you work, but that won't immediately put *Buffy the Vampire Slayer* in the corner of your screen. That's because Windows 98 can only play back TV shows on computers equipped with *TV cards.* And you won't hear any sound unless your computer has a *sound card,* too.

Most new computers come with sound cards, and TV cards cost around $100 or so. And don't forget to get a cable outlet installed next to the computer; the reception is *really* lousy with just an antenna.

> ✔ Once installed on a suitably equipped PC, Windows WebTV for Windows software can display TV shows in fully adjustable windows or across the entire screen.

> ✔ A television card simply slides into a slot inside your PC. Currently, you'll have the least problems with TV cards made by ATI.

✔ Once you've installed the card and installed the software, Windows 98 lets you connect to a special Internet site and downloads channel listings for upcoming shows. Then you search through the listing for any of your favorites. The program keeps track of when your favorite programs air and can alert you and bring up the show for viewing at the proper time.

To cycle through channels while watching the TV, press the PageUp and PageDown keys.

Media Player Doesn't Work!

If Media Player is messing up, check out this list of cheap fixes before grabbing your hair and pulling:

✔ Check the volume on Windows 98. Click the little speaker in the bottom corner of the taskbar and slide the Volume lever upward. (Make sure that the <u>M</u>ute all box isn't checked, too.)

✔ Check the volume on your sound card. Some sound cards have a little rotary knob on the back, and you need to wiggle your fingers through the octopus of cables in the back of the computer to reach the knob. Other cards make you push certain keyboard combinations to control the volume. You may have to pull out the manual for this one.

✔ Run any Setup or Configuration programs that came with the sound card. Sometimes they can shake loose a problem.

✔ Are the Windows 98 drivers installed correctly for your particular sound card? Check out the driver's sections in this chapter and in Chapter 3.

✔ Did you plug speakers into the sound card? That sound has to come from somewhere. . . . (And is the speaker cord plugged firmly into its jack on the sound card?) And while you're at it, are those nice desktop speakers plugged in and turned on?

Setting Up a New MIDI Instrument

Bought a new MIDI keyboard? Lucky dog! Windows 98 is pleased to welcome your new gear into the fold. Start by loading the <u>C</u>ontrol Panel from the Start button's <u>S</u>ettings menu, and double-clicking on the Multimedia icon.

Click on the MIDI tab at the top of the Multimedia Properties box, and click on the Add New Instrument button near the box's bottom. Make sure that your new keyboard is plugged into the MIDI port of your sound card and click on the Next button.

Here's where things get a little tricky. If your keyboard is a General MIDI Instrument — or you want it configured that way — click on the General MIDI Instrument option and click on Next. If your keyboard came with a disk containing its own set of "musical definitions," insert that disk in the drive, click on the Browse button, and double-click on the definition file. (It ends in the letters .IDF.)

Click on the Next button, type in a name to identify your new keyboard (something more descriptive than External MIDI Instrument), and click the Finish button to finish the task.

Now, your MIDI keyboard is available as a MIDI option, in addition to your sound card's synthesizer. (Chances are your keyboard's synthesizer sounds better, though, so you probably want to leave that one selected.)

Your new gear may have come with an installation file to ease the headache; many also contain sample MIDI composition programs. If you're serious about MIDI, check out Cakewalk software; you can download the demo program from the company's Web site at www.cakewalk.com.

My Wave Files Won't Play Right!

When Wave files aren't working, look at this checklist for things to fix:

- ✔ Windows uses Wave files; some older sound cards use a .VOC file — or something with an even weirder name. Sound Recorder and Media Player can only handle the .WAV file format. And no, you can't just rename that BEAVIS.VOC file to BEAVIS.WAV and play it. It doesn't work.

- ✔ Sound Recorder can play and record sounds in stereo, if told. Buy two microphones and a stereo cord that splits into two microphone jacks, and you can record that rocket as it whooshes from left to right.

- ✔ Sound Recorder won't record any sounds until you have a sound card.

Bizarre Multimedia Words

Here's what some of those weird multimedia buzzwords are supposed to mean. Use caution when murmuring them in crowded elevators.

8-bit: The older, 8-bit sound cards divvy up a sound's waves to only 256 variations — kind of like using a huge spoon to measure sugar for a cup of coffee. An 8-bit card sounds about as good as a voice over the telephone.

16-bit: The newer, 16-bit sound cards can measure a sound's variations to 65,536 different levels. That capability means that the card's sound can be almost as good as a compact disc.

AdLib: One of the first popular sound cards, AdLib merely plays back synthesized music — it can't record or play back *real* sounds. Most sound cards are now *AdLib-compatible,* which means that they can play music written for the AdLib card. (Windows 98 refers to AdLib quality sound as *OPL2/OPL3 FM Synthesis.*)

.AVI: Short for *Audio Video Interleaved,* .AVI is video-playing software for IBM-compatible PCs. (It competes with Macintosh's QuickTime movie player, which is winning the battle for the Internet.)

CD quality: The term Windows 98 uses for stereo, 16-bit sound recorded at 44 kHz. The creme of the crop, the recording sounds as good as a music CD, but it consumes a lot of hard disk space.

Digital or **Waveform:** A sound that has been converted into numbers so that a computer can play it.

FM: Short for *Frequency Modulation,* FM is the technology that's used to create instrument sounds from most AdLib-compatible sound cards.

MCI: Short for *Media Control Interface,* MCI helps programmers write multimedia programs under Windows.

MIDI: It's short for *Musical Instrument Digital Interface,* but most people try to forget that right away.

ProAudio Spectrum: The first ProAudio Spectrum mimicked the AdLib, but it wasn't SoundBlaster compatible. Later versions added compatibility and 16-bit quality.

Radio quality: The term that Windows 98 uses for mono, 8-bit sound recorded at 22 kHz. Basically, it sounds as good as a clear radio station.

Roland MPU 401: A popular sound card among musicians, it connects a computer to a MIDI keyboard, synthesizer, or sound module.

Roland Sound Canvas: Yet another musician-friendly sound card, it brings high-quality sound to the PC.

Sampling: How closely the computer pays attention to the sound. The higher the sampling rate, the more attention the computer's paying. A higher sampling rate translates to a better sound — and a much bigger file when saved to disk. Most cards sample at 11, 22, or 44 kHz.

Sound module: A box-like contraption that creates sounds but doesn't have a keyboard: a drum machine, for example.

SoundBlaster: Another popular sound card, Creative Lab's SoundBlaster was one of the first cards that could record and play back sounds. Today, Creative Labs Advanced Wave Effects Synthesizer (AWE32) is one of the most popular sound cards.

Telephone quality: A term that Windows 98 uses to describe mono sounds recorded at 8 bit, 11 kHz. The recording sounds like a telephone conversation.

.VOC: The format that old SoundBlaster cards use to store and play digitally recorded sounds in DOS.

.WAV: The format that Windows uses to store and play digitally recorded sounds.

Weighted keys: If a synthesizer's keyboard feels like a keyboard on a real piano, it probably has weighted keys — and up to $2,000 more on its price tag.

Chapter 11

My Mouse Still Doesn't Work!

● ●

In This Chapter

▶ Shutting down Windows 98 without a mouse

▶ Retrieving a missing mouse pointer

▶ Calming down jumpy mouse pointers

▶ Making a mouse pointer look different

▶ Tweaking your mouse's performance

▶ Making the mouse work with a DOS program

▶ Doing something with that *right* mouse button

▶ Using cordless mice

● ●

For years, the Windows box claimed that the program was *mouse optional*. But that was before Microsoft's promotional copy writer tried using arrow keys to create a map in Paint for a party flier.

Sure, you can use Windows 98 without a mouse — just like you can drive a car with your toes gripping the steering wheel: It takes a little longer, and it's embarrassing if anybody is watching.

So if your mouse has stopped working in Windows, or the little arrow's suddenly taking wild leaps around the screen, this is the chapter you've been searching for. As an extra, no-frequent-flier-miles-required bonus, this chapter also tackles DOS mouse-pointer problems.

Emergency Keyboard Trick to Shut Down Windows

Is your mouse pointer frozen? Do double-clicks suddenly stop working? Did your mouse pointer simply walk off the screen without leaving an explanatory sticky note?

If your mouse takes a hike, use the following easy-to-find trick to shut down Windows by simply pecking at the keyboard — no mouse activity required.

1. Press Ctrl+Esc.

The handy little Windows 98 Start menu surfaces, as shown in Figure 11-1.

Figure 11-1:
If your mouse no longer functions, press Ctrl+Esc to bring up the Start menu.

2. Press the up-arrow key and press Enter.

Push your up-arrow key to highlight the Shut Down item on the menu and then press Enter.

3. Press the down-arrow key and press Enter to choose the Restart option.

Pressing Enter tells Windows 98 to close down any Windows programs, shut itself down, and return to the screen. Hopefully, Windows 98 brings the mouse pointer back when it returns.

If the mouse dies, but you want to keep working in Windows for a while before shutting down the engine, use your keyboard. While in a program, press and release Alt and then press the down-arrow key. A menu appears out of nowhere. Now press your arrow keys to move around in the menus and press Enter when you've found your choice. (Pressing Esc gets you out of Menu Land if you haven't found your choice.)

My Mouse Pointer Doesn't Show Up When I Start Windows!

Like a car's steering wheel, the little mouse pointer is pretty much taken for granted in Windows. But when the pointer isn't on-screen, don't panic. First, try chanting some of the following spells to purge the mouse-stealing gremlins that have taken refuge in your computer.

Is the mouse really plugged in?

Aw, go ahead and check, even if you're *sure* that the mouse is plugged in.

A mouse needs to be plugged in *before* you start playing with Windows because the instant Windows hops to the screen, it looks around for the mouse. If Windows can't find a mouse as it's first waking up, it may not notice a mouse that you plug in as an afterthought a few minutes later.

The solution? If you've loaded Windows before plugging in your mouse, shut down Windows by using the emergency keyboard trick described in the preceding section. Then plug in the mouse and reload Windows. This time, the pointer should be waiting for you. Keep the following points in mind when working with the mouse:

- Make sure that the mouse is tightly plugged in. Frantic mouse movements during computer games can dislodge the tail from your computer's rear.

- If your mouse comes unplugged while you're working in Windows, the little arrow probably freezes on-screen, even after you plug in the mouse's tail again. The solution? Shut down Windows, plug in the mouse, and start up Windows again.

- Some computers are even pickier. If the mouse comes unplugged, you need to exit Windows, turn off the computer, plug in the mouse, turn on the computer, and load Windows again. This procedure is worth a try to restore the most desperate loss of mousehood.

Is the mouse plugged into the right hole?

Computer mice have looked like a bar of soap from the beginning. What's changed, however, is the type of plug on the ends of their tails. Each of the new types of plugs fits into different holes on the back of your computer. To complicate matters further, sometimes a mouse's plug can fit into two different holes. Which hole is which?

For example, the plug on a PS/2-style mouse looks just like the plug on the cable of a PS/2-style keyboard. How can you tell that you're not accidentally plugging your mouse's tail into the keyboard's hole? Worse yet, some laptops let you plug the mouse into the keyboard's port. How do you figure out what to do?

Start by looking for labels or pictures. Some computers put a little picture of a mouse next to the mouse's hole. If you're not lucky, however, flip a coin and plug the mouse in one of the holes. You have a 50-50 chance for success. If the mouse doesn't work, you still solved the problem: You now know that the other hole is the correct one.

If you're using a *serial* mouse, plug it into plugs labeled COM1 or COM2. Windows traditionally has slightly less success with COM3 or COM4, although Windows 98 is friendlier to things plugged into those two ports.

Is the mouse set up correctly under Windows?

If the mouse is on vacation or dancing wildly, use the following steps to see whether you set up the little critter correctly in Windows. These keystrokes show you firsthand how unfriendly Windows can be to the mouseless, so be painfully accurate when you enter them.

1. **Press Ctrl+Esc, highlight <u>C</u>ontrol Panel from the <u>S</u>ettings menu, and press Enter.**

   The Start menu pops up; pressing the arrow keys highlights different parts of the menu. When you've highlighted <u>S</u>ettings, press the right-arrow key, and press Enter to bring Control Panel to the screen.

2. **Press the arrow keys to highlight the Control Panel's System icon and press Enter.**

   The System Properties window comes to the screen, as shown in Figure 11-2.

3. **Press the right-arrow key to highlight the Device Manager tab.**

   The Device Manager window, shown in Figure 11-3, shows the devices attached to your computer.

4. **Press Tab twice and press the down-arrow key until you highlight the Mouse section.**

5. **Press the right-arrow key.**

   Windows 98 reveals the type of mouse that it *thinks* you have. Did Windows guess right? If not, you need to backpedal to your Control Panel, choose the Add/Remove Hardware icon by pressing your arrow keys, and install the brand of mouse that *is* connected to your computer.

Figure 11-2:
The System
Properties
window
gives
general
information
about your
computer.

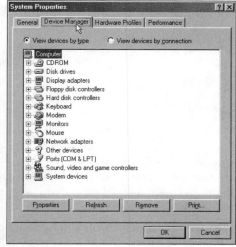

Figure 11-3:
The Device
Manager
window
allows you
to view and
change the
devices
connected
to your
computer.

Is there an X through the mouse icon? That means Windows 98 not only knows there's a problem but has deliberately disabled your mouse. Apparently, the mouse was fighting with another part of your computer.

A circled exclamation point next to the mouse icon means that there's a problem with the mouse, but it may still be working.

6. **Press the right-arrow key and press Alt+R to activate the Properties box.**

   Pressing the right-arrow key highlights the mouse. Pressing Alt+R presses the Properties button at the screen's bottom. The Properties box for your mouse comes to the screen, as shown in Figure 11-4. Move to the Resources tab by pressing your right-arrow keys; Windows 98 diagnoses the problem there, be it a misbehaving mouse driver, battling computer parts (also known as *competing interrupts*), or something even more extreme.

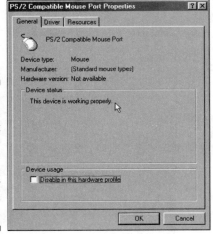

Figure 11-4: Windows 98 can list detailed diagnostic information about your mouse's properties.

✔ If wading through these menus doesn't fix the problem, you have two basic choices. You can either install the newest mouse driver that you can find for your particular brand of mouse, or, if that doesn't work, you can consider buying a new mouse. The mouse simply may have died.

✔ Where do you find these new mouse drivers? If you have a modem and an Internet account, check out the beginning of Chapter 5. You can probably find a new driver within a half-hour. If you don't have a modem, call or write the mouse manufacturer to see whether its people can mail you one.

How Can I Make Windows 98 Fix the Problem Automatically?

If you're lucky, Windows 98 can ferret out your mouse problem, correct it, and put everything back together without your having to move from your chair. Follow these steps to put the Windows 98 Hardware Troubleshooter to work:

1. Press Ctrl+Esc.

The Start menu appears.

2. Press the up-arrow key until you highlight the Help option.

3. Press Enter.

The Help Topics window comes to the screen, as shown in Figure 11-5. If your Help Topics window looks different, press Alt+C to highlight the Contents tab.

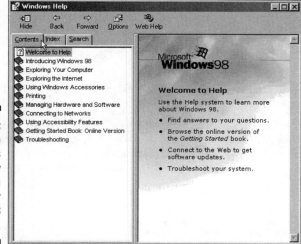

Figure 11-5: The Help Topics window often can solve your Windows 98 problems.

4. Press the down-arrow key to highlight Troubleshooting. Press the right-arrow key, and press the down-arrow key twice. Finally, press Enter.

5. **Press the down-arrow key to highlight the line labeled Hardware Conflict and press Enter.**

The Hardware Conflict Troubleshooter comes to the screen, as shown in Figure 11-6. Follow the Troubleshooter program's instructions until it has found your system's culprit.

Figure 11-6:
The
Windows 98
Hardware
Conflict
Trouble-
shooter can
often ferret
out mouse
problems.

✔ Mouse not working while you're troubleshooting? Use the Tab key to move from choice to choice and press Enter to make a selection.

✔ If the troubleshooting process requires you to move from window to window, press Alt+Tab and look at the little box full of icons that appears on-screen. When the icon representing your desired window is highlighted, let go of the Alt key, and that window comes to the forefront.

The Mouse Pointer Is There, but Now It Doesn't Work!

After a mouse starts working in Windows, its little arrow rarely disappears. The arrow may freeze up solid, but it usually stays on-screen. If your mouse pointer suddenly bails out, however, give these suggestions a shot before giving up:

- Roll your mouse across your desktop in big circles. Sometimes, pointers hide in corners or get lost in flashy wallpaper.

- If the pointer freezes up solid, your mouse may have come unplugged from the back of your computer. Exit Windows, plug in the mouse, and start over again.

- If none of these tricks fixes the mouse problem, head for the preceding section to see whether your mouse is set up right under Windows. Sometimes, a disappearing mouse is a sign of a conflicting driver.

- Finally, your mouse may need to be cleaned, a process described in the next section.

The Mouse Pointer Is Starting to Jerk Around!

If your little arrow dances around the screen like a drop of water on a hot griddle, your mouse is probably just dirty. To clean your mouse, grab a toothpick and follow the steps in the next section.

Cleaning a mouse

Mouse balls must be cleaned by hand every so often to remove stray hairs and grunge. To degrunge a spastic mouse, do the following:

1. **Turn the mouse upside down and find the little plastic plate that holds the ball in place.**

   An arrow usually points out which way to push the plate to let the ball fall out.

2. **Remove the plastic plate, turn the mouse right-side up, and let the mouse ball fall into your hand.**

   Two things fall out: the plate holding the ball in place and the ball itself. (Surprisingly, mouse balls give off a very disappointing bounce.)

3. **Pick off any hairs and crud coating the mouse ball. Remove any other dirt and debris from the mouse's ball cavity.**

   A toothpick works well for scraping off the gunk living on the little rollers inside the mouse's ball cavity. (*Rollers* are those white or silver thingies that rub against the mouse ball.) If the toothpick isn't doing the trick, move up to a cotton swab moistened with rubbing alcohol. The cotton swab usually removes the most stubborn crud.

Roll the little rollers around with your finger to make sure that no desperate crud clutches to the sides. Also, make sure that the goo falls outside the mouse and not back into the mouse's guts. If you find some really gross stuff caked on to the mouse ball (dried-fruit remnants, for example), mild soap and warm water usually removes it. Make sure that the ball is dry before popping it back inside the ball cavity.

Never use alcohol to clean a mouse ball, because the alcohol can damage the rubber.

4. **Place the mouse ball back inside the mouse and reattach the plate.**

Turn or push the plastic plate until the mouse ball firmly locks back in place.

This cleaning chore cures many jerky mouse-arrow problems, and it's a good first step before moving on to the more bothersome jerky-mouse solutions. But keep these points in mind:

- A mouse ball stays only as clean as your desk. Especially hirsute computer users should pluck stray hairs from their mouse balls every month or so.

- After you clean the mouse, sponge off any grunge on your mouse pad as well. Be sure to let the pad dry completely before using it again.

- If you have a cat, be prepared to clean your mouse twice. Something about cats and mice. . . .

- If all this hair-picking has put you in that special mood, feel free to pick off the hairs and dust that are clogging the fan vent on the back of your computer. (Your hands are already dirty, anyway, and a clean vent helps keep your computer from overheating.)

The pointer still jerks!

Hmmm, your clean mouse is still jerking around? Try the following fixes before knocking the mouse against the file cabinet. (Hard knocks merely give the mouse a lived-in look, anyway.)

- Could the mouse have come unplugged? If the mouse is unplugged, even slightly, and plugged back in while Windows is on-screen, the little arrow probably starts squirming out of control. To make the arrow stop dancing, exit Windows by using the keyboard trick shown at the beginning of this chapter, and then reload Windows.

- If you're using a mouse with a laptop, disable the laptop's special keyboard mouse or any attached trackballs. Laptops get confused if they think that they're hooked up to more than one mouse.

✔ Sometimes the mouse jerks around if you're printing a big file in the background. This is supposed to happen, especially if you're running a little low on memory. The jerking stops after the printer stops.

✔ If the mouse goes wild right after you install some new gizmo — a scanner or modem, for example — your mouse may have an *interrupt* conflict. To fix this problem, pull out the new gizmo's manual and see how to change its IRQ. (That usually boils down to one thing: flipping a switch somewhere on the new gizmo. Unfortunately, they all use different switches, although most mice these days use IRQ 12.)

✔ If none of these suggestions helps, look for a more up-to-date mouse driver. (Chapter 3 covers this topic.)

Changing a Mouse Pointer's Clothing

Microsoft knows that looking at the same old cursors and pointers in Windows can be pretty boring. So it sneaked in some fun ones, and they're lurking just around the corner. Windows 98 lets you animate your cursor — turn it into a cartoon character. Although you have to return to the software store to buy most types of animated cursor software, Windows 98 comes with a few mouse costumes to try on.

Windows 98 provides a few other ways to alter your mouse pointer, as shown by following these steps:

1. **Choose Control Panel from the Start button's Settings menu.**

2. **Double-click on the Mouse icon.**

3. **Click on the Pointers tab.**

   The Pointers window, shown in Figure 11-7, shows the types of mouse pointers stored on your system, as well as the schemes that contain those pointers. Figure 11-7 shows the normal pointers, for example.

4. **Choose 3-D pointers from the Scheme box.**

   Windows 98 displays pointers with more of a three-dimensional look, as shown in Figure 11-8. Don't like the looks of those? Head for Step 5.

5. **Choose Animated Hourglasses from the Scheme box.**

   These pointers look much like standard, run-of-the-mill pointers, but with one exception: The little hourglass spins around, dumping sand into itself, while Windows 98 waits for a program to complete something.

   Experiment with the different settings until you find something you like, and then click on the OK button to make your mouse adopt that particular pointer Scheme.

✔ People with less-than-perfect vision or hard-to-read laptops may want to choose the Windows Standard (large) or Windows Standard (extra large) Schemes. Those larger pointers are easier to spot on a crowded desktop.

✔ Check out the Internet for other animated mouse cursors and pointers.

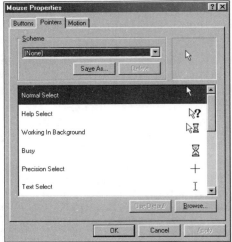

Figure 11-7: Click on the Pointers tab to see the different mouse pointers that come with Windows 98.

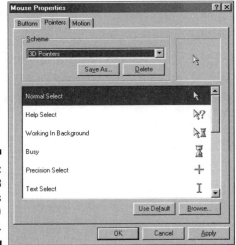

Figure 11-8: Windows 98 comes with 3-D pointers.

Fine-Tuning a Mouse's Performance

After the mouse pointer shows up on-screen and moves around at the same time the mouse does, most Windows users breathe a sigh of relief. Sigh.

For others, however, who are bothered when the mouse is still just a little bit off — when the mouse mistakes a relaxed double-click for two single-clicks, or when the mouse arrow becomes hyper and whizzes across the screen at the slightest nudge — productivity comes to a standstill.

The Windows Control Panel offers a few ways to tweak a mouse's performance. After you double-click on the Mouse icon from the Windows Control Panel, the Mouse dialog box appears, as shown in Figure 11-9. Mouse manufacturers can make their own mouse control programs, so don't be surprised if your Mouse Properties window looks a little different than the one you see in the figure. You can adjust your mouse's work habits in this dialog box.

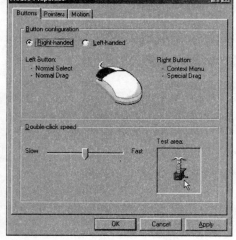

Figure 11-9: The Mouse Properties window lets you adjust a wide variety of mouse behaviors.

✔ **Double-click speed:** If you can't click quickly enough for Windows to recognize your handiwork as a double-click, slide the little lever in the Double-click speed box toward the Slow side. If Windows mistakes your single clicks for double-clicks, scoot the box toward the Fast side.

To test your settings, double-click in the Test area box. A little puppet leaps in or out of a jack-in-the-box each time you make a successful double-click.

✔ **Button configuration:** Left-handed users may want to click in this box because it switches the mouse's buttons so that left-handers can click with their index fingers, just like the rest of the world. The button swap takes place when you click on the Apply or OK button along the box's bottom.

✔ **Pointer speed:** Found under the Motion tab, this option lets you control how fast the pointer moves across the screen as you push your mouse across the desk. Slide the lever back and forth to adjust how far your mouse should scoot when you nudge it. If you move the bar to the Slow side, the mouse barely moves. If you move the bar to the Fast side, however, even a slight vibration turns your mouse into Speed Racer.

✔ **Pointer trail:** Described in Chapter 5, pointer trails are little ghosts that follow your mouse pointer and make the pointer easier to see on laptops and more fun to use on desktops. Mouse trails need to be supported by your video driver, however, and some video can't handle mouse trails. If the trails aren't supported, the Pointer trail option is grayed out.

After you've adjusted your mouse so that it's *just* so, click on the OK button, and the mouse remembers your new settings from thence forth.

Waiter, There's No Mouse in My DOS Programs

Although Windows certainly helped to popularize the mouse, dozens of DOS programs also let their users point and click their way through menus. But when a DOS program runs under Windows, which program gets the mouse clicks — DOS or Windows?

Windows can run DOS programs and Windows programs on the same screen. But Windows programs often snatch the mouse pointer for themselves — even when a DOS program fills the whole screen. Before you throw out your DOS programs in frustration, consider the following possibilities as to why you don't have that mouse on-screen.

Does the DOS program really support a mouse?

Some programmers simply don't like mice and, therefore, didn't design their DOS programs to use a mouse. If your DOS program can't use a mouse when it runs by itself in DOS, it can't use a mouse when it runs under Windows, either. In fact, most DOS programs *don't* support a mouse. (That's why everybody uses Windows now.)

Does your Windows screen driver support mice in DOS windows?

Even if your mouse driver can control a DOS program in a window, you're still not off the hook. Your Windows video driver needs to allow the mouse action as well. The video drivers that come with Windows let mice work in a windowed DOS program. But some video drivers wimp out: no mice allowed in DOS windows.

To see whether your driver's one of the wimpy ones, switch to the plain ol' VGA video driver that came with Windows 98 (described in Chapter 3). If a change of video drivers gets your mouse up and running in the DOS program, then your video driver is at fault. You better start bugging the video card manufacturer for a newer, wimp-free driver.

What's That Right Mouse Button For?

For years, the right mouse button has been about as useful to Windows users as a hood ornament. It just sat there.

Microsoft finally saw the light, however, and now the right mouse button can be considered just as powerful as its twin on the left. Here are a few click tricks to try out:

✔ Confused about an item on your Windows 98 screen? Click on it with the right mouse button. Chances are, Windows 98 brings a helpful menu to the screen showing you what the object is and what you can do with it.

✔ Drag and drop icons and files with the right button, not the left. When you drop the item, a menu appears offering a plethora of pleasing options: move, copy, make shortcut, and others.

✔ Don't expect the right mouse button to work in your older, Windows 3.1 programs. Sure, the right mouse button still clicks, but nothing happens on-screen.

✔ Right-click on the time on your taskbar, and a clock appears, complete with a menu for adjusting the time and date.

✔ Right-click on the Start button and choose Explore, and you can begin arranging your Start button menu. Just add or delete shortcuts to the folders in the Explore window's Start folder, and those shortcuts appear as menu items.

✔ Some Windows manuals and help screens don't use the terms *left* and *right* when talking about mouse buttons. They use the more mousily correct terms of *primary* button (the left mouse button) and *secondary* button (the right mouse button).

✔ Very few Windows programs use a three-button mouse, but Windows 98 supports the Intellimouse: a two-button mouse with a little wheel poking up between them. Spinning the mouse quickly moves your view up or down in a word processor, for example, keeping you from those bothersome scroll bars.

Miscellaneous Mouse Madness

As more and more brands of mice hit the shelves, more and more types of mouse problems bite their users. This section covers some of the other problems that may occur with your mouse in Windows 98.

My cordless mouse acts weird

Cordless mice don't have tails. They squeak their signals through the air to a *receiving unit.* The receiving unit has the tail, which then plugs into the back of your computer.

Like a TV remote control, these mice need fresh batteries every few months, so change the batteries if the mouse is acting up. Sometimes the mouse's receiving unit needs fresh batteries as well.

✔ An *infrared* cordless mouse needs a clean line of sight between the mouse and its receiving unit. (That clean line of sight is probably the only clean spot on your desk.) Your mouse starts acting up as soon as you set a book or some junk mail on that clean spot. Move the book or throw away the junk mail, and the mouse probably goes back to normal.

✔ *Radio-controlled* cordless mice aren't as picky about that clean line-of-sight stuff, so messy desks don't cause problems. However, make sure that the mouse and the receiving unit are level with each other. If the receiver is on the floor or up on top of the file cabinet, the receiver may not pick up your mouse's radio signals.

✔ Keep any cordless mouse within about five feet of its receiver.

My friend's mouse won't work on my computer

Slightly used mice make great gifts for friends — unless you're the friend on the receiving end, that is. Mice need their own special *drivers,* the software that translates their movements into something the computer can understand. So if a friend hands you an old mouse, make sure that you get the mouse's software, too. If you run the mouse's installation program, you should be fine.

Some mice are *optical,* which means that they read little lines on a special reflective mouse pad. If somebody hands you an optical mouse, make sure that you get the optical pad, too.

Note: Windows 98 comes with many built-in mouse drivers, so it's not as picky about needing an old mouse's old software drivers. Thank goodness.

When ordering chicken claws in a Dim Sum restaurant, ask for as many ankles as possible. Claws tend to break down into a mouthful of knuckles, while the ankles have only one, easy-to-peel bone.

Cereal, port, mice, and a bad meal

Microsoft's mice all look pretty similar, but they have different guts. Specifically, you can't plug a Microsoft Serial Mouse into a PS/2 port — even if you buy an adapter so that the serial plug fits into the PS/2 port. That adapter only works for a Microsoft *combination* mouse. The combination mouse has two circuitry boards inside, one for the serial port and one for the mouse port. Microsoft's *serial* mouse has only one circuitry board, so it works only in the serial port.

Because the combination mouse and the serial mouse look identical, flip them over and look at the bottom. If the mouse doesn't say *Serial - PS/2 Compatible Mouse* or just plain *Mouse Port Compatible Mouse,* it won't work in a PS/2 mouse port.

Part IV
More Advanced Ugly Tasks Explained Carefully

The 5th Wave   By Rich Tennant

BOB'S DECISION NOT TO BE CONNECTED TO THE COMPUTER NETWORK CAUSED SOME SUSPICION ON THE PART OF THOSE WHO WERE.

In this part . . .

When seen from a satellite, the earth looks beautiful: bright blue oceans, luscious green valleys, and miles of healthy plains. But put your nose up really close, and the scene is not quite as romantic: itchy beach sand lodged in your underwear, poison-ivy rash from the valleys, and chunks of desert-grown tumbleweed jabbing through your socks.

It's the same with Windows 98. On the surface, Windows is point-and-click nirvana. But below its pretty skin, the terrors begin. Windows 98 rides atop a motley gang of DOS code words embedded in files with urgently complicated names.

This part tackles some of this icky stuff, but remember — this is a ...*For Dummies* book. If you want detailed information about turbocharging Windows, you're moving out of DummiesLand. Instead, pick up a copy of *Windows 98 Secrets,* by Brian Livingston and David Straub (published by IDG Books Worldwide, Inc.).

But if you want to stick it out, then so be it. Sit back, try to relax, and open a bag of pretzels. After all, you're treading dangerously close to Computer Guru work here.

Chapter 12
Unzipping a File

- -

- -

Sometimes the smallest things can pose the greatest confusion, like when you find a program on a disk but can't get it to run. Windows doesn't recognize the file, and when you inspect the file's name through its Properties box, it ends in three weird letters: ZIP. What's the deal?

This chapter shows what those .ZIP files mean and, more important, how to get to the good stuff hidden inside them.

All Right, What's a Compressed Archive?

Back in the good old days, a computer program was just that: a single file that would run a program. You'd type the word TANKS, the Tanks program would hop onto the screen, and you could start blowing things up. Quick and easy, especially with a smooth, broken-in joystick.

Today's programs have lost their simplicity. In fact, most programs have their files spread out across several floppy disks or an entire compact disc.

To solve these basic problems — huge programs that contain bunches of files — some smart guy invented a new type of program called an *archiving* program.

An archiving program grabs a bunch of files, squishes them between its palms, and saves the results as a single file called an *archive.* That new archive file is *lots* smaller than all the original files put together.

- ✔ To open that archived file, you need an archive decompression program. This program lets the files pop back out unharmed. Really.

- ✔ Because these compressed files (archives) take up less disk space, they're great for storing programs on floppy disks.

- ✔ Archiving programs can squeeze *data* files as well as program files. That makes them handy for storing stuff that you don't need very often, like last year's record of frequent flyer miles.

- ✔ Although several varieties of file compression programs are popular, the most widely used is called WinZip, described in the next section.

- ✔ Compressed archive files are often referred to as *zipped, squeezed,* or *compacted* files.

- ✔ The act of decompressing an archive is sometimes called *unzipping, unsqueezing, extracting, unarchiving,* or *exploding.*

- ✔ Don't confuse an archiving program with other disk-compression programs like CompressionAgent, DriveSpace, or Stacker. Those types of programs automatically compress *everything* on a hard drive and then decompress files on the fly when they're needed. Archiving programs like WinZip compress only selected files into one big file. Then, to use that big file again, you decompress it.

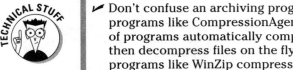

What's This Useless File Ending in .ZIP?

When people want to compress a bunch of files into a single smaller file, they head for a compression program, which is one of the doohickeys described earlier.

And chances are, compression fans are heading for a program called WinZip from Nico Mak Computing. A file that ends in the letters .ZIP probably has been compressed with WinZip — it's been *zipped,* as they say in computer lingo.

The point? You can't do anything exciting with a zipped file until you *unzip* it.

- ✔ Can't tell what letters your file ends in? Click on it with your right mouse button, choose P̲roperties from the menu, find the MS-DOS name listing, and look at the filename's last three letters.

✔ You can find WinZip on most computer bulletin boards and online services, as well as the Internet at www.winzip.com. If you have a modem, you can *download* it onto your computer from the Internet, as described in Chapter 5.

✔ WinZip is a shareware program (see Chapter 2 for more on shareware programs). Basically, *shareware* means that you should mail the programmer a check if you find yourself using the program.

✔ If you compressed your hard drive with CompressionAgent, DriveSpace, or Stacker, then don't bother using WinZip to save space when storing files on the hard drive. Because the hard drive itself is already compressed, WinZip doesn't really help save any space. (The same holds true for files of pictures or movies; the image's format calls for the files' contents to be squished down to minimum size.)

What's an .ARC, .ARJ, or Compressed .EXE File?

Although WinZip is the most popular program to compress files, it's certainly not the only one. Table 12-1 shows a list of compressed file extensions and programs to bring the files back to normal.

If you come across a file ending in one of these wacky acronyms, you need the appropriate decompression program to bring the file back to life. Luckily, these older formats don't come up very often these days.

Who cares about a file that ends in .ZIP?

Browse any of the most popular file libraries on the Internet and you notice one thing: Almost all the files are zipped.

Because a zipped file is much smaller than an unzipped file, zipped files don't eat as much precious real estate on the owner's Web site.

Also, because zipped files are so much smaller, they don't take nearly as much time to download. And when you download a file, you sometimes pay by the minute to your Internet service provider.

Table 12-1	Compressed Files and Their Decompressors
Files Ending in These Letters . . .	**Need This Program to Be Brought to Normal Size**
.ZIP	WinZip. A shareware program distributed by Nico Mak, WinZip can be found on the Internet at www.winzip.com, as well as other online services.
.ARJ	ARJ240A.EXE. An older way to store files, this DOS shareware program compresses files in a different style than WinZip. Only ARJ240A.EXE can decompress a file ending in .ARJ; WinZip won't do the trick.
.ARC	ARC-E. Yet another DOS shareware program, the .ARC format is one of the oldest around.
.LZH or .LHZ	LHA213.EXE. Created by mathematician Haruyasu Yoshizaki (Yoshi), this program is free.
.EXE	None. A self-extracting archive is a program that automatically decompresses itself. Increasingly popular, they can also be increasingly confusing: You often have no way of knowing whether your program can simply start running or start decompressing itself when you double-click on its icon. So to be on the safe side, place it in an empty folder before double-clicking on it.

Setting Up Windows to Unzip Files

Before you can unzip a file in Windows, you need one major thing: a copy of the WinZip program. Here's how to install the program so that you can begin releasing your zipped files from bondage:

1. **Get a copy of WinZip.**

   If you don't have WinZip, check out this chapter's earlier section on zipped files for some tips on how to grab a copy.

2. **In Windows Explorer, create a new folder called Trash on your desktop.**

   Don't know how to create a folder? Troop to Chapter 2 if you're a little fuzzy on the subject.

TIP

Just as most people keep "In Baskets" on their desk to hold incoming information, most people should make a "Trash" or "Temporary" folder on their Windows 98 desktop as well. Whether you call it "Trash" or "Temporary," this folder is a handy place to store incoming files before you decide where to put them on a permanent basis. Plus, it keeps a new file *self-contained.* If the new file is a self-extracting archive, it releases all its contents within that folder, where the contents won't get mixed in with your other files.

3. Copy your new WinZip program file to the new Temporary or Trash folder.

Again, hit Chapter 2 if you're unsure how to copy files.

4. Double-click on the WinZip program's icon in the Temporary or Trash folder.

The screen flashes and a box comes to the screen, shown in Figure 12-1. This means that the WinZip program is about to install itself permanently onto your hard drive.

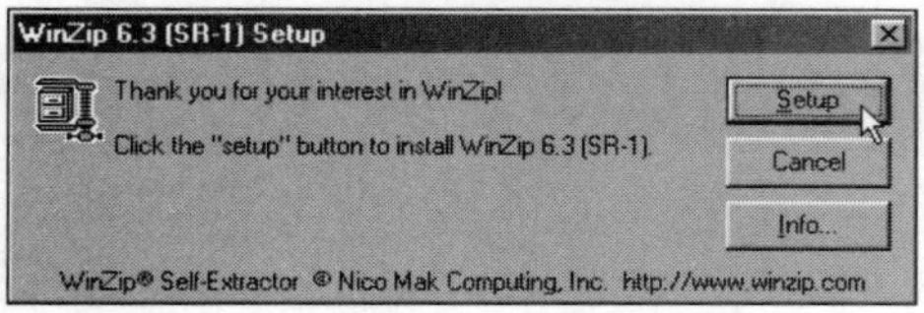

Figure 12-1:
WinZip
comes
with an
installation
program.

> **WinZip 6.3 (SR-1) Setup**
>
> Thank you for your interest in WinZip!
>
> Click the "setup" button to install WinZip 6.3 (SR-1).
>
> [Setup]
> [Cancel]
> [Info...]
>
> WinZip® Self-Extractor © Nico Mak Computing, Inc. http://www.winzip.com

5. Click on the program's Setup button.

The program installs itself into the folder listed in its Install to box. (If that folder doesn't already exist, the program usually asks for permission to create it.) Follow the program's instructions to copy it to your computer.

6. Delete the WinZip file from your Temporary or Trash folder.

After the program has installed itself — putting its programs into your computer's folders — you no longer need the packaging. If you kept a copy of the program on a floppy disk, then go ahead and drag the WinZip file to your Recycle Bin for deletion.

7. Close the WinZip window from your desktop.

✔ That's it. You've now set up Windows so that it can easily unzip any of those .ZIP files without ever leaving warm and fuzzy Windows-land. I describe the easy, step-by-step process to unzip .ZIP files in the very next section.

✔ When Windows 98 recognizes a file, it assigns a distinguishable icon to it. That recognizable icon lets you know that you can double-click on the icon to launch the program that's linked to it. So because Windows 98 can now recognize .ZIP files, it assigns the icon shown in Figure 12-2 to any file that you can unzip.

✔ Remember, WinZip is shareware. If you use WinZip, you're honor-bound to send Nico Mak a check. (It cost $29 the last time I checked.)

Figure 12-2:
An icon
for a
zipped file.

Zippery

Unzipping a File from Within Windows

Getting Windows *ready* to unzip a file, described in the previous section, is the hard part. But after you follow those seven steps, you're in like Flynn. Now, unzipping a file is as fun and easy as rolling a coconut down a bumpy hill.

Here's how to unzip a file ending in .ZIP:

1. **Set up Windows for unzipping a file.**

   Make sure that the WinZip program is installed on your computer. That's described in the preceding section. Done all that? Then head for Step 2.

2. **Place your .ZIP file in its own folder.**

   Move that .ZIP file into an empty folder on your desktop called Trash.

3. **Double-click on your .ZIP file.**

   From inside the Trash folder, simply double-click on your .ZIP file. WinZip hops onto the screen, as shown in Figure 12-3, giving you a peek at the files packed inside your .ZIP file.

4. **Choose the files you'd like to extract — or press Ctrl + / to select them all — and click on the Extract button from the toolbar; another page appears, as shown in Figure 12-4.**

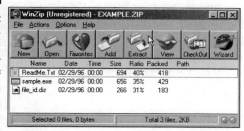

Figure 12-3:
Double-
click on a
.ZIP file for
a view of
the files
contained
inside.

Figure 12-4:
Choose
Extract from
the Unzip
menu to
begin
extracting
the zipped
files.

5. **Choose the files' destination by clicking on a new folder, or just click on the Extract button to extract the files to your Trash folder.**

   WinZip dutifully extracts the zipped file's files to your chosen folder, and then remains on the screen.

6. **Close down the WinZip program.**

   Like any other Windows 98 program, a click in its upper-right corner does the trick.

   ✔ WinZip leaves your zipped program — as well as its newly extracted files — in your desktop's Trash folder. Go ahead and install the program as described in Chapter 2.

   Keep a copy of the zipped program on a floppy disk for a backup and then delete it from your Trash folder. (And after installing your new program, delete its files from your Trash folder, as well.)

   ✔ After you unzip a file, feel free to delete the .ZIP file from your hard disk. The .ZIP file is just taking up space. (Make sure that you keep a copy of the .ZIP file on a disk, however, in case you need it again.) The same wisdom holds true for self-extracting archive files.

 ✔ If you have a self-extracting archive file, place it in your Trash folder and double-click on it. That makes the file expand.

 ✔ If you have a virus-scanning program, feel free to scan for viruses *after* unzipping a strange new file. A virus-scanning program can't detect any concealed viruses until *after* they've been unzipped.

Chapter 13

Getting Rid of It!

• •

In This Chapter

▶ Uninstalling a program from Windows the easy way

▶ Uninstalling a clingy Windows program

▶ Removing a program's listing from your Start button menu

• •

In a moment of clear vision, programmers made most Windows programs pretty easy to install. Just put the disk in the drive, rev up the program's Setup file, and the program nestles itself into your hard drive.

In fact, that's the problem. Most Windows programs nestle themselves down so comfortably that you can't get 'em *off* your hard drive, even with a crowbar.

This chapter picks up where the crowbar falls down. It tells how to remove old or unwanted programs from Windows, should the romance ever fail. And, as a bonus, it also tells how to remove the hidden remnants of those programs.

Why Get Rid of Old Programs?

Just like some people who don't clean the backseats of their cars, some people don't bother deleting old programs from Windows. But you should purge old programs from your hard drive for two reasons. First, they take up hard disk space. You have less room for the latest computer games. Plus, Windows runs more slowly on a crowded hard drive.

Second, old programs can confuse a computer. Two competing versions of the same program can befuddle even the most expensive computer.

When you *do* choose to delete a program, just simply delete the program's Shortcut icon off your desktop, and it's gone, right? Nope. *Shortcut icons* are merely push-buttons that *start* programs. Deleting a shortcut from your desktop or menus doesn't remove the program, just like your house stays standing when the doorbell button pops off.

✔ Here's the bad news: Removing an old Windows program can require a lot of effort. Many Windows programs spread their files across your hard drive pretty thickly.

✔ In addition to spreading their own files around, some Windows programs also add bits and pieces of flotsam to other Windows files.

✔ Unlike Windows programs, DOS programs are usually much easier to purge from your hard drive. The steps in the next section get rid of DOS programs as well as Windows programs.

Deleting a Program the Easy Way

If you're lucky, you won't have to spend much time in this chapter. That's because certain tricks make it easier to delete programs that have outlived their usefulness. To see if you qualify, read the next three sections.

Telling Windows 98 to delete a program

Windows 98, bless its heart, comes with a delete program built in. Yep — programmers can create programs that put special hooks into the Windows 98 delete program. Then when you go to the Windows 98 Program deletion area, you can simply click on the file's name to send it scurrying off your hard drive.

But many programmers, curse their little jowls, didn't think anybody could possibly want to delete their programs. So they didn't bother to install the special hooks.

Follow the steps below to see if the program you despise is listed in the Windows 98 special deletion area.

1. **Choose <u>C</u>ontrol Panel from the Start button's <u>S</u>ettings menu.**

2. **Double-click on the Add/Remove Programs icon.**

   The Add/Remove Programs Properties window comes to the screen, as shown in Figure 13-1.

3. **Click on the name of the program you want to delete.**

4. **Click on the Add/<u>R</u>emove button at the screen's bottom.**

5. **Follow the instructions to remove your program.**

   That's it. Although different programs make you jump through different hoops — usually asking if you're *sure* that you want to delete such a precious program — they usually wipe themselves off your hard drive without a trace.

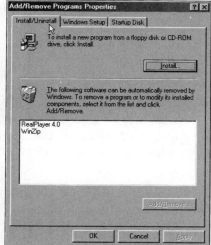

Figure 13-1:
The Add/
Remove
Programs
area
lists the
programs
that
Windows 98
can delete
automatically.

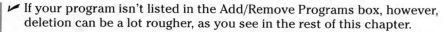

✔ If your program isn't listed in the Add/Remove Programs box, however, deletion can be a lot rougher, as you see in the rest of this chapter.

✔ Even after you delete a program, you can still put it back on your hard drive if you decide you really *did* like it there. Just run its Setup program to install it again. Chances are, you have to customize it again; all your personal settings are lost.

Telling the program to delete itself

Some programmers bypass the Windows 98 deletion program and handle matters themselves. They toss an uninstall program in with their own wares.

WinZip, for instance, described in Chapter 12, places an Uninstall WinZip icon right next to the Start menu icon that starts the program. Should you tire of WinZip, a click on the Uninstall WinZip icon, shown in Figure 13-2, whisks WinZip from your hard drive.

Figure 13-2:
The WinZip
program
comes with
an Uninstall
program.

These custom-made uninstall programs do the best job. Because they were created by the same people who made the program, the uninstall programs know exactly what crevices of your hard drive need to be swept.

Buying and installing an uninstall program

If your unwanted programs don't appear on Windows 98's Add/Remove Programs area and they don't come with their own uninstall program, you're not out of luck yet.

Go to the store and buy an uninstall program, such as Quarterdeck's CleanSweep, shown in Figure 13-3.

Figure 13-3:
Quarterdeck's CleanSweep Deluxe watches all your programs when they install themselves so it can uninstall them later.

CleanSweep and similar programs, such as CyberMedia's UnInstaller, can scan your computer's hard drive for any remnants an unwanted program has left behind. In addition, they can find and remove parts of Windows 98 that aren't needed by your particular computer setup.

The latest versions of both programs can effectively remove pieces of the greatest hard drive clogger: the Internet. Chances are, your Internet browser stores just about everything you see on the screen. Some programs keep the detritus around for longer than others; uninstall programs enable you to filter through the trash for the good stuff and dump the trash.

✔ CleanSweep can safely move a program from one directory to another. You can't do this by simply copying or moving that program's folder to a different location, because programs put too many claws in different parts of your hard drive. CleanSweep rounds up the claws so everything gets moved properly.

✔ Uninstall programs can seek out and destroy duplicate files from your hard drive, as well as files you haven't used in a very long time. (It can back up those files to a floppy disk for you.)

✔ If your program isn't listed on the Windows 98 Add/Remove Programs box and you don't have an uninstall program and your unwanted program didn't come with its own uninstall program, you're stuck. The rest of this chapter shows how to remove as much of the program as possible without getting into trouble.

Uninstalling a Clingy Program

Ready to pry off a particularly obstinate program from your hard drive? The next few steps show where to apply the putty knife and how hard to scrape. Be sure to read all the warnings, however; you don't want to damage any of the existing stucco.

1. Click on the Start button with your right mouse button and choose Open from the pop-up menu.

The My Computer program pops to the screen, as shown in Figure 13-4, displaying your Programs folder inside.

Figure 13-4:
The Programs folder contains the contents of your Start button's Programs area.

2. Double-click on your Programs folder.

The folder opens up, as shown in Figure 13-5, and the contents should look familiar: They're the same entries that you see in the Start menu's Programs area.

Figure 13-5:
Double-click on the Programs folder to see the contents of your Start menu.

3. Locate your program's shortcut icon.

See the shortcut icon that launches your program from the Start menu? Then move along to Step 4. If you don't spot the shortcut icon, however, keep opening the folders until you spot the icon for the program that you're trying to remove.

4. Click on the program's shortcut icon with your right mouse button and choose Properties.

When the unwanted program's Properties box comes up, click on the Shortcut tab, shown in Figure 13-6.

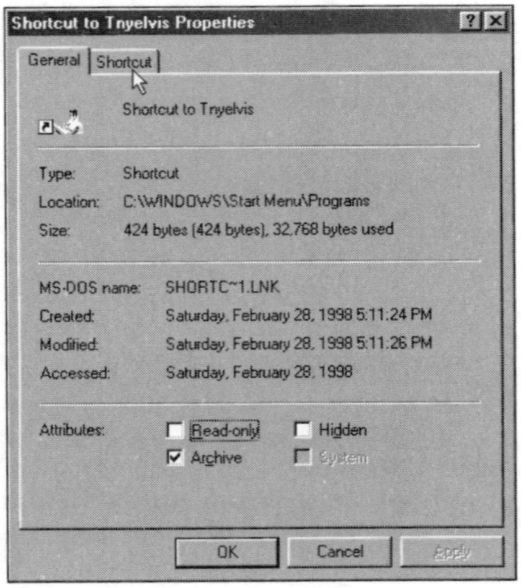

Figure 13-6:
Click on the Shortcut tab to find where a program is located on your hard drive.

5. **Take note of the folders listed in the Target box.**

The Target box may still use the old DOS language, but it tells you where your file lives on your hard drive. In Figure 13-7, for example, the Tiny Elvis file lives in the Tiny Elvis folder, which lives in your Program Files folder, which is on drive C.

The Target box also spells out the program's name: TNYELVIS.EXE.

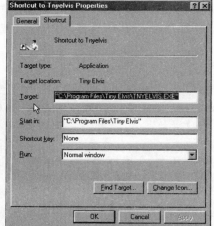

Figure 13-7:
The Target box spells out where the program lives on your hard drive.

6. **Close the Properties window, delete the program's icon, and close down the other windows.**

You no longer need the Properties window, nor the other windows that popped up from the Start menu. Close them down with the traditional click in the upper-right corner.

Plus, because you're removing the unwanted program, you can safely remove its icon from your Start menu with this step.

7. **Load the My Computer program.**

It's that icon on your desktop that looks like a computer (see Figure 13-8).

Figure 13-8:
The My Computer icon.

8. **Double-click on the drive and folders where the program lives.**

   In this case, you'd click on these drives in this order: the drive C icon, the Program Files folder, and the Tiny Elvis folder.

   Your program's folder appears on the desktop, revealing all its files.

9. **Choose** **Edit** **and then choose Select** **All.**

   Windows 98 highlights all the icons in the folder. Before moving any further, however, make sure that you don't have anything important stored in the folder by mistake.

10. **Drag and drop the icons to the Recycle Bin.**

    Drag and drop one icon to the Recycle Bin; because all the icons are selected, they all tag along.

11. **Drag and drop the program's empty folder to the Recycle Bin.**

    That's the last bit of tidying up. You removed as much of the program as possible without getting your hands too dirty.

    ✔ When Windows starts up, sometimes it complains about not being able to find your newly deleted file. If so, head for Step 2 in the preceding list. Then open the StartUp folder. You may need to delete a shortcut to your recently deleted file from that folder.

    ✔ Even after all this uninstall hassle, bits and pieces of the program may still linger on the hard drive, cluttering up the place. Some programs toss files into your Windows directory after they're installed, but the programs don't tell you. You simply can't tell which files belong to which program. Chapter 16 holds a few clues as to what file does what, but your best bet is probably to buy an uninstall program.

Installing a Program the Right Way

Chapter 2 shows how to install programs in Windows, but now is the time to repeat something:

When installing a new program, create a new folder for it and dump the new files in there.

As you can see from this chapter, this simple step makes the program a *lot* easier to get rid of later if you decide that it really stinks.

TECHNICAL STUFF

What is this "C:\Program Files\Tiny Elvis\TNYELVIS.EXE" stuff?

When you click on the Shortcut tab in Step 4 of the preceding steps, the Target box says that your Tiny Elvis program lives in this area of your hard drive: C:\Program Files\Tiny Elvis\TNYELVIS.EXE. Those words are old-DOS computer code for the program's *path*, which boils down to the following:

✔ The C: part stands for drive C:, the hard drive. DOS likes to see colons after letters when it talks about hard drives.

✔ The \Program Files part stands for the Program Files folder on the hard drive. DOS likes to put a \, commonly called a *backslash,* between directories and between hard drive letters and directories.

✔ The \TNYELVIS part stands for the Tiny Elvis folder, complete with the mandatory backslash.

✔ Finally, the TNYELVIS.EXE part stands for the Tiny Elvis program file. (It, too, needs a backslash to separate it from the folder behind it.)

This complicated DOS structural stuff pops up in Windows 98 every once in a while. It's there to remind you that Windows 98 is merely the latest layer of flesh riding uncomfortably over some particularly sharp DOS bones.

Removing a Program's Name from the Start Button Menu

The first few steps of the Uninstalling a Program section show how to remove a programs icon from the Start button. But if you just want to know the quickest way possible, follow these steps:

1. **Click on the Start button with your right mouse button and choose Explore.**

   The Windows Explorer program hops to the screen, displaying your Start button's menu. The Start button menu is really just a folder full of shortcuts called "Start Menu" that lives in your Windows folder.

2. **Double-click on the Programs folder.**

   Explorer opens up the Programs folder, shown in Figure 13-9, to reveal all the categories on your Start menu.

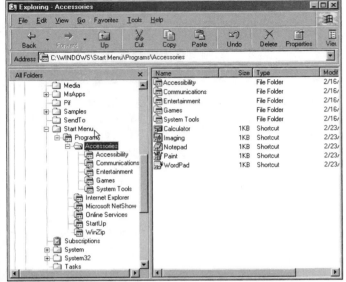

Figure 13-9:
The Start
button
menu is
merely a
folder full of
shortcuts in
your
Windows
folder.

3. Find the shortcut for the program that you want to delete from the Start menu.

You may need to double-click on some of the folders to find the program's shortcut icon, especially if that program is buried deep within your Start menu.

4. Delete the shortcut.

Click on the shortcut icon and press the Delete key. Or drag and drop the icon to the Recycle Bin. Either way, you've effectively trimmed that icon off your Start menu.

✔ While you have the Start menu open and ready to be rearranged, feel free to move your folders around to organize them. For example, you can create a new folder for your CDs, and drag and drop all the Start menu's icons for your compact disc programs into that folder.

✔ To make a program start itself automatically whenever Windows 98 starts up, move its shortcut icon into the Program folder's StartUp folder.

Chapter 14

Making Games (Er, DOS Programs) Run Right

In This Chapter

▶ Understanding .PIFs

▶ Deciding when a .PIF is necessary

▶ Writing your own .PIFs

▶ Filling out a DOS program's Properties form

*T*he word *.PIF* sounds like a dainty sneeze, suppressed politely in a crowded elevator. But .PIFs carry a *lot* more impact on your computer. Basically, a *.PIF* (Program Information File) is the DOS version of a common Windows 98 shortcut — it tells Windows 98 where the DOS program lives on your hard drive.

But a .PIF gives Windows much more information than that. By telling Windows 98 all about a DOS program's nutritional requirements, a .PIF can fool cranky old DOS programs and high-powered DOS games into running under Windows.

To create a .PIF, Windows 98 makes you fill out a form uglier than a health insurance claim. This chapter points out which parts of the .PIF form you can safely ignore and which parts you need to play with to convince a reluctant DOS game, er, business program, to run under Windows 98.

What's a .PIF?

Windows 98 is designed to run flashy new *Windows 98* programs. But some Windows users can't give up their favorite DOS programs of yesteryear. Plus, most of the best computer games are still DOS programs — Windows simply can't provide the graphics horsepower needed for quick 'n' dirty blast-em-ups.

Luckily, most DOS programs work just fine under Windows 98. If the program *doesn't* work, however, you need to do the work: You need to fill out a Program Information File. Like a chart hanging on a hospital bed, the .PIF contains special instructions for Windows on how to treat that DOS program.

✔ Because Windows has grown so popular, many new DOS programs come packaged with a .PIF in their folder, free of charge. The .PIF icon almost always looks like an MS-DOS Prompt icon with a shortcut. If you find one, you're safe: Just double-click on it, and the program should take off.

✔ Also, Windows 98 automatically creates a .PIF for the more than 400 DOS programs it can recognize.

✔ A .PIF is really just a fancy Windows 98 shortcut. It not only serves as a button for starting the program, but it tells Windows 98 how to treat the program after the program gets moving.

✔ A program's .PIF usually sounds just like the program, but ends with the letters PIF. For example, a .PIF for your Blastoid program would be called Blastoid.PIF.

✔ To see what extensions are tacked onto your files, choose Folder Options from the View menu of My Computer or Windows Explorer. Click on the View tab and make sure that there's no check mark in the box that says Hide file extensions for known file types.

✔ To load your DOS program, double-click on its PIF *shortcut*, not the program. For example, to load Blastoid, double-click on Blastoid.PIF — not Blastoid.exe.

✔ Or if you — or the program's installation program — put the DOS program's icon on your Start menu, that icon should refer to the program's .PIF. For example, the icon for your Blastoid program should refer to Blastoid.PIF, not Blastoid.exe. (Programs almost always put their proper .PIF on your Start menu, so you usually don't need to worry about this one.)

Do I Really Need a .PIF?

Most DOS programs aren't picky enough to require a .PIF. To find out whether your DOS program needs a .PIF, take this simple test:

Try to run the DOS program from within Windows.

If your program runs fine, you're safe. Ignore this chapter and concentrate on more important things, like whether it's time to switch to whole wheat English muffins. If your DOS program didn't run — or it ran kinda funny — stick around; this chapter may help out.

✔ .PIFs can fine-tune a DOS program's performance. For example, a .PIF can make a DOS program start up in a window rather than filling the whole screen. (Be forewarned, however: Some DOS programs refuse to be squeezed into a window — even with the most powerful .PIF.)

✔ By fiddling with a program's .PIF, you can make the program run smoother, as well as clean up after itself: No empty window for you to close when the program says that it's "Finished" running.

Creating a DOS Program's .PIF

Creating a program's .PIF is easy. Simply fill out the program's Properties form: To turn an option on, click in its little box within the form. An X appears inside the box to indicate that the option is turned on. Click in the box again to turn that option off.

So what's the hard part? Deciding which boxes to click in. Because the Properties form is designed to handle rough DOS problems, it forces you to play arbitrator among the ugliest DOS disputes: memory access, DOS modes, and equally unfriendly geek turf. A .PIF is loaded with bizarre terms like *Fast ROM emulation* and *Dynamic memory allocation*.

To begin filling out a DOS program's Properties form, click on the program's icon with your right mouse button and then choose Properties from the pop-up menu. The program's Properties form appears, as shown in Figure 14-1.

Figure 14-1:
Click on the
program's
icon with
your right
mouse
button and
choose
Properties
to begin
filling out
its form.

The Properties form consists of six sections, all marked along the top with their own tab: General, Program, Font, Memory, Screen, and Misc. The next few sections explain which parts of the form you need to worry about and which ones you can safely ignore.

Help! Forgot what does what? Then click on the little question mark in the Properties box's upper-right corner. A question mark fastens itself to your mouse pointer. Now click in the confusing area, as shown in Figure 14-2. Windows 98 brings up a snippet of helpful information, as shown in Figure 14-3, explaining the purpose of that box or button.

Figure 14-2: Click on the question mark in the upper-right corner and then click on a confusing part of the Properties screen.

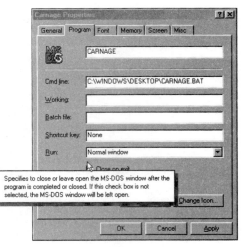

Figure 14-3: And helpful information appears.

The General tab

The General tab, shown along the top of the Properties form, provides basic information about the program: the program's name and size; the folder it's living in; and the date the program was created, changed, or last accessed. (Merely calling up the program's Properties makes Windows 98 access the program, so the access date is always the current date.)

The most common use for the General tab? Simply to see the program's name listed under the MS-DOS name section, as shown in Figure 14-4.

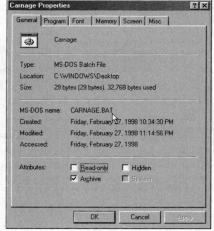

Figure 14-4: Check the program's name under the MS-DOS name section to find out the program's file extension.

 To make sure that you're creating a .PIF file for the right program, look at the name listed under MS-DOS name. If that name doesn't end in the letters BAT, EXE, or COM, you're probably filling out the Properties form for the wrong program.

 Don't fiddle with a program's Attributes settings unless you're absolutely sure what you're doing. Windows 98 can become seriously confused and spread that confusion around to its users.

The Program tab

The Program tab, shown in Figure 14-5, moves quickly into some of the more complicated areas. It starts out easy, though: Type the name of the program into the box next to its icon near the top-left corner of the screen.

Boring attributes

Files come with four special toggle switches known as *attributes*. The General tab enables you to toggle all four of these attributes either on or off.

Read-only: A check mark in this box means that the file can be read, but not changed and saved. Click this tab on important files that you don't want changed accidentally. If you try to delete a Read-only file, Windows 98 warns you that you're about to delete an important, Read-only file.

Although Windows 98 warns you when you try to delete Read-only files by pressing the Delete key, it doesn't warn you if you drag and drop the file into the Recycle Bin. Be careful.

Archive: An attribute you probably won't ever have to mess with. The Archive toggle is used by some backup programs to decide whether that file should be backed up. A check mark usually means that the backup program has slated that file for backup.

Hidden: Sneaky ol' Windows 98 likes to hide files from its users. Most of the time, it's hiding boring program information you don't need to see anyway. But a check mark in this box makes a file disappear from your desktop, My Computer, and Explorer programs.

Windows 98 can let you see files, even if they've been set as Hidden through their attributes. Simply choose Options from a window's View menu, click on the View tab, and click on the Show all files button.

System: Windows 98 doesn't even let you play with this attribute, which it reserves for its holy System files. Windows 98 needs these files to run properly, so don't mess with them.

Cmd line: Short for command line, this is what you'd be expected to type into your computer if it ran under DOS. That means you'd type your program's *path* — a collection of folder names leading to the program's location on your hard drive — followed by the program's name. (See Chapter 12 for more information about paths.)

Working: Does the program load its program files from folders other than its own? Then list those folders in here, using the same syntax as shown in the Cmd line box. (Leave this blank for most programs.)

Batch file: This enables you to run a batch file before your DOS program takes charge. *Batch files* are strings of DOS commands — the kinds of things you find in Dan Gookin's superb *MORE DOS For Dummies* book (published by IDG Books Worldwide, Inc.). Be sure and read his last chapter.

Shortcut key: A shortcut key lets you quickly start a program at the touch of a key — no mousing through menus required. For example, you could assign Ctrl+Alt+! to a favorite DOS program. Then press Ctrl+Alt+! to automatically load the program and bring it to the screen. Be careful that you don't assign the same shortcut keys to different programs, though, or Windows gets confused.

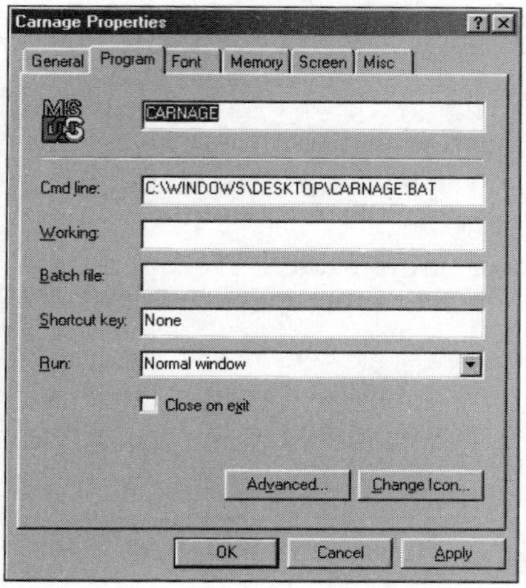

Figure 14-5:
The Program tab contains some of the more advanced areas for tweaking DOS programs.

Run: This defines whether the program starts running in a normal window, a maximized window, or in minimized mode along your taskbar.

Close on exit: After they finish running, most DOS programs just sit in a window, saying "Finished" across their top. To make them clean up after themselves, closing their empty window automatically, click in this box.

Change Icon: Click here to choose a different icon. (Chapter 3 shows where to find some doozies.)

Advanced: Here's where things get sticky, as you can see in Figure 14-6. Basically, this area allows you to choose between three modes:

- **Prevent MS-DOS-based programs from detecting Windows:** Some DOS programs didn't like earlier versions of Windows. So before those programs ran, they'd check to see if Windows was running in the background. If they found Windows, the DOS programs wouldn't run. Checking this box keeps those DOS programs from finding a version of Windows in the background so they're more apt to run under Windows 98.

- **Suggest MS-DOS mode as necessary:** This setting tells Windows to detect whether the program could run better in MS-DOS mode. If so, it switches to MS-DOS mode automatically.

- **MS-DOS mode:** Choosing this one is like choosing Shut Down and Restart in MS-DOS mode from the Start button. No other programs run in the background, and your DOS program has the computer to itself. If you choose MS-DOS mode, the following four options become available as well:

• **Warn before entering MS-DOS mode:** Check here, and Windows 98 warns you before closing down all programs and entering MS-DOS mode.

• **Use current MS-DOS configuration:** Windows normally uses your normal AUTOEXEC.BAT and CONFIG.SYS files to run your DOS program, so this box is normally checked.

• **Specify a new MS-DOS configuration:** The opposite of the listing above, this one lets you add a few lines to your AUTOEXEC.BAT or CONFIG.SYS files.

• **Configuration:** This handy button lets you choose some convenient DOS options to be loaded automatically whenever your new MS-DOS configuration takes effect.

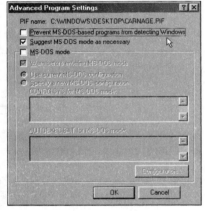

Figure 14-6: The Advanced area lets you choose between three modes for running DOS programs.

The Font tab

Not much to talk about here, especially because you can change all this on-the-fly while the program's running. But click on the Font tab, shown in Figure 14-7, to choose the size of the letters you want the program to use when displaying text in a window.

✔ Normally, you want to stick with TrueType fonts because they have fewer jagged edges than the Bitmap fonts. Click on a font size in the Font size window, and the Font preview window below shows you what your choice looks like.

✔ If you choose Auto in the Font size window, Windows 98 automatically makes the fonts shrink or grow, depending on what size looks best in your window. In fact, Windows even changes the font's size as you change the size of the window. (That's why you can usually stick with the Auto setting and not have to bother with all this stuff.)

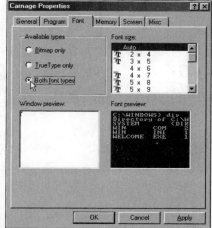

Figure 14-7:
The Font tab lets you change the size of fonts used by text-based DOS programs.

✔ To choose a different font while your program's running, click on the button with the big letter A along the top of the program's window. The Font page appears, letting you change the size of the letters used in the program.

The Memory tab

Although this page looks like a doozy, as shown in Figure 14-8, you don't have much to fill out. You almost always want to leave every setting set to Auto. Windows is usually smart enough to dole out memory in the right proportions, and if Windows can't guess right, then you should be running that program in MS-DOS mode, anyway.

If your DOS program makes Windows crash a lot, try clicking in the Protected box in the Conventional memory area. That can keep DOS programs from trying to grab at parts of your computer memory that Windows likes to hang onto.

The Screen tab

Although DOS programs normally take the whole screen for themselves, they can run in windows on your desktop, just like real Windows programs. You see a few differences, though, and the Screen tab, shown in Figure 14-9, enables you to fiddle with them.

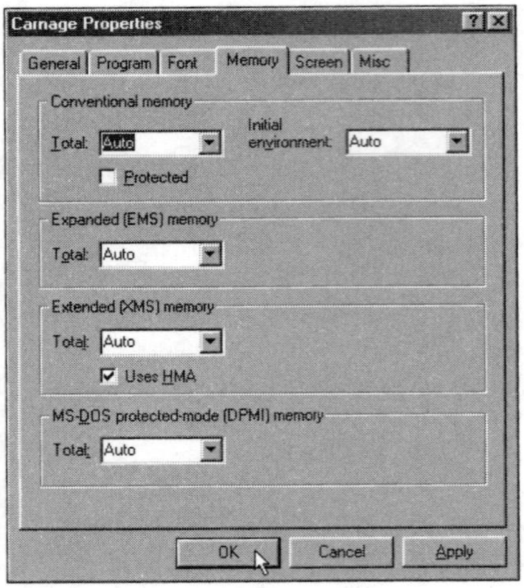

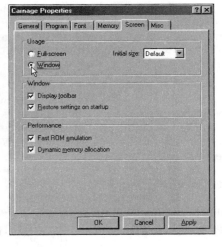

Figure 14-8:
You can
usually get
away with
leaving
everything
set to Auto
in the
Memory
tab area.

Figure 14-9:
The Screen
tab lets you
determine
how the
screen
should
run in a
window or
if it should
run full-
screen.

Usage: Click on the Full-screen option, and the program takes the entire
screen when it runs, just like normal. Choose Window, by contrast, to make
the program run itself in a window upon startup.

Initial size gets a little trickier. Although most text-based DOS programs
show 25 lines of text when they arrive on the screen, others can handle
more. If your computer's video card can show more than 25 lines of text
on the screen, you can change this setting to two other common modes:
43 lines and 50 lines. (Not all DOS programs can handle these modes,
though — your video card and program both need to cooperate for anything
magic to happen. Otherwise, nothing happens.)

Window: Want Windows to display that handy toolbar across the top —
those little buttons for quickly cutting and pasting, adjusting font size,
changing properties, and more? Choose the Display toolbar option. The
other option, Restore settings on startup, means that the program always
reverts to the settings stored in its PIF, no matter how much you changed
them the last time the program ran.

Performance: Word processors often run faster if the Fast ROM emulation
box is checked. But if something goes wrong — the mouse acts up or
garbage appears on the screen — change it back. DOS programs that don't
switch between graphics and text modes can have the Dynamic memory
allocation box checked, leaving a little extra memory free for other programs to share.

The Misc tab

A plethora of potpourri, shown in Figure 14-10, the Misc tab contains
unrelated switches that really don't fit anywhere else.

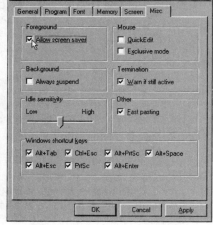

Figure 14-10:
The Misc tab
contains
unrelated
settings that
don't fit
anywhere
else.

Foreground: Do you want your screen saver to pop up in your DOS program? Then click in the Allow screen saver box. An unchecked box leaves
your screen saver disabled.

Background: Check the Always suspend box, and the DOS program stops
working when you switch back to Windows.

Don't choose this mode when running any DOS-based communications programs, or you may lose your connection or data.

Idle sensitivity: Windows is a merry-go-round of simultaneously running programs. As it constantly divvies up its attention to each program, it constantly checks to see if the DOS program is busy. Setting Idle sensitivity to Low keeps Windows from constantly checking to see if it can sap resources from the DOS program. The result? The DOS program runs faster. Setting Idle sensitivity to High makes the DOS program run more slowly because Windows is always tapping on its shoulder.

Mouse: If your DOS program doesn't use the mouse, choose QuickEdit. Then you can copy and paste information from your DOS window without having to click on any buttons on the toolbar. If your DOS program uses the mouse, though, don't check this box. If your DOS program not only uses the mouse but has to have complete control over it, choose Exclusive mode. This mode doesn't let Windows use the mouse while the DOS program's in the forefront, but hey, at least your DOS program can use it.

Termination: Done with your DOS program? The Good DOS User always shuts down the DOS program the right way — by pressing the keys that tell the DOS program to shut down. Lazy Windows users often click on the DOS window's upper-right corner to close the DOS program, however. Because jerking DOS programs off their feet like that isn't very nice, Windows 98 sends a terse message asking whether you're sure that you saved your work and that you know what you're doing. To make Windows stop sending this message, click on the Warn if still active box.

Other: Some DOS programs never expected people to type faster than 85 words per minute. Windows can squirt information into a DOS program much faster than that, however. If your DOS program has trouble keeping up with the flow, remove the check mark from the Fast pasting box.

Windows shortcut keys: Windows uses a bunch of keystrokes for performing certain tasks. Pressing Ctrl+Esc brings up the Start menu, for example; pressing Alt+Tab cycles through your currently open programs. But if a DOS program tries to use those same keystrokes, you're in trouble. To break up the conflicts, click in the boxes next to the keystrokes that you want to reserve for the DOS program. The remaining boxes — the ones with the check marks — are keystrokes that Windows 98 gets to use.

What Should I Fiddle with If This Happens?

Don't want to search through the rules in the preceding section to find a quick answer? Maybe you'll get lucky and find help in the following sections.

My DOS program wants its own AUTOEXEC.BAT and CONFIG.SYS files!

When Windows 98 puts itself into MS-DOS mode to accommodate DOS programs, it loads the two mainstays of DOS-dom: The AUTOEXEC.BAT and CONFIG.SYS files. In a funky, bare-bones language, the files tell the computer what devices are attached to it, how to manage its memory, and how to treat the programs that are about to run.

Normally, Windows 98 uses "default" AUTOEXEC.BAT and CONFIG.SYS files that live in the root directory of drive C. And, normally, those files are all you need. But if a DOS program gets picky and needs specific settings in those AUTOEXEC.BAT or CONFIG.SYS files, you can put those settings in the program's .PIF.

Then when you load the program and Windows jumps into DOS mode, it uses that program's own special version of AUTOEXEC.BAT and CONFIG.SYS. When the program's running and Windows 98 comes back to life, everything's back to normal.

> ✔ In fact, you can set up a different set of AUTOEXEC.BAT and CONFIG.SYS files for all your DOS programs.
>
> How? Head for the Advanced button on the PIF's Program tab, click in the MS-DOS mode check box, click in the Specify a new MS-DOS configuration box, and start customizing the program's settings in the boxes.
>
> ✔ DOS program memory management can be terribly complicated, however. If your particular game doesn't specifically state what settings to use, you may want to check out Dan Gookin's *MORE DOS For Dummies* (published by IDG Books Worldwide, Inc.).

My DOS game won't work!

Check the following settings carefully; DOS games seem to be the most sensitive to them.

✔ Try clicking on the Start button, choosing Sh<u>u</u>t Down, and choosing Restart the computer in <u>M</u>S-DOS mode. Then run your program as if you were in DOS. That's usually your best chance of success.

✔ In the .PIF's Advanced Program Settings box, choose <u>P</u>revent MS-DOS based programs from detecting Windows. Some DOS games actually look into your computer's memory to see whether you have Windows running in the background. If they see any signs of Windows, they refuse to load. This box keeps Windows hidden.

✔ In the Screen menu, make sure that you've checked <u>F</u>ull-screen. Most DOS programs insist on running in full-screen mode, and some can't even handle Windows' slight delay while it switches them to full-screen mode. Choosing this mode from the start avoids potential problems.

✔ Under the Misc tab, don't click on Always <u>s</u>uspend, slide the Idle sensiti<u>v</u>ity lever to Low, and make sure that you're not reserving any Windows shortcut keys that your DOS game could use.

Chapter 15

Fun Windows 98 Products to Rush Out and Buy

*W*indows 98 is an enormous program, consuming up to 300MB of your hard drive, if you let it. It comes with more than two dozen freebie programs. But strangely enough, most new buyers want to buy even *more* Windows 98 software, accessories, and rechargeable batteries within a few weeks of tapping the keyboard.

Some of these programs help you control your computing where Windows 98 lets you down. Utilities perform some housecleaning, for example. Other programs can take apart Windows.

Other Windows 98-linked products are just plain fun: digital cameras that dump pictures onto a computer screen for later processing, for example. Digital postcards!

Uninstall Programs

Windows 98 comes with its own Uninstall program. Just click on the Control Panel's Add/Remove Programs icon, and Windows 98 automatically lists the programs that it can remove.

However, people are still snapping up uninstall programs for Windows 98, making these programs some of the most popular on the market. Why? Two reasons. First, many companies ignore the Windows 98 Uninstall feature. After all, who would possibly want to uninstall their fine software? So software companies don't write the uninstall stuff necessary for their program to appear on Windows 98's Uninstall menu.

Second, many uninstall programs can do much more than simply wipe an unwanted program off your hard drive. Quarterdeck's CleanSweep Deluxe, for example, shown in Figure 15-1, purges your hard drive of programs that have lost their charm. But it can also weed out Internet debris — miscellaneous temporary files your Internet browser forgot to erase from your hard drive.

Figure 15-1:
Quarterdeck's
CleanSweep
Deluxe can
do much
more than
other
uninstall
programs.

CyberMedia's MicroHelp Uninstaller, shown in Figure 15-2, also pries away unwanted programs from your hard drive; it removes duplicate files, cleans up Internet remnants, and moves programs to other folders on your computer, a task that Windows 98 usually can't handle by itself.

✔ Simply deleting the program's folder often isn't enough; Windows programs tend to spread bits and pieces of themselves in a wide variety of folders and special areas. Only an uninstall program knows where to look and what to remove.

✔ In fact, most uninstall programs take careful notes as your new programs install themselves. Then when you're ready to dump a program, the uninstaller looks at its notes to decide which files stay and which files go.

Figure 15-2:
CyberMedia
Uninstaller
takes
detailed
notes as to
how an
incoming
program
changes
your system
so that
removing
the program
is easier
later down
the road.

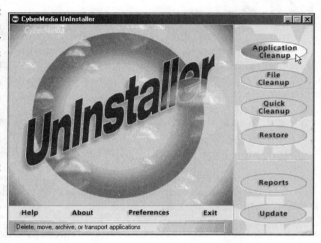

Norton Utilities

A computing mainstay for years, Norton Utilities has helped millions of users out of their computing mishaps. Norton Utilities isn't really a program; it's a bundle of programs designed to do the things that your operating system doesn't. When your computer can't undelete a file, for example, Norton Utilities can often pull it back from the abyss.

Damaged data on the hard drive? The stern Mr. Norton usually unfolds his arms, rolls up his sleeves, and salvages at least part of the good stuff. Even though Windows 98 provides many of the utilities that Norton came up with a decade ago, the program still comes in handy.

- ✔ Windows 98 comes with many of the same types of programs that Norton Utilities does. Windows 98 can scan your disk, defragment it, and undelete your files. But Norton's tools invariably work better, faster, and more reliably.

- ✔ Even if you don't fiddle with your computer much, a copy of Norton Utilities on your hard disk makes your computer easier to repair when a friend comes over to help get you out of a help!-I've-lost-every-important-file jam. Your friend can read Norton's records of where data is stored on your hard drive and increase the odds of recovering it.

Virus Detection Utility

Evil people with too much spare time create computer programs designed to damage information stored on computers. Some of these programs, known as *viruses,* are harmless: A certain message pops up on a certain day. Others are more painful: The program suddenly reformats a hard drive, taking all its information down with it.

Viruses usually come from two places: floppy disks and the Internet. Today's virus-detection utilities can automatically scan floppy disks for viruses, as well as keep an eye on any programs entering through the Internet.

Windows 98's newfound close ties to the Internet bring a new susceptibility to the evil programs. Luckily, several programs can sniff out and destroy viruses before they've had a chance to do any harm.

✔ One of the grandfathers of the virus-crushing business, McAfee's VirusScan is a popular choice. It can recognize a wide variety of viruses and automatically receives an updated "Wanted" list warning of new finds. The program includes a year of free upgrades and a lifetime of free updates, conveniently downloaded from the Internet.

✔ Others prefer Norton's antivirus program; check recent computer magazine reviews on the Internet and make up your own mind.

Microsoft's PowerToys (And They're Free!)

Microsoft's programmers simply couldn't be stopped. After they slaved away to whip out Windows 98, the momentum kept rolling. So they released Tweak UI — a collection of "tweak" programs to give more-advanced users better control over Windows 98. Although the programs are created and copyrighted by Microsoft, they are given away for free. The softhearted corporate giant isn't *that* generous, though. The company doesn't offer any help if you can't get them to work right.

First, install the program:

1. **Head for the CD's Tools folder, open the reskit folder, and open the powertoy folder.**

2. **Right-click on the notepad icon with a single icon embedded in it, and choose Install from the pop-up menu.**

   Tweak UI leaves an introductory window on the screen.

3. **Read the pleasant introductions or close the window and jump right in.**

   The program is pretty self-explanatory.

4. **Tweak UI also leaves its permanent icon in the Control Panel. Double-click on the icon, and the program jumps to the screen, as shown in Figure 15-3.**

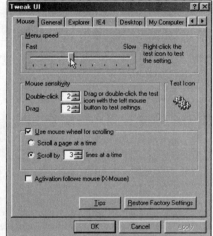

Figure 15-3:
Tweak UI customizes nearly every aspect of Windows 98.

A few of the more commonly used settings appear in the following list.

✔ The General tab controls effects, like animation and beeping on errors, but there's more. Type in the Internet search engine that Internet Explorer should use when you type **go casserole** during a craving for Italian food.

✔ Ever had an icon you wanted to get rid of, but Windows just wouldn't let you remove it from the desktop? The Desktop tab lets you choose who gets to ride and who stays behind.

✔ Click the little arrows seen in Figure 15-3's upper-right corner to see even more tabs like the Control Panel tab. Designed to track the icons in your Control Panel, it weeds out remnants from other programs.

✔ Check out the New tab. Drag a template for your stationery onto the window, and your stationery appears as a convenient option under <u>N</u>ew when you right-click on your desktop.

✔ When things look grim, unleash the repair robots waiting in the Repair tab. They do their best to rebuild icons, repair Associations and font folders, and do their fix-up work on Regedit, your important system files, temporary Internet files, and your ever-important-but-often-overlooked URL History.

> ✔ Don't want anybody seeing what you just did on your computer? The Paranoia tab deletes all evidence of your session: Nobody will know where you just logged on at the Internet. The Start menu's list of recently opened files is wiped clean.

TV Tuner Card

Windows 98 comes with TV software. It can download local listings from the Internet, automatically send out reminders when favorite programs begin, and sort programs into convenient lists of upcoming movies.

But until you get that TV tuner card, you can't see a picture on your screen. Shortly after Windows 98 comes out, TV tuner cards will be much cheaper than a television itself. Go for it.

> ✔ At the office, you can get important business and financial headlines during the day, and soap operas at lunch.

> ✔ In the home, a TV tuner card brings a small TV into a home office or family room.

> ✔ Plus, if you're the type who enjoys programming VCRs, you'll enjoy the software's auto-record feature — and the setup that it requires.

Chapter 16
Are These Files Important?

*A*fter about a year or so, that familiar ring of keys comes to life and begins burrowing a hole through a pants pocket. The solution, quite simply, is to get rid of some of the keys.

But which keys? What's this key for? The old apartment? The coffee machine cabinet in the *old* office? Did this key work on the *old* bike lock? Does this key open *anything?*

This chapter shows you how to separate the important Windows files from all the junk Windows files living on your hard drive. You discover which of those suspicious-looking Windows files are important and which ones can be peeled off and tossed aside.

What's This File For?

Although computers may seem like bundles of geekisms, they're *organized* bundles of geekisms.

For example, most Windows programs tack three letters onto the name of every file they create. Whenever Notepad saves information in a file, that file's name ends in the letters TXT. Called an *extension,* those three letters serve as a file's thumbprint: Those extensions, as well as the file's icon, identify which culprit created which file.

Excavating extensions

Windows 98 normally hides a file's extension, gracefully displaying a file's name as Placebo rather than its computer-language name of PLACEBO.TXT. But sometimes seeing those extensions can provide valuable clues to a file's origin, making it easier to decide that file's fate when cleaning the hard drive.

The extensions of some files reveals them to be detritus, for example; programs often leave temporary files littering your hard drive when the computer loses power unexpectedly.

To make Windows 98 display each file's extension, choose Folder Options from the View menu of either My Computer or Windows Explorer. Choose the View tab and click in the Hide file extensions for known file types box.

Click on OK, and your file's extension magically begins appearing in your programs and menus.

To quickly look at a file's extension without messing with the Options section, click on the file with your right mouse button and then choose Properties. In the MS-DOS name area, as shown in Figure 16-1, the file's last three letters reveal its extension.

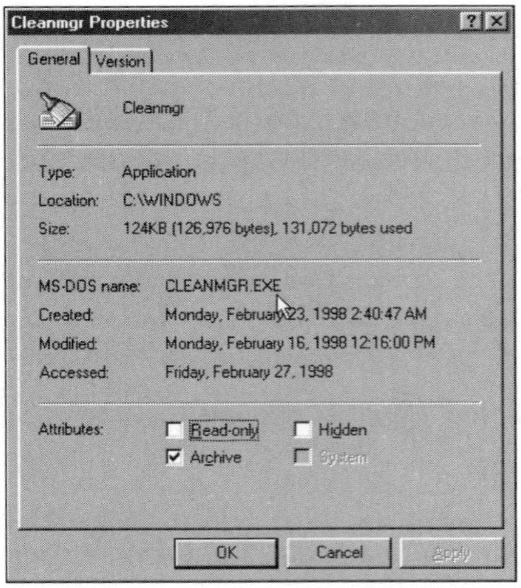

Figure 16-1: The last three letters listed in the MS-DOS name area are a file's extension, which Windows 98 uses to determine what program created what file.

Table 16-1 identifies some of the most common file extensions you may spot on your hard drive, as well as their icons and creators.

Table 16-1   Who Dunnit? Which Programs Use Which Extension?

Files Ending Like This . . .	*Usually Do This*
.3GR	Short for *grabber,* this helps Windows display text and graphics.
.ANI	Short for *animated,* these contain special "whirling" mouse pointers.
.AVI	Contain movies in a special format that's playable through Media Player. (You don't need special hardware to view the movies, but movie *makers* usually need expensive *video grabbing* cards.)
.BAT	Short for *batch* files, these contain lists of DOS commands, including commands to load DOS programs. (Rarely used in Windows.)
.BFC	Short for *briefcase,* these contain a Briefcase full of files to move back and forth between a desktop computer and laptop. (See Chapter 5.)
.BMP	Short for *bitmap,* these contain pictures or illustrations, usually created by Paint.
.CAL	Short for *calendar,* these contain appointments created by Calendar, a calendar program that came with older versions of Windows.
.CBT	Short for *Computer Based Training,* these usually contain tutorials for Microsoft products.
.CDA	Short for *CD Audio Track,* these stand for the songs playable by CD Player.
.CDF	Short for *Channel Directory File,* these contain information for channels that launch you to special spots on the Internet.
.COM	Short for *command,* these almost always contain DOS programs.
.CPE	Fax cover sheets for the Fax Cover Page Editor.
.CRD	Short for *card,* these contain the names and addresses created by Cardfile — a program that came with the old version of Windows.

(continued)

Table 16-1 *(continued)*

Files Ending Like This . . .	Usually Do This
.CUR	Short for *cursor,* these contain animated cursors that can be changed along with your mouse settings.
.DAT	Short for *data,* these usually contain information for programs, not people, to peruse.
.DLL	Short for *Dynamic Link Library,* these are like miniprograms. Other programs often peek at these .DLL files for help when they're working.
.DOC	Short for *document,* these usually contain text stored by a word processor. Microsoft Word saves files ending in .DOC, for example. Unfortunately, a .DOC file created by one word processor can't always be opened by another word processor.
.DRV	Short for *driver,* these files help Windows talk to parts of your computer, like its keyboard, monitor, and various internal gadgetry.
.EPS	Short for *Encapsulated PostScript* file, these contain information to be printed on *PostScript* printers. PostScript is a special format for expensive printers to read and print information created by expensive PostScript-compatible programs.
.EXE	Short for *executable,* these contain programs. Almost *all* Windows programs end in .EXE; most DOS programs do, too.
.FLI	These files contain animation — high-tech cartoon/movies — often made with programs by a company called Autodesk. They're not compatible with .AVI, so you can't watch 'em in Media Player. (See ".AVI.")
.FND	Short for *Find,* these contain a list of the files turned up through a search using the Start menu's Find program.
.FON	A font that's not *TrueType* compatible (see .TTF). Windows uses these fonts mostly for its menus, error messages, and other system information.

Files Ending Like This . . .	Usually Do This
.GIF	Short for *Graphic Interchange File,* these contain pictures stored in a space-saving format invented by modem hounds on CompuServe. Paint can't view GIFs, although several shareware Windows programs can.
.GRP	Short for *group,* these files let Program Manager — a remnant from Windows 3.1 — remember which icons belong in which of its groups. When you double-click on a .GRP file, Windows 98 displays the contents in a My Computer window.
.HLP	Short for *help,* these contain the helpful information that pops up when you press F1 or choose <u>H</u>elp from a program's menu.
.HT	Short for *HyperTerminal,* these contain the settings HyperTerminal uses for dialing up other computers with your modem.
.HTM or .HTML	One of these files contains the instructions — written in *HyperText Markup Language* — for the computer to put together a Web page.
.ICO	Short for *icon,* these contain — you guessed it — icons. (See Chapter 3.)
.IDF	Short for *Instrument Definition File,* these contain the settings Media Player uses with your sound card or synthesizer.
.INF	Short for *information,* these usually contain text for programs, not humans. Programs often grab information from .INF files when they're first installed. For example, a file called OEMSETUP.INF often lives on a program's floppy disk; Windows looks at the OEMSETUP.INF file for help when installing that program's drivers and other special goodies.
.INI	Short for *initialization,* these files contain code-filled text for programs to use, usually so that they can remember any special options a user has chosen. Unlike .INF files, described earlier, humans can fiddle with an .INI file's content to make programs work better — or worse.

(continued)

Table 16-1 *(continued)*

Files Ending Like This . . .	Usually Do This
.JPG	Short for *Joint Photographic Experts Group,* these contain pictures, similar to files ending in .GIF, .BMP, and .PCX. Paint can't view them, but Internet Explorer can.
.LNK	Short for *shortcut,* this file contains information on how to access another file on your computer.
.MDB	Microsoft's database program, Access, tosses numbers into these files.
.MID	Short for *MIDI,* these files tell sound cards or synthesizers to play musical notes in a certain order. If everything goes right, the musical notes sound like a pretty song. (See Chapter 3.)
.MOV	Short for *Movie,* this contains a QuickTime file — the format Apple Macintosh computers use to store their files. Windows 98 can't view them; you need to get a QuickTime movie player program. (See Chapter 7.)
.MPG	Short for *MPEG,* these are like .JPG files except they contain movies. Nope, Media Player can't view them, but some other Windows programs can.
.PCX	These contain pictures viewable in Paint. Paint can't save pictures in this format, however.
.PIF	Short for *Program Information File,* these contain special instructions for Windows to treat DOS programs. (See Chapter 13.)
.PPT	Short for the program that created them, *PowerPoint,* these files contain instructions for the computer to behave in a certain way during a demonstration.
.RTF	Short for *Rich Text Format,* these contain ASCII text with special codes. The codes let different brands of word processors swap files without losing groovy stuff like margins or italics. (Used by WordPad, Microsoft Word for Windows, and many other programs.)

Files Ending Like This . . .	Usually Do This
.SCR	Short for *screen,* these files contain a screen saver program. Copy .SCR files to your Windows folder, and they appear on the Screen Saver menu in Control Panel's Desktop area. (Chapter 3 offers much more elaborate instructions.)
.SHS	Short for *scrap,* this file contains a chunk of another file that's been dragged and dropped out of another program. For example, if you highlight a paragraph in Word and then drag and drop that paragraph onto your desktop, the paragraph is saved as a scrap on the desktop.
.SYS	Short for *system,* these contain information designed for your computer or its programs — not for humans.
.TMP	Short for *temporary.* Some Windows programs stash occasional notes in a file but forget to erase the file after they're done. Those leftover files end in .TMP. Feel free to delete them *if you're sure that Windows isn't running in the background.*
.TTF	Short for *TrueType Font,* a type of Windows font that can change its size smoothly.
.TXT	Short for *text,* these files almost always contain plain old text, often created by Notepad.
.VXD	Windows 98 looks at these files when controlling parts of your computer, like its printer or display. Similar files end in .VPD (a printer driver) or .VDD (a display driver).
.WAV	Short for *waveform* audio, these simply contain recorded sounds. Both Media Player and Sound Recorder let you listen to Wave files.
.WKS	The Microsoft Excel spreadsheet can read and write files in these format.
.WPD	Short for *Windows PostScript Driver,* these files help Windows talk to those expensive PostScript printers. WordPerfect files also use this extension.
.WPG	Short for *WordPerfect Graphics,* these files contain images stored in the graphics format used by WordPerfect.

(continued)

Table 16-1 *(continued)*

Files Ending Like This . . .	Usually Do This
.WRI	Short for *Write,* these contain text created in the Write word processor — a WordPad-like word processor that came with earlier versions of Windows. WordPad can read and write files in this format.
.XLS	Excel, Microsoft's spreadsheet, spreads its numbers into this file.
.ZIP	These contain a file — or several files — compressed into one smaller file. (See Chapter 11.)

Find any identifiable file extensions on your own hard drive? Jot them down here for further reference. (Finally — you're *allowed* to write in books.)

_____

_____

_____

✔ Unfortunately, these file extensions aren't *always* a sure identifier; some programs cheat. For example, some plain old text files end in the extension .DOC — not .TXT.

✔ Most of the file extensions listed in Table 16-1 are *associated* with the program that created them. That means when you double-click on that file's name in My Computer or Windows Explorer, the program that created the file brings it to the screen. A double-click on a file named Navel.bmp, for example, makes the Paint program pop to the screen, displaying the Navel bitmap file.

✔ Although Table 16-1 lists most of the extensions you may come across when using Windows, feel free to write down any others that you discover in the space provided. Many of your own programs are using their own special code words when saving files.

What Are Those Sneaky Hidden Files?

Many of the files on your computer's hard drive are for your computer to play with — not you.

So to keep its computer-oriented files out of your way, Windows 98 flips a little switch to make them invisible. The filenames don't appear in My Computer or Windows Explorer, nor do they show up in any menus.

Most hidden files are hidden for a good reason: Deleting them can make your computer stop working or work strangely. Don't delete hidden files without serious reason, and even then, chew your lower lip cautiously before pushing the Delete key.

Table 16-2 shows a few of the Sneaky Hidden Files you may stumble across in the dark.

Table 16-2	Under Rare Circumstances You May Encounter These Hidden Files
These Hidden Files or Folders . . .	**Do This**
IO.SYS, MSDOS.SYS	These files, hidden in your computer's *root directory,* contain the DOS life force that enables Windows 98 to run older programs without a problem.
DBLSPACE.BIN, DRVSPAC.BIN	Windows uses these files when you choose one of the Windows disk compression programs.
Recycled	This invisible folder is your Recycle Bin, which contains all your deleted files.
BOOTLOG.TXT, BOOTLOG.PRV, SETUPLOG.TXT, DETLOG.TXT, DETLOG.OLD	If Windows 98 crashes, it looks at these files — and other files containing the word *LOG* — after it is reloaded in an attempt to figure out where it went wrong.
Any files ending in DLL, SYS, VXD, 386, or DRV	These files help Windows 98 talk with its programs or parts of your computer.

Identified any other hidden files? Feel free to write their names and identities in the space below.

_____

_____

_____

✔ Ever wiped an unidentifiable smudge from the coffee table? Well, that's why hidden files are hidden: To keep people from spotting them and deleting them, thinking that they're as useless as a smudge.

✔ For the most part, hidden files stay hidden. But Windows 98 lets you spot them if you're sneaky. Choose Folder Options from the View menu in either My Computer or Windows Explorer and then click on the View tab. Finally, click on the Show all files button in the Hidden files section and click on OK to close the window.

✔ When the novelty of seeing hidden files wears off, head back to the same page and click on the Do not show hidden or system files button. There's not much point in looking at hidden files, anyway.

✔ When you delete a folder, you delete *all* the files in that folder — even the hidden ones. Be sure to look inside the folder with the Show all files option turned on so that you can see for sure what you're about to delete.

✔ When your computer hides a file by flipping the file's "hidden" switch, computer nerds say the computer has changed that file's *attribute*.

Purging the Unnecessary Files

Windows comes with slightly more than three trillion files, all poured onto your hard drive. After a few months, that number increases exponentially. But which files can you wipe off your hard drive without making everything tumble down?

The next two sections contain tips on what files you can get rid of.

Removing any leftover temporary files

While it's humming away, Windows 98 creates some files for its own use. Then when you shut Windows down for the day, Windows is supposed to delete those *temporary* files. Unfortunately, it sometimes forgets.

Sometimes it doesn't even have a chance to forget. A power outage can leave an interrupted program's files scattered across your hard drive, for example. After a while, the dead files add up.

That means that you have to start purging those temporary files yourself. To see what temporary trash Windows has stored permanently on your hard drive, follow these steps.

1. **Open the Files or Folder area from the Start button's Find area.**

2. **Type *.tmp into the Named box.**

   That's an asterisk, a period, and the letters TMP, as shown in Figure 16-2.

3. **Click on the Find Now button.**

4. **Look at the dates of the files that turn up.**

   Spot any files that are older than a week or so? Copy them onto a floppy disk for protection, and then drag and drop them into the Recycle Bin.

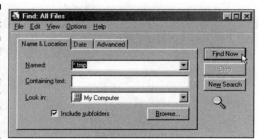

Figure 16-2:
Type ***.tmp**
into the Find
program to
find any
leftover
temporary
files.

✔ To be on the safe side, don't *ever* delete any files with the current day's date. Wait a couple of days — just to make sure that they don't contain anything important. And even then, make sure that you save a copy of the file on a floppy disk in case a program starts begging for it a few days later.

✔ Windows often stuffs its temporary files in your DOS folder; you may find some deletable remnants there.

✔ Also, check your Windows Folder for a Temp folder; sometimes Windows stashes its junky leftovers in there.

Dumping unwanted fonts

At first, fonts are fun, wacky ways to turn boring letters into weird arty things.

After a while, though, the fun can wear thin. Too many fonts can clog up the hard drive something fierce. Plus, they make Windows take longer when loading.

Here's how to dump the fonts you've grown sick of. For example, you can remove your Happy-Holiday-Card fonts in January and reinstall them next December.

1. **Open the Control Panel from the Start button's Settings area.**

2. **Double-click on the Fonts icon.**

   A new boxful of fonts appears, like the one in Figure 16-3.

3. **Double-click on any fonts that you don't use or no longer like.**

   Whenever you double-click on a font, Windows lets you see what it looks like, as shown in Figure 16-4.

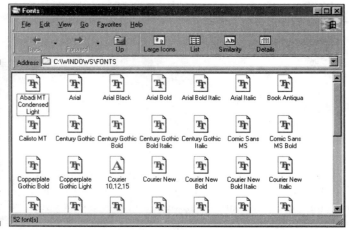

Figure 16-3: Double-click on the Control Panel's Fonts icon to see the fonts on your computer.

Figure 16-4: Double-click on a font's name to see what it looks like.

4. Hold down Ctrl and click on the names of *all* the unwanted fonts.

Windows removes those fonts when you complete Step 5.

> **WARNING!**
>
> Don't delete fonts starting with MS, like MS Sans Serif or MS Serif. Also, don't delete any fonts with red letters in their icons. Windows 98 and its gang of programs often use those fonts in their menus.

5. Drag and drop the fonts into the Recycle Bin.

That's it; they're gone.

If you've found some cool replacement fonts, Chapter 3 shows you how to put them on your hard drive. If you've deleted the wrong font, however, open up the Recycle Bin as soon as possible, click on its name with your right mouse button, and choose Restore for a quick resuscitation.

Chapter 17

Networking (Not Working) with Windows 98

● ●

In This Chapter

▶ What's a network?

▶ What computer parts do I need to buy for a network?

▶ Installing the parts of a network

▶ Configuring Windows 98 to use a network

▶ Allowing networked computers to share hard drives and folders

▶ Allowing networked computers to share printers

▶ Sending networked information in Windows 98

● ●

A network is simply a bunch of computers that somebody wired together. Like most technologies, this can be both good and bad.

Some people find networks to be a nightmare, and with good reason: A mean-spirited boss plops them in front of the computer and tells them to "log in" and start "using the network" to process the files Jerry couldn't finish last Friday.

Other, more network-savvy people find the convenience of a network to be a dream: Instead of copying oodles of files to a handful of floppies and carrying them down the hall to Jennifer, Steve can simply copy the files to Jennifer's computer over the network. (And while he's connected, he can strike up a computerized "chat" to ask her how the cat's doing.)

Windows 98 comes with all the software you need to create your own network, as long as you provide the right cables and hardware. This chapter explains why you'd want a network, how to set one up, and how to use the network once you've got the thing running.

What's a Network?

The concept of a network is pretty easy to grasp. A network is two or more computers that have been wired together so that they can share information. But computer networks have more subtleties than nervous high schoolers on their first date.

For example, how do you tell if a computer's on a network? Who's allowed on the network? Which computers are on the network? Are *all* parts of Computer A available to Computer B, or just Computer A's CD-ROM drive? Should networked computers be allowed to kiss without passwords?

All these technical decisions need to be made beforehand, usually by the network administrator — somebody who often looks as harried as the high school principal at the prom.

A simple network consists of three main parts: The *hardware,* the *software,* and the *administrator* — the person who decides how the hardware and software behave. (Unfortunately, installing the network yourself transorms you into the administrator.)

✔ Likewise, simple networking hardware consists of *cable* to connect the computers and *cards* that plug inside the computers and give the cable something to connect to.

✔ Networking software comes built into Windows 98; you don't have to buy anything extra. The software merely needs to have its settings adjusted by a human — the administrator — in order to work with the cable and cards.

✔ The network administrator, in addition to making sure that the software and hardware work well together, flips the switches to decide everybody's level of access. For example, you — the network administrator — can let everybody access everybody else's computer. Or you can merely let people read files from a single computer — nobody can snoop on anybody else's computer. You have complete control over who gets to do what on your computers.

Computers aren't the only things that can be networked. Printers, CD-ROM drives, and modems can be put on a network as well. This way, everybody on the network can send their files to a single printer or modem. When two people try to send their files to a printer simultaneously, one computer on the network simply holds onto the incoming files until the printer is free and ready to deal with them.

LAN stands for *Local Area Network,* and it describes computers linked directly by cables. Computers that sit closely together — in the same room or small building — usually use a LAN. (This chapter talks about LANs.)

WAN stands for *Wide Area Network,* and it describes computers linked through phone lines and modems. A WAN can link computers that are located miles away from each other. (This chapter doesn't talk about WANs. The Internet is a WAN, however, and it's covered in Chapter 5.)

What Computer Parts Do I Need to Set Up a Network?

If you're trying to set up a lot of computers — more than five or ten — you need a more advanced book: Networks are very scary stuff. But if you're just trying to set up a handful of computers in your home, home office, or small business, this chapter may be all you need. (And if your network is already installed, count your blessings and move on ahead in this chapter for information about making it work.)

So without further blabbing, here's a no-fat, step-by-step list of how to set up your own small and inexpensive network to work with Windows 98. The steps in the following sections show you how to link your computers so that they can share hard drives and printers. (After you're networked, you can play those cool network games like Descent and Doom that are all the rage!)

Deciding on the cable

This part sounds strange at first, but hear me out. The first step in creating a network is choosing the type of network cable your computers need. And the type of cable you need depends on how much you can spend and where your PCs are located throughout your room.

What *don't* I need for a Windows 98 network?

Windows 98 comes with its own built-in networking software. This networking software works with plain old Windows 3.11 (also known as Windows for Workgroups), as well as Windows NT (both Version 3.51 and Version 4.0).

You don't need to buy any other networking software you may have heard about, like Novell Netware, Banyan-Vines, Lantastic, or Microsoft LAN Manager. All the software you need comes with Windows 98.

In fact, *don't* install the network software that comes with your network card — the Windows 98 built-in software should work faster and more reliably. You should turn to the network card's software only as a last resort — if Windows 98 has failed miserably.

See, PCs can be connected by one long cable that stretches from PC to PC. Or they can be connected in a spider-like configuration, where each PC gets its own "leg" of cable.

Look at the way your own PCs are arranged and try to picture which setup would be easier — stringing a single cable from PC to PC (as shown in Figure 17-1), or setting a "hub" in the middle of your PCs and connecting a separate cable from the hub to each PC (as shown in Figure 17-2).

Figure 17-1:
Thin Coax cabling looks like cable TV wire and links computers in a long line.

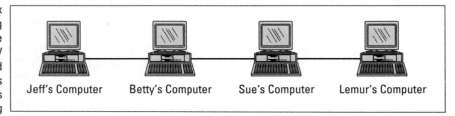

Jeff's Computer   Betty's Computer   Sue's Computer   Lemur's Computer

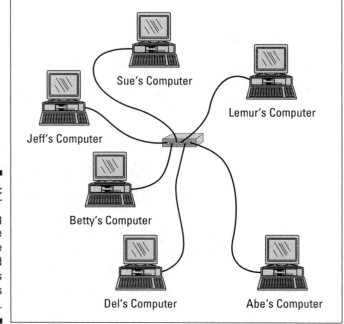

Figure 17-2:
10BaseT cabling looks like telephone wire and links computers in a hub.

Each of these two setups uses a different type of cable, and the two types of cable have weird names: *Thin Coax* and *10BaseT.*

✔ If you prefer to set up the PCs with a single cable, you need to use cable called *Thin Coax* network cable. This cable looks sort of like cable-TV wire, and it runs from computer to computer, creating a long "back-bone" with PCs latched onto it like ribs.

The Thin Coax cable is also known by a wide variety of names, including thin-Ethernet, Thinnet, and BNC.

✔ If you'd do less tripping over cables by using the "spider" approach, you should opt for the *10BaseT* cable. Resembling telephone cable, this cable works better where computers will be moved around a lot, like in modular office settings. Because each computer gets its own cable that plugs into a central hub, moving a computer to a different location is no big deal — you're not trying to bend a "backbone" of linked computers.

The 10BaseT cable is known by a wide variety of names, including RJ-45, TPE (Twisted Pair Ethernet), Twisted Pair, and 10BT. But when looking for it at the store, just say you want the kind that "looks like telephone cord instead of cable TV cord."

✔ Neither type of cable is particularly better than the other. Your decision should be based pretty much on how your computers are located throughout the room.

Piddling little Thin Coax and 10BaseT details

Cable decisions involve a little more effort than deciding whether your PCs are arranged like spokes in a wheel or like a broomstick. Depending on your type of cable, you need to pick up a few extra goodies at the software store. (Don't worry; these add-ons are usually pretty cheap.)

Networks using Thin Coax cable (the stuff that looks like TV cable) need two more little goodies: *T-connectors* and *terminator plugs.* Each PC on the network needs a *T-connector.* The T-connector is a little metal pipe shaped like the letter *T.* One end plugs into the network card in the back of your PC, leaving two ends open for the cable to plug into. Finally, you push one terminator plug onto each end of the cable linking the PCs. As shown in Figure 17-3, this essentially "plugs" the cable so that the data doesn't leak out.

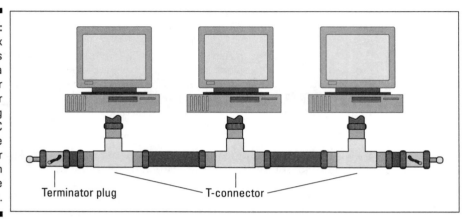

Figure 17-3:
Thin coax networks need a T-connector for connecting to each PC and one terminator plug at each end of the main cable.

People using 10BaseT cable (the cable that looks like phone wire) need an extra, more expensive goody called a *hub,* which is the device all the net-worked computers plug into. Unlike Thin Coax users, who can simply snake their single cable from PC to PC, 10BaseT users need to snake each of their multiple cables to a single hub. Without the hub, shown in Figure 17-4, the network won't work right. (More complex networks can often link hubs, but I'm deliberately leaving the complicated stuff out of this book.)

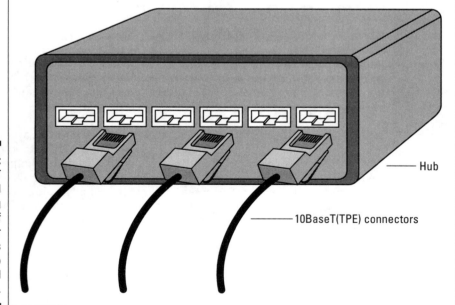

Figure 17-4:
10BaseT users need to plug each of their computer's cables into a central hub.

Deciding on the card

Decided where your PCs will be located in your network setup, as described previously? Then you've probably already decided between the Thin Coax and 10BaseT cable.

Now it's time to decide on a *network card* — the thing that plugs into one of your computer's internal slots and provides a place for the cable to plug into. Luckily, many network cards accept both types of cable, making it easy to change your mind should your needs change down the road. When you choose a card, keep these things in mind:

- ✔ The card must be an *Ethernet* card that supports your cable.

- ✔ The card must fit into one of your computer's unused slots. If you don't know what type of slot your PC uses, it may be worth finding out. A PCI bus card can shoot information through a network the fastest, if your computer's bus supports those cards.

To see what type of bus and slots your computer uses, right-click on My Computer and choose P̲roperties. Click on the Device Manager tab, followed by the plus sign next to System devices, to see a list of your computer's pertinent internal organs.

Almost all computers come with an ISA slot; most Pentiums have a PCI slot, and most laptop computers have a PC Card slot, formerly known as a PCMCIA slot. If you're not particularly slot savvy, consider picking up a copy of *Upgrading & Fixing PCs For Dummies* (published by IDG Books Worldwide, Inc.).

When buying anything for Windows 98, look for a "Designed for Windows 98" Plug and Play logo. Lacking that, look for a Windows 98 Compatible sticker. Cards and software with those logos and stickers are the easiest to install.

The fastest network card for Windows 98 is a 32-bit card on a Pentium's PCI bus. But 16-bit cards in ISA slots can usually connect a half dozen or so computers in a small-office setting.

Buying the parts

Picked out the cable? Decided on the cards? Then it's time to make the shopping list.

The Thin Coax cable network shopping list

Made the decision to install a network using Thin Coax cable? Then here's a list of all the stuff you need to buy at the computer store:

✔ One Thin Coax-supporting Ethernet card for each computer on your network

✔ One T-connector for each computer on the network

✔ Two terminator plugs

✔ One length of cable for each PC-to-PC connection. To connect four computers on a desktop, for example, you need three six-foot lengths of cable.

Confused as to how much cable to buy? Figure 17-1 shows how three pieces of cable can link four computers. And Figure 17-3 shows how two pieces of cable can link three computers.

✔ Six-foot and 12-foot lengths of cable usually do the trick. Buy a few extra lengths of cable to keep on hand in case you add a computer or two later.

✔ Buy a few extra T-connectors, too. You need one of those for every extra computer you want to pop onto your network.

✔ If you plan to add a laptop, make sure that you buy a Combo or Thin-Coax-supporting network PC Card. This lets you connect to computers using either type of networking system.

The 10BaseT (also known as UTP) cable network shopping list

Going to install a network using the 10BaseT or UTP (unshielded twisted pair) cable? Then here's a list of everything you need to pick up at the computer store:

✔ One 10BaseT-supporting Ethernet "Plug and Play" card for each computer on the network

✔ One hub that has enough ports for each computer — plus some extra ports for a few computers you may want to add at a later time

✔ A 10BaseT cable for each computer, and make sure that it's long enough to reach from the computer to the hub. (Refer to Figure 17-2 for a picture.)

Two important and unrelated last-minute facts: The 10BaseT type of cable looks like telephone line, and "Plug and Play" cards are the easiest to install.

Installing the Network's Parts

Buying groceries is the easy part; you can just toss stuff into the cart without thinking of the aftereffects, like those extra calories from the His and Hers frozen dinners, the squished eggs from the guy who bagged your groceries, or the problem of where to store the watermelon.

The same goes with installing a network. Buying the parts is relatively easy. Installing those parts into your computer can be pretty rough, though. Buying network hardware is always much easier than installing it and getting it to work right.

This part of the chapter describes the two ways to install network hardware — the easy way and the hard way. If you're lucky, you can snake through with the Easy Way section.

If you're *not* lucky, pick up a copy of *Windows 98 Uncut* by Alan Simpson (published by IDG Books Worldwide, Inc.). His detailed book shows you how to struggle through installing the network stuff the hard way.

Installing network cards the easy way

Windows 95 introduced a concept called *Plug and Play* to computerdom. According to the theory, people could simply plug their new computer parts into their computers: Windows would recognize them, install them, and rev them up. Windows 98 continues Plug and Play technology by recognizing a wide variety of network cards.

Unfortunately, not all computer parts are Plug and Play, so Windows 98 can't install them all automatically. But if you're installing a Plug and Play network card, here's the way things are supposed to work:

1. **Find your original Windows 98 compact disc; you need it.**

2. **Turn off and unplug all the computers on your soon-to-be network.**

   Turn 'em all off; unplug them as well.

3. **Turn off all the computers' peripherals — printers, monitors, modems, and so on.**

4. **Insert the network cards into their appropriate slots.**

   Remove the computer's case and push the card into the proper type of slot. Make sure that you're inserting the proper type of card into the proper type of slot — for example, inserting an ISA card into an ISA slot.

   If a card doesn't seem to fit into a slot, don't force it. Different types of cards fit into different types of slots, and you may be trying to push the wrong type of card into the wrong slot.

5. **Replace the computer's case and connect the network cables to the cards.**

6. **Connect the cable's doodads.**

For example, plug the T-connectors into the network cards, and string the Thin Coax cables between all the T-connectors. Finally, plug the unconnected ends of the T-connectors on the first and last computers on the network with the terminator plugs. (Refer to Figure 17-3 for a picture.)

If you use the 10BaseT cable, connect the computers' cards to the hub with the cable, as shown previously in Figure 17-2. (Most hubs have power cords that need to be plugged into the wall as well.)

7. **Turn on the computers and their peripherals.**

   Turn on the computers and their monitors, printers, modems, and whatever else happens to be connected to them.

   ✔ If all goes well, Windows 98 wakes up, notices its newly installed network card, and begins installing the appropriate software automatically. Hurrah!

   ✔ If all doesn't go well, click on Windows 98's Start button, choose Control Panel from the Settings option, and double-click on the Add New Hardware icon. Click on the Next button and choose Yes to make Windows try to "autodetect" the new network card.

   ✔ If Windows *still* doesn't recognize your card, call up the Control Panel's Add New Hardware program and click on the Next buttons on the first two screens. Choose No, I want to select the hardware from a list, and click on Next. Double-click on Network adapters and choose your brand of network adapter from the list. Click on the OK button, and click on the Next button in the next window. When you click on Finish, Windows 98 has finished installing your network card. (You probably need to restart your computer to activate the new card.)

   ✔ If your card comes with DOS or Windows for Workgroups software, don't install it. Windows 98 comes with its own network drivers built in, which are much better than the ones provided by the card's manufacturers.

   ✔ If your card still doesn't work, you can't install it the easy way, unfortunately. Better check out the "Installing network cards the hard way" section coming up next.

Installing network cards the hard way

Don't fret if this network installation stuff seems over your head. It's over the heads of just about everybody who hasn't turned computers into a career (or a number-one hobby) or who doesn't live a complete cyber-lifestyle.

If your network card doesn't work right — or it's not designated as being Plug and Play — you probably need to adjust the card's settings. And these adjustments can become dreadfully complicated.

The card is probably trying to use a setting that your computer has already reserved for another card inside your computer — a sound card, for example, or perhaps a communications port.

One of the most important of these settings, called an *Interrupt* or *IRQ*, serves as a doorbell for getting your computer's attention. Your network card needs its own IRQ. And unfortunately, your computer has only a handful of IRQs to dish out.

To see what IRQs your computer is already using for other devices, right-click on the My Computer icon, choose Properties from the pop-up menu, and click on the Device Manager tab. Click on the Properties button, and Windows 98 shows you a list of devices and the IRQ settings they've grabbed. Figure 17-5, for example, shows how most of the available IRQs have been assigned to various gadgetry; only Interrupts 9 and 10 are available.

In this case, let's assign the network card an IRQ of 10. But how? Different cards enable you to change their IRQs in different ways. Some make you use software that comes with the card; others make you flip little switches on the card itself. Because cards' designs vary, you have to grab the card's manual for the answer to this one.

Some cards also want an "I/O (Input/output) address;" Windows 98 lists these on the same Computer Properties page as it lists the IRQs, as shown in Figure 17-6. Click on the Input/output (I/O) button, shown in Figure 17-6, to see the available settings and the parts of your computer currently using those settings.

Figure 17-5: Windows 98 can show you which IRQs are already in use, making it slightly easier to configure your network card to use a vacant IRQ.

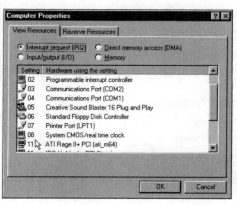

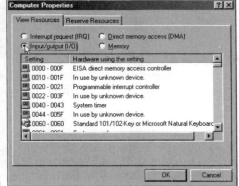

Figure 17-6:
Windows 98
shows you
which I/O
addresses
have been
used by
other parts
of your
computer.

You may have to experiment quite a bit before finding an available IRQ and
I/O setting for your particular card. Don't be afraid to ask a knowledgeable
computer friend for advice; this is some of the most complicated stuff in
computing.

Configuring Windows 98's Sensitive Networking Areas

Bought the network cables and cards? Installed them? After you install
everything, Windows 98 eventually makes you reboot the computer. When it
restarts, a window appears asking you to "log on" to the system, as shown in
Figure 17-7. Congratulations! You're experiencing your first flavors of
network life.

Figure 17-7:
After you
install
networking
cards and
configure
the
software,
Windows 98
makes you
"log on" to
the system.

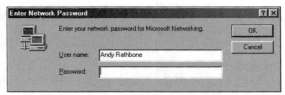

You're not through yet, however. The next few sections explain how to "log on" for the first time, as well as how to set up your computers so that they can begin talking to each other.

Identifying yourself to the network

When Windows 98 asks you to log on for the first time, you need to do two things: type your name and type your password.

Don't ever tell anybody your password, or that person can do evil things to your computer files.

- ✔ Typing your name is easy enough; most people can remember their own names. You can type just your first name, or your first and last names. The computer needs to know your name so that it can recognize you. That way, your computer knows who's using it, and the computer knows how to treat that person.

- ✔ If you're the only person who'll be using your computer and your network, you don't have to type a password at all. Just press Enter, and Windows 98 lets you into the computer without a password from then on. (You can add a password later by double-clicking on the Passwords icon in the Control Panel window.)

- ✔ In fact, if you're the only person who's going to be using the network, a password may be merely a bother. Passwords come in handy when several people work on the same PC in an office setting, however.

- ✔ When the screen clears and Windows 98 appears, look for the Network Neighborhood icon. That's a symbol that Windows 98 knows a network card has been installed. If you don't see that icon, pictured in Figure 17-8, your card must not be configured correctly because Windows can't find it.

Figure 17-8:
The
Network
Neighborhood
icon.

Network
Neighborhood

Identifying your computers to the network

After you log into your new network, you need to make sure that your network knows the right information about your computer. The following steps show you how to introduce your computers to the network and vice versa.

1. **Click on Network Neighborhood with your right mouse button and choose P̲roperties from the menu.**

   The Network dialog box appears, as shown in Figure 17-9.

2. **Check for missing components.**

   Make sure that the following items are listed in the Configuration box:

   - Client for Microsoft Networks
   - Client for Netware Networks
   - IPX/SPX-compatible Protocol
   - NetBEUI
   - TCP/IP
   - Your network card (For example, Figure 17-9 shows my Linksys Ether16 LAN Card.)

3. **Add any missing components.**

   Click on the A̲dd button and add any of the components that are missing.

4. **Click on the Primary Network L̲ogon box.**

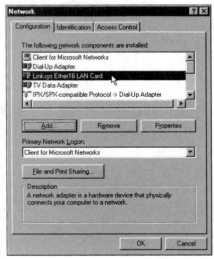

Figure 17-9:
The Network dialog box lets you adjust the settings for your network.

5. **Choose Client for Microsoft Networks.**

6. **Click on the File and Print Sharing button.**

7. **Make sure that the two options are checked, as shown in Figure 17-10.**

   These two options allow other computers on the network to share the files and printers connected to this computer.

8. **Click on OK to close the File and Print Sharing box.**

9. **Click on the Identification tab.**

10. **Type a name for your computer in the Computer name box.**

   I've named my computer *Pentium,* as you can see in Figure 17-11. Other people use friendlier names, like *Huey* or *Dewey.* The name you use here appears on the menus of other computers on the network.

   Computer names can't contain spaces, and they can't be longer than 15 characters.

Figure 17-10:
Make sure
that other
computers
can share
the files and
printers
on each
computer.

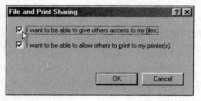

Figure 17-11:
Type a
different
name for
each
networked
computer
in the
Computer
name box,
but type the
same name
in the
Workgroup
box.

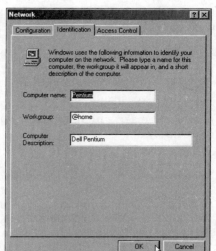

11. **Type a name for your network in the Workgroup box.**

   All the computers in your network must use the same Workgroup name. Make sure that you type the name exactly the same for each PC. Just like computer names, Workgroup names can't contain spaces, nor can they be longer than 15 characters.

12. **Type a short description of your PC into the Computer Description box.**

   The least important setting, the description merely adds a little identifying information about the computer when it appears on a network's menu.

13. **Click on the Access Control tab.**

14. **Click on the Share-level access control button.**

   Basically, this keeps things simple by letting you assign one password to each resource — be it a hard drive or a printer or an entire computer — on your network.

15. **Click on the OK button.**

16. **Log in to each of the computers on your network and repeat all these steps.**

   Be sure to choose a different name for each of your computers in Step 10, and be sure to choose the same Workgroup name for all your computers in Step 11.

   If everything went well, you can double-click on the Network Neighborhood icon and see all the computers on your network, as shown in Figure 17-12.

   When you double-click on the computers, however, a blank window appears. Why? Because you haven't told the network what parts of those computers should be shared with the other computers. (That stuff's in the *next* section.)

If the names of your computers aren't all listed, however, try these things:

   ✔ Open and close the Network Neighborhood folder icon. Do the same with the Entire Network icon that lives inside that folder.

   ✔ Shut down all your computers and make sure that the network cables are plugged into the cards securely.

   ✔ Make sure that you typed the same name into the Workgroup box in Step 11, and make sure that each computer on the network has its own unique name.

   ✔ If you're not even seeing a Network Neighborhood icon, your card probably isn't installed right. You may have to fiddle with its IRQ and I/O settings, unfortunately.

   ✔ Don't worry if these things take time. You only have to do them once.

Figure 17-12:
After you successfully configure your network, double-clicking on the Network Neighborhood icon should list all the computers connected to your network.

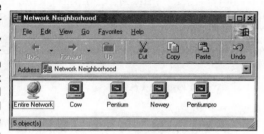

Making Your PCs Share Their Goodies

Congratulations! You've made yet another of many successful steps toward successful networking. But when you double-click on any of your computers now listed in your Network Neighborhood folder, a blank window appears. That's because those computers haven't been told that they're supposed to *share* their information.

Sharing — a bit of thievery referred to as "sharing resources" in the networking world — is covered in this section.

Sharing hard drives

To keep things simple, this section shows you how to do the easiest type of networking: Letting any computer on the network grab anything from the hard drive of any other computer on the network.

Admittedly, it's not going to be the most secure system. Anybody in the office can grab anything else. But it's an easy way to understand how networks work so that you're more prepared to restrict access later (and still be able to get into the network yourself).

To start small, here's how to designate a single hard drive on one computer as being *shared,* or "available to everybody else on the network."

If you're feeling burnt out after all the previous network atrocities, don't worry; this part is really easy — finally.

1. **Double-click on the My Computer icon of the computer containing the hard drive you want to share.**

   Make sure that you're sitting down at a computer that's placed on your network. When you double-click on the My Computer icon, its window opens, as shown in Figure 17-13, revealing all the hard drives and CD-ROM drives used by that computer.

2. **Right-click on the drive you want to share with the rest of the computers on your network.**

   A menu pops up, as shown in Figure 17-14.

3. **Click on the Sharing option.**

   A Properties box for that drive appears, as shown in Figure 17-15.

4. **Click on the Shared As button.**

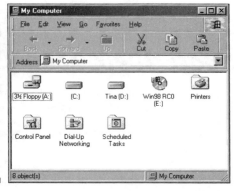

Figure 17-13: Double-click on the My Computer icon to see the drives used by a computer.

Figure 17-14: Computers on a network have a "Sharing" option on their drive's pop-up menu.

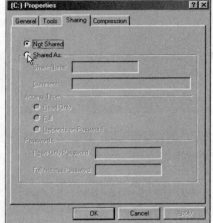

Figure 17-15:
The
Properties
box lets you
assign the
levels of
access
granted to
people on
the network.

5. **In the Share Name box, type a name for the drive.**

Windows 98 usually helps you out by calling your C drive *C,* but you can call it "drive C" or something else, if you like. This is the name of the drive that other people see on the network.

6. **In the Comment box, type a short description.**

Just type some helpful, descriptive information here if you think that it's necessary.

7. **Designate the Access Type.**

You can allow people three types of access, all designated by choosing among the following buttons:

• **Read Only:** This option lets people read and copy files from the drive, but not delete or move them.

• **Full:** This option lets people read, copy, delete, or move the files.

• **Depends on Password:** This option offers some networkers Read Only access but gives other networkers Full access, depending on the password status you choose in the next step.

8. **Designate the passwords.**

If you want people on your network to use passwords to access your files, click here and type the appropriate password they need to use.

If you leave it blank, they won't need any passwords.

9. **Click on the OK button.**

The My Computer window reappears, but with the drive C icon showing a subtle difference, as shown in Figure 17-16.

Figure 17-16:
Hard drives available for sharing on a network have a little hand beneath their icon.

✔ Feel free to repeat these steps on any of the hard drives on any of the computers on your network. Then, when you double-click on that computer's name in the Network Neighborhood folder, you won't be calling up a blank window. Instead, you see that computer's shared hard drives listed as available folders.

✔ I set up all my hard drives as shared. That makes it easier to grab files from any place on any computer.

✔ If your networking needs are more complex, you might consider Windows NT. Described in this book's appendix, it's more powerful, secure, and configurable than Windows 98.

Sharing printers

Having several computers around the house but only one printer is not uncommon. In fact, it's the source of marital strife in some computer-oriented households: Who gets to have the printer hooked up to his or her computer?

With a network, the answer's easy: everybody. Simply connect the printer to the network, and everybody can send files to it without having to get up.

To put a printer on the network, follow these simple steps:

1. **Double-click on the My Computer icon of the computer currently connected to the printer.**

   The My Computer window appears.

2. **Double-click on the Printers folder.**

   The Printers window pops onto the screen, as shown in Figure 17-17.

3. **Right-click on the icon of the printer you'd like to share and choose S̲haring from the pop-up menu.**

   The printer's Properties window appears, showing its Sharing page (see Figure 17-18).

4. **Click on the S̲hared As button and then click on the OK button to finish.**

   That's pretty much it — simplicity itself. You can get a little more elaborate if you want. For example, you can type a password into the Password box in Step 4 if you want to restrict printer access to password-knowing networkers only.

Figure 17-17:
The Printers window shows the printers currently available to that computer.

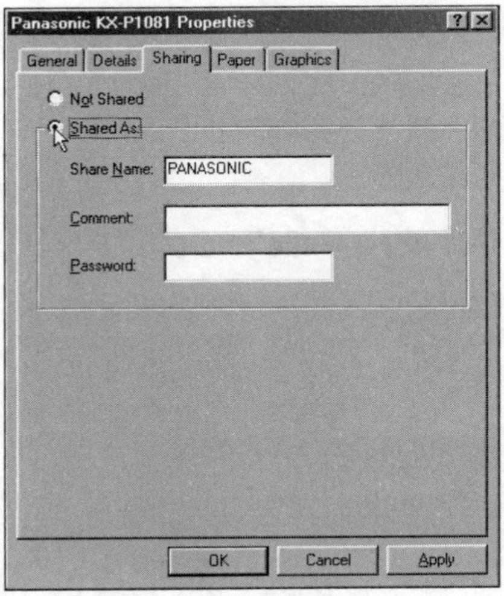

Figure 17-18:
Click on the Shared As button to share your printer with other computers on the network.

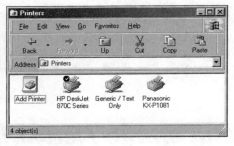

✔ You can also type a name for your printer in Step 4, like *Fred,* or *Paper Jam.* Whatever you type in the Share Name box is the name that appears as the printer's name to the other networked users on their computers. If you don't type anything, Windows 98 simply uses the first word in the printer's icon name.

✔ Anything you type into the optional Comment box of Step 4 also shows up on the network as an additional description.

Sharing individual folders

You don't have to put an entire computer on a network. You can just designate one of its drives as "shared," for example, or just its CD-ROM drive. In fact, you can even put a single folder on the network.

Just click on the folder or CD-ROM drive, choose Sharing from the pop-up menu, and fill out the Properties form, just as if the folder or CD-ROM drive were a hard drive. (That stuff is described in the "Sharing hard drives" section a little earlier in this chapter.)

Copying Files Around on the Network

After you've spent hours installing a network, telling your computer about the new network, introducing the other computers to the network and each other, and telling the network what parts of the other computers they can access, you're ready to reap the rewards of your efforts: You can start grabbing files from other computers without getting up.

Accessing a file on another computer

After you've spent a few hundred dollars networking your computers, you're ready to do fun stuff, like copying files around. The following steps show you how to copy a file from one computer to another:

1. **Double-click on the Network Neighborhood icon.**

   The Network Neighborhood window appears, listing all the computers on the network.

2. **Double-click on the icon of the computer containing the file you want to access.**

   A window for that computer opens, listing the resources available on the computer. If you've made all its hard drives available, for example, you see a folder for each hard drive. Or if you shared only a single folder on that computer, you see only that single folder.

3. **Double-click on the folder containing the file you'd like to access.**

Keep clicking on folders until you find the file you want.

4. **Access the file.**

You can copy the file to your own computer by dragging and dropping it there. Or you can simply double-click on the file to start editing it while leaving it physically on the other computer.

✔ If you can't move the file, perhaps you only have Read Only access to that computer's drives or folders. Better check out this chapter's "Sharing hard drives" section for information on how to give yourself more access.

✔ After you open the window to access another computer on the network, Windows 98 treats that computer as if it were a plain old folder on your desktop. You can copy your own files onto that computer by dragging and dropping them onto that folder. You can even run programs off other computers by double-clicking on them.

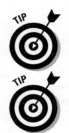

When you put your CD-ROM drive on the network as a shared hard drive, all your computers can grab information from it.

Feel free to make shortcuts to your most-often-used folders and files on your networked computers. That saves the time and hassles of running through the Network Neighborhood each time you want to grab something popular.

Accessing a printer on a network

Accessing a networked printer is a mite more complicated than accessing shared hard drives or folders, but it's not too much of a pain. When accessing a hard drive or folder, you can get in immediately because you've already done the setup work.

But when you want to access a printer, you need to jump through a few hoops — even though you've made the printer available as a shared resource, as described in the "Sharing printers" section a few pages back in this chapter.

The next few steps show you how to set up Computer A so that it can use a printer that's been connected to Computer B.

Highly paid computer administrators refer to the computer that's connected to the printer as the *print server*. The other computers are called *print clients*. Similarly, whenever you grab a file from a computer, the computer that's grabbing is the *client;* the computer that's dishing out the files is the *server*.

1. **Make sure that you made the printer on Computer B available as a shared resource.**

   This mild-mannered task was described earlier in this chapter.

2. **Double-click on the My Computer icon on the computer where you want to print the file.**

   The My Computer window appears.

3. **Double-click on the Printers folder and double-click on the Add Printer icon, shown in Figure 17-19.**

   The Add Printer Wizard magically appears.

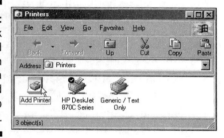

Figure 17-19: Double-click on the Add Printer icon to add a networked printer to your system.

4. **Click on the Next button.**

5. **Click on the <u>N</u>etwork printer button and click on Next.**

6. **Click on the B<u>r</u>owse button to find the printer.**

   A list of computers hooked up to your system appears; double-click on the one with the printer hooked up to it, and you see the networked printer, as shown in Figure 17-20.

Figure 17-20: Clicking on the Browse button lets you find your printer more easily.

7. **Click on your printer's name and click on the OK button.**

8. **Tell the Wizard whether or not you print from DOS programs.**

   If you print from MS-DOS programs, click on the Yes button; if you're strictly a Windows user, click on the No button.

9. **Click on the Next button.**

10. **Type a name for the printer.**

    Or to keep things simple, accept the name that Windows uses.

11. **Decide whether to make this printer the default printer.**

    If you want this computer to use this network printer all the time, click on the Yes button; if you plan on using another computer more often, click on the No button.

12. **Click on the Next button.**

13. **Click on Yes and click on the Finish button.**

    Clicking on Yes tells that computer to send a test page over the network for the printer to print. That's a good way to make sure that the thing works *before* Jeffy has to print out his report on Florida manatees at 7:30 Monday morning.

   ✔ You may have to grab your original Windows 98 CD so that your computer can copy the printer drivers. (It's a good thing you kept that Windows 98 box handy, eh?)

   ✔ From now on, that computer uses the networked printer, just as if it were connected to it. And, in effect, it *is* connected to it. The cable just makes a lot of stops along the way.

   ✔ After you connect a computer to a printer — make the computer the *print server,* in more geekish terms — you can see it in the Network Neighborhood. The printer doesn't have a little hand under it; a little cable runs through it, as shown in Figure 17-21.

Figure 17-21:
Click on the print server to see the printer's icon.

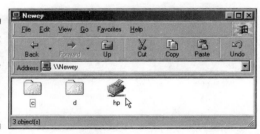

Part V
More Shortcuts and Tips Galore

The 5th Wave   By Rich Tennant

"I WISH SOMEONE WOULD EXPLAIN TO PROFESSOR JONES THAT YOU DON'T NEED A WHIP AND A LEATHER JACKET TO FIND A LOST FILE."

In this part . . .

After a few years of driving a city's streets, a cabbie knows all the shortcuts: which side streets bypass freeway traffic, what hours the airport is clogged, and when the train station is a better market for quick fares.

Grizzled cabbies usually don't like to share their secrets; their livelihood's at stake. But Windows users? You can't *stop* them from talking about shortcuts.

Put two Windows users together, and you not only hear about secret places to click, but you also hear about what key to press *while* you're clicking.

Toss in a few tips on how to cheat at Minesweeper, and you've got an idea of what you can find in this part of the book.

Chapter 18

A Grab Bag of Tricks

The programmers who created Windows 98 tried to make things easy. For example, opening a file in most Windows programs is relatively simple — on the surface, at least.

But after the programmers finished putting things on the menus, they started hiding some secret stuff in the cracks.

This chapter yanks the suspiciously secret stuff out of the cracks and puts it on the coffee table for easy viewing.

Her Version of Windows 98 Has More Stuff Than My Version!

Not all versions of Windows 98 are alike — for several reasons. Don't get me wrong — only *one* version of Windows 98 is out there. The difference boils down to what *parts* of that version are installed on your computer.

When Windows 98 installs itself onto your computer, it doesn't install all of its many programs and options. If it did, it could easily eat up 300MB of space on your hard drive. So Windows 98 leaves a lot of its programs sitting on its floppy disks or compact disc. In fact, that's why Windows 98 gives you four options when it installs itself: Typical, Portable, Compact, and Custom.

Typical is your best bet; if your computer has a large hard drive, choose *everything*. Some of those programs may seem over your head now, but the system maintenance programs come in handy later for any neighborhood teenagers who may be able to fix your computer.

To see which parts of Windows 98 made it onto your computer during installation, double-click on the Add/Remove Programs icon from the Control Panel. Click on the Windows Setup tab; programs with a check mark next to them have been installed. If you don't see a check mark, or the box has a gray check mark, that program or batch of programs hasn't been fully installed.

A Compact Disc Isn't Very Compact

Windows 98 may be a huge program, but it's not big enough to completely fill a compact disc. The programmers took advantage of this freak of nature by piling loads of Windows 98 "extras" onto the compact disc version.

You can find most of these goodies in the Control Panel's Add/Remove Programs icon. Others hide in folders on the disc itself — and nobody told you about them.

Table 18-1 shows some of the items that still lingered on the Windows 98 CD during the later stage of its production. Chances are, your CD is laid out similarly.

Table 18-1	Extra Goodies on the Windows 98 Compact Disc	
What It's Called	*Where It Is*	*What It Does*
Interactive CD Sampler	On the installation CD's initial menu	A slick promo vehicle for Microsoft products, this fancy menu enables you to choose videos describing software in the Microsoft family (the flight simulator's fun).
Cool videos	On the installation CD's initial menu	More commercials, but no fancy menu: Point and click on the video files. (And yes, that's *the* Barney.)
Browse this CD	On the installation CD's initial menu	Brings up an Explorer's eye view of the CD and its contents.

What It's Called	Where It Is	What It Does
Add/Remove Software	On the installation CD's initial menu	Installs Windows 98 or various parts of it.
add-ons	Click on the main menu's Browse this CD button to find this folder, as well as the other folders in this table.	Check out ClipBook for viewing clipboard contents, storing the contents as bitmap images, and sharing ClipBook objects over the network.
betaonly	*Ibid.* (I've always wanted to use that word in a book so I could feel important.)	A motley crew of utilities, including fat32win, which estimates the disk space savings it offers to your hard drive. Windows 98's fax program lurks here, too.
cdsample	Same	The background files required to run Microsoft's slick Interactive CD Sampler (described at the top of this table).
drivers	Same	Customized software that enables Windows 98 to communicate with computer parts like sound cards and printers.
tools	Same	A handful of well-worn DOS commands, handy utilities for computer gophers.
win98	Same	The files required to install Windows 98.

Make Programs Print Just the Right Way

Most Windows programs enable you to choose Page Setup from the File menu. With that option, you can change how a page looks when you print it. Should the page have numbers along the top or bottom, for example? Or should a title be across the top of each page?

Unfortunately, few programs are very clear about how to add that stuff to a page. So here's the trick:

By inserting special symbols into the Header and Footer boxes in most Page Setup areas, you can make the date, time, filename, page numbers, or personal text appear across the top or bottom of each of your printed pages.

Those special symbols — and what they do — appear in Table 18-2.

Table 18-2	Special Codes and Their Printing Effects
Adding This Symbol to the Header or Footer Box...	**Adds This to the Printed Page**
&&	Ampersand
&d	Current date
&t	Current time
&p	Page numbers
&f	Filename
&l	Any text following this code starts at the left margin
&r	Any text following this code starts at the right margin
&c	Any text following this code is centered between the margins

Running Out of Memory?

No matter how much memory you have stuffed inside your computer, Windows always seems to want more. Here are a few tricks for fighting back:

✔ If Windows says that it doesn't have enough memory to do something and you're sure that your computer *does* have enough memory, check your Clipboard. If you copied a big picture to the Clipboard, delete it: That picture may rob Windows of the memory that it needs to do something else.

✔ If you're scrimping for memory, don't use big photographs for your wallpaper. Tiling smaller images across the screen uses a lot less memory.

✔ If you use a lot of DOS programs, make .PIFs for them, as described in Chapter 14. Sometimes Windows gives too much memory to DOS programs; a .PIF can get some of that memory back.

Highlighting Text Quickly

I don't know why this trick works, but here goes:

When highlighting a bunch of text in Notepad and moving the pointer from the bottom toward the top, wiggle your mouse around above Notepad's window. That speeds up the marking process.

That trick works when highlighting information in other Windows programs, too. Weird.

Cheating at Minesweeper

You'll be master of the Minesweeper tournaments! Well, until everybody else sees you do the trick. Anyway, this Minesweeper-cheating secret is handy for people who prefer to play Minesweeper under less stressful conditions.

1. **Open Minesweeper from the Start menu and select your usual skill level.**

   No skill level yet? Just move to Step 2; Minesweeper starts you at the beginner level.

2. **Click on a square to start Minesweeper's game timer.**

   The clock starts ticking away in the upper-right corner.

3. **Hold down both mouse buttons and press Esc.**

   A 3 x 3 block of squares indents itself when you press the buttons; the timer stops ticking when you press Esc.

You can now finish the game at a more leisurely pace, rising only to show the neighbors how you finished the game at Expert level in merely three seconds.

Plugging It In Right Side Up

This tip doesn't have *that* much to do with Windows, so it's slipped in here unannounced toward the end, free of charge.

After your computer's up and running, with all the cables plugged into the right places, put a dot of correction fluid on the top of each cable's plug. That makes it easier to plug the cables back in right-side up when they fall out.

Character Map

Windows Character Map, found in the Start menu's System Tools area (which lurks in the Programs area's Accessories area), lets you add accented characters to funky foreign words like *à votre santé*. But when Character Map comes to the screen, all the letters and characters are small and hard to read.

Here's the trick:

- ✔ Hold down your mouse button while moving the pointer over the characters in Character Map.

- ✔ When you *hold down* the mouse button, a magnified view of the characters pops to the forefront for easy viewing.

- ✔ Or just click once on any of the characters. Then when you move your arrow keys, a magnified view of the foreign character pops up wherever you move your arrow keys.

- ✔ Don't have the Character Map on your computer? Head to the Control Panel's Add/Remove Programs icon; you can install the program there.

Chapter 19
Speedy Menu Shortcuts

● ●

In This Chapter

▶ Drag-and-drop shortcuts

▶ Quick-clicking tips

▶ Choosing items quickly from a list

▶ Replacing highlighted text

● ●

*B*efore you can do just about *anything* in Windows 98, you need to click on a menu.

So the quicker you can click, the quicker you can breeze through Windows and move on to the more important things in life.

This chapter shows some of the best quick-click tips.

Moving through Menus Quickly

When choosing something from a Windows menu, people usually follow the most logical course:

1. **Click on the option along the program's top and watch as the little menu falls down.**

2. **Then click on the desired item from the little menu.**

That's two clicks: The first one brings down the menu, and the second chooses the item from the menu. However, you can reduce your finger action to a *single* click.

When you click somewhere to open a menu, *keep holding down your mouse button.* When the menu drops down, slide the mouse pointer until it rests over the item you want. Then *release* the mouse button to choose that item.

That simple trick turns a two-click operation into a single-click, cutting your click work in half.

Press the First Letter of an Item in a List

Windows often presents lists of a zillion options. In fact, some lists have too many options to fit on-screen at the same time. So to scroll up or down the list of options, people usually click on little arrows.

To reach an item in the bottom of the list, you could press PgDn several times, or click on the scroll bars a couple times. But here's a faster way:

When Windows lists too many items to fit on-screen at once, press the first letter of the item you want; Windows immediately jumps to that item's place in the list.

For example, Figure 19-1 lists all the deleted files decomposing in the Recycle Bin. To immediately jump to the deleted file named Launch TV Viewer, press the letter L. Windows immediately jumps to the first file beginning with L. Slick, huh?

Figure 19-1:
When faced with a long list of items, press the first letter of the item you want; the highlight jumps to the first item beginning with that letter.

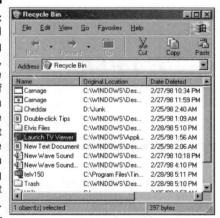

Secret Places to Click

Much of Windows consists of aiming carefully with the mouse and clicking the mouse button — pointing and clicking on a menu to choose something, for example. Or clicking in a box to put an X inside it.

But here's a secret, welcomed by those with big fingers: You don't have to aim carefully with your mouse. The next few sections show some *sloppy* places to click that work just as well.

Skipping past downward-pointing arrows

Some menus come packaged inside little boxes. And they're hidden. To make the menu drop down, you need to click on the little downward-pointing arrow next to the box. But you don't need to be overly precise, as shown in Figure 19-2.

Figure 19-2:
Instead of aiming precisely for a box's arrows, aim and click inside the easier-to-reach box itself to reveal the drop-down menu.

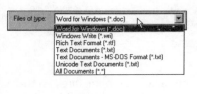

 Instead of aiming directly for the downward-pointing arrow next to a box, click inside the box itself. A click inside the box also makes the menu drop down, and the box is easier to aim at than the arrow. (This trick works only for "drop-down" list boxes: the lists with the little arrows. It doesn't work for boxes in which you can type or for lists without arrows.)

Avoiding tiny check boxes and circles

Some menus make you click inside a tiny circle — also known as a *radio button* — or check box to change an option. For example, to switch to extra-large, ultra-visible icons on your desktop, right-click on your desktop, choose P̲roperties, and choose the Effects tab.

At first glance, you may think that you would click in the tiny square next to Use l̲arge icons, as shown in Figure 19-3. Or would you?

Figure 19-3: Clicking on an option's title does the same thing as clicking in the option's little check box.

Instead of clicking on the tiny button next to an item, click on the name of the item itself. That chooses the item, just as if you clicked inside the tiny circle or box.

Replacing highlighted text

To replace text in a word processor, the usual course is to highlight the text, press the Delete key, and type in the new text. But here's a quicker way.

After highlighting some text that you'd like to replace, immediately begin typing in replacement text. Your first keystroke deletes the highlighted text, just as if you had pressed Delete.

Chapter 20

Tips for Windows Explorer and My Computer

*U*ntil you get used to its cold approach, Windows Explorer is probably the most raggedy part of Windows. It's the hole in the comfortable Windows blanket, letting the cold air of file management blow in.

Windows 98 For Dummies covers the basics of file slinging, so you won't find that stuff in this chapter. Instead, you'll find tips and shortcuts for pointing and clicking your way through Windows 98's baffling catacombs of icons, menus, and filenames.

Selecting Files and Folders Quickly

If you have My Computer or Windows Explorer on-screen, you're most likely looking for some files or folders to click on. Table 20-1 shows some shortcuts for grabbing bunches of 'em, quickly.

Table 20-1	Shortcuts for Selecting Files and Folders in Windows Explorer and My Computer	
To Grab These . . .	**Do This**
A single file or folder	Click on it.
Several files or folders	Hold down Ctrl while clicking on them.
Several files or folders sitting next to each other	Click on the first file, hold down Shift, and click on the last file.
A file or folder beginning with a specific letter	Press that specific letter.

Uh, How Big Is This File?

Face it, My Computer and Windows Explorer don't volunteer much information about your files, folders, or hard drive. Most of the time, they merely list file and folder names in alphabetical order.

And that's fine when you're first starting out with Windows. But after a while, you need to know *more:* How big is that file? Is this file *older* than that file? And how much space do you have on your hard drive, anyway?

These tips let you see all the gory information about files, folders, and disk drives.

✔ While holding down Alt, double-click on any file, folder, shortcut, or icon on your desktop. A box opens on-screen and reveals that little doodad's *properties:* its size, name, birthdate, and the date it was last saved. You also find a list of its *attributes:* technical information about the file's various technical switches.

✔ If you click on a shortcut, however, the properties box only tells you information about the shortcut. To see information about the real thing — the file, folder, or drive that the shortcut points to — click on the properties box's Shortcut tab and click on the Find Target button. That sequence brings the real thing to the screen.

✔ Tired of poking through Windows Explorer to find all your Paint files? Then tell Explorer to sort your files by their *file types*. Just click on the tab marked Type along the Explorer's top edge. Explorer sorts your files alphabetically by their type, from Application files to Zip files.

Where'd they go?

Got a sneaking suspicion that Windows Explorer and My Computer aren't showing you *all* the files in your folder? You're right — they aren't. Some of the files are for the computer to use, not you. So Microsoft made them invisible. To see the files that Windows 98 has hidden from you in Explorer or any folder, choose Folder <u>O</u>ptions from the <u>V</u>iew menu.

Click on the View tab and look for the Hidden files area of the Advanced settings box.

Finally, click in the <u>S</u>how all files area. Click on the OK button, and Windows 98 begins showing you all the files in its folders.

Clicking in this area bypasses that "Hidden" attribute seen on the first page of the Properties page, meaning that all your files and folders show up, whether you check the Hidden box or not.

Making My Computer Work Like Windows Explorer

Windows 98 can manage files in two ways. Some people like the icon-and-window based look and feel of My Computer with its easy-to-see folders. Others prefer the basic "File Manager" approach of Windows Explorer. Windows 98 doesn't give you a choice on your desktop, however: Whenever you double-click on a folder on your desktop, you're stuck with the My Computer view of icons.

If you prefer Windows Explorer's way of looking at things, you can make Windows 98 default to Explorer's way of displaying files.

1. **Open Windows Explorer and choose Folder <u>O</u>ptions from the <u>V</u>iew menu.**

2. **Click on the File Types tab along the top and scroll down to the entry for "Folder."**

3. **Click on the <u>E</u>dit button, highlight the explore option, and click on the <u>S</u>et Default button.**

Now My Computer — as well as any folders sprinkled on your desktop — begins displaying its contents using Windows Explorer's look and feel. To switch back to the My Computer style of displaying a desktop folder's contents, follow these same steps, but set the default back to the open option rather than the explore option.

Uh, Am I Moving or Copying This File?

Can't remember whether you're *moving* or *copying* a file as you drag it from window to window? Then the tips below may help.

✔ As you begin dragging a file's little icon, look inside the icon. If it contains a plus sign, you're *copying* the file. If the icon doesn't have a plus sign, you're *moving* the file.

✔ If you're *copying* a file when you want to *move* it — or vice versa — then press or release Ctrl. One of these two actions toggles your action between copying or moving.

All the Letters Are Too Small!

Windows Explorer is full of tiny words in tiny little rows and columns, but it doesn't have to be. Windows 98 allows you to view your drive's filenames and folders using a wide variety of font sizes.

For example, the tip below can make Windows Explorer's letters exceptionally large and easy to read on a groggy Monday morning.

1. **Click on a blank area of your desktop with your right mouse button and choose Properties.**

   The Display Properties screen appears.

2. **Click on the Settings tab, click on the Advanced button, and examine the Font Size box.**

   If your Font Size currently says Small Fonts, go to Step 3. If it says Large Fonts or Other, go to Step 4.

3. **Click in the Font Size box, choose Large Fonts, and click on the OK button.**

   Depending on your brand of monitor, Windows 98 may want to restart itself to come up with larger fonts. Follow the on-screen directions to let Windows 98 shut itself down and come back to life with larger fonts.

4. **Make sure that the Font Size box currently reads Other.**

   By choosing the Other option, you can tell Windows 98 to "scale" the fonts to be a large percentage of their current size.

5. **Choose 125% from the box and click on the OK button.**

   Windows 98 probably wants to restart your computer; just click on Yes when Windows 98 asks whether you're ready for the restart.

   Regardless of the method you choose, Windows 98 wakes up with larger-sized fonts on the screen.

Cleaning Up Those Strings of Folders

When you double-click on a folder (or single-click, if you're running in Active Desktop's Web mode), Windows 98 opens it, leaving a window on the screen. Click a folder within that window, and yet another window appears to display its contents.

Dig inside some folders to find one that's buried deep within your filing system, and you end up with a string of folders cluttering your desktop. But it doesn't have to be that way, as these two tips show.

Hold down Ctrl while double-clicking on a folder. Instead of opening a new window to show that folder's contents, Windows 98 simply displays the new folder's contents in the existing folder's window. That feature enables you to dig deeply into your folder structure without opening any extra windows.

This last tip doesn't really belong here, but it's too useful to leave out:

Isn't it infuriating when you're stuck with a folder or window on the screen that's pretty close to the one you want — but is actually one level beneath the one you want? For instance, you have the Asparagus folder open but you *really* want to see the Vegetables folder — the one that *contains* the Asparagus folder. Here's the solution: Just press the Backspace key. Each time you press Backspace, Windows 98 opens the folder just above the one that's currently open.

Making All Folders Behave the Same Way

It can take days — even weeks — to adjust folders so that they open up showing just the view you like: all large icons arranged by name, for example, or a more detailed view spilling over with information about the file.

1. **From the Yiew menu, choose Folder Options.**

   The Folder Options window appears, ready for you to change the looks of your folders.

2. **Click on the View tab, and then click on the Like Current Folder button.**

   It's a big and clunky button; you can't miss it.

If things don't work out — you don't like that current folder after all — return to the Folder Options window and choose the Reset All Folders button.

Chapter 21

Desktop Tips and Tricks

● ●

In This Chapter

▶ Making programs load themselves as icons

▶ Making programs load automatically — or not

▶ Fitting more icons on the desktop

▶ Organizing the Start menu

▶ Adding the Control Panel's icons to the desktop

● ●

The Windows 98 desktop, like any good desktop, can be organized in a wide variety of ways to help you get your work done. Some people like desktops messy, some like them organized, and some like to use the bottom edge for storing chewing gum.

This chapter shows you how to fiddle with the Windows 98 desktop until it's working the way you want it to work.

Programs That Load Themselves as Icons

Whenever you load a program, it usually hops onto a window on the desktop, ready for work. But some programs get lazy. Instead of hopping into windows, they minimize themselves along the taskbar, where they're hard to spot.

Sometimes, however, this laziness can be handy. For example, you can tell Windows 98 to load all your programs as icons along the taskbar when you sit down at your computer. Then your programs are champing at the bit and ready to go.

Here's the secret switch that tells Windows 98 whether to load a program in a window, load a program as an icon along the taskbar, or load the program so that it fills the entire screen.

1. **Right-click on your Start button and choose Open.**

   A faintly familiar window appears; it's the first tier of your Start menu.

2. **Right-click on the program and choose Properties.**

3. **Click in the Run box.**

   The box usually says Normal Window.

   - To make the program load itself as an *icon* on the taskbar, choose Minimized.

   - To make the program load itself in a *window,* choose Normal window.

   - To make the program fill the screen as it loads, choose Maximized.

Don't remember how to put a program into the StartUp area of your Start menu? Just put the program's shortcut into the StartUp folder found in your Programs folder, which lives in your Start Menu folder, which lives in your Windows folder. (Whew.)

Bypassing Your StartUp Folder

If you place a program's shortcut into the StartUp section of the Start button's Programs area, Windows 98 automatically loads that program each time you load Windows 98.

But what if you suddenly change your mind, and you don't *want* those programs to pop up when you turn on your computer this morning? Easy solution.

When Windows 98 starts to load, press and keep holding down Shift. That tells Program Manager not to load any of the programs listed in its StartUp folder.

Cramming More Icons onto the Desktop

Face it, having shortcuts for your favorite programs on the desktop is handy. Some people put shortcuts to all their disk drives along one edge, for example; others put shortcuts to To-Do lists and calendars.

After a while, the desktop can get crowded — especially when you run at a lower, 640 x 480 resolution on a small monitor. The solution is to make

Windows 98 pack the desktop shortcuts a little closer together, like sardines in a can. Here's how:

1. **Click on an empty portion of your desktop with your right mouse button and choose P<u>r</u>operties from the pop-up menu.**

2. **Click on the tab marked Appearance.**

3. **Click in the box marked <u>I</u>tem.**

4. **Click on the Icon selection.**

5. **Adjust the numbers in the Si<u>z</u>e box.**

✔ When you make the numbers smaller, Windows 98 makes the icons smaller, too. For example, if you change the Size number from 32 to 16, the icons are half their regular size, and you can pack twice as many of them into the same space.

✔ You can keep the icons the same size, but make Windows pack them closer together by playing with the two Icon spacing entries in the Item box as well. Making the Si<u>z</u>e number bigger makes Windows space the icons farther apart on the desktop; decreasing the number makes Windows move the icons closer together. Try different numbers until you find the spacing that looks best on your own desktop.

✔ For best results with closely packed icons, shorten the icon's titles. (Just click on the titles twice, slowly, to rename them.) Shorter titles keep the words from overlapping. Oh, and you can get away with deleting the words "Shortcut to" from the titles as well. That little arrow on the icon shows you that it's a shortcut, and Windows 98 always remembers.

Organizing Your Start Menu

Sometimes, everything in Windows 98 seems fast and automatic. For example, many brand-new Windows programs install themselves, create a new entry in your Start menu, and slip their own icons inside. How polite! And that new icon is easy to find, resting alone in its own offshoot from your Start menu.

But after you've added five or six more new Windows programs, the novelty wears off. In fact, with so many programs packed into the Start menu, finding the program you want can be hard. You can combat the crowding in a couple of ways.

✔ Keep your Start menu organized. Instead of having a bunch of utility programs listed under your Programs area, for example, make a Utility area under your Programs area and move all the utility programs there.

✔ When installing a new program, don't let each new program create its own offshoot from the Start menu. If the program is polite enough to ask where you'd like its icon to be installed, take advantage of that — tell it to put its icon in the same area as similar programs.

✔ When your Start menu starts looking crowded, start weeding. Click on the Start menu with your right mouse button and choose Open from the menu. A window appears, packed with folders and shortcuts. Each folder represents an area in your Start menu; each shortcut represents an entry. Move around the shortcuts until they're set up the way you like them. (And feel free to delete the ones you no longer use.)

✔ Prefer using Windows Explorer? Then use the preceding trick but choose Explore from the pop-up menu.

Making Control Panel Open Sections Automatically

Some chores take a couple of steps. To change wallpaper, for example, you simply right-click on the desktop and choose the Properties tab. Other chores, however, take a little longer. If you need to, say, calibrate a joystick or change your mouse's settings, you need to bring up the Control Panel.

Or do you? Actually, you can create a desktop shortcut to any of the Control Panel's icons.

1. **Call up the Control Panel.**

   You can find it waiting in the My Computer folder or the Start menu's Settings area.

2. **Drag and drop any of Control Panel's icons to your Desktop.**

   Click on Yes when a menu pops up asking whether you want to create a shortcut.

If you constantly readjust your keyboard for different languages, consider putting a keyboard shortcut on your desktop. The same holds true for some Windows 98 programs that put their settings adjustments into your Control Panel.

Some Control Panel icons are already easy to bring up. For example, just double-click on the little speaker in the bottom-right corner of your taskbar to bring up the Multimedia volume control, where you can adjust the volume for all your sound card's components individually.

Chapter 22

Whoops! Make It Go Back the Other Way!

Something gone horribly wrong in Windows? This chapter shows how to make Windows go back to the way it was when you first installed it. (And without having to reinstall it, either.)

Undoing a Mistake

Whoops! Deleted the wrong paragraph? Entered the wrong information into a box? All is not lost.

As soon as you notice you've made a mistake, press Ctrl+Z or Alt+Backspace. Your Windows program tries to immediately undo whatever action you've just done.

I Deleted the Wrong File!

Relax — that's what the Recycle Bin is there for. And, fortunately, the Recycle Bin is usually a little bit lazy about emptying the trash. To see whether your file is there, run through the following steps.

1. Double-click on the Recycle Bin icon.

The Recycle Bin window leaps to the screen showing a list of the deleted files that are still salvageable (see Figure 22-1). If you spot your file, simply drag and drop its icon onto your desktop. Whew! Don't spot its name? Or perhaps you don't remember its name? Then move to Step 2.

Figure 22-1:
The
Recycle Bin
can sort
through
your
deleted files
to display
them by
name,
location,
deletion
date, file
type, and
size.

2. **Click on Details from the View menu, and then choose the Date Deleted button.**

   Remember when you threw it out? Viewing files by the date they entered the garbage can makes it easier to extract them. Still can't find it? Move along to Step 3.

   If you don't remember the name of the file that you deleted, but you remember the day you deleted it, tell Recycle Bin to sort by deletion date. Then you can easily look at the names of files deleted on certain days.

3. **Click on the Type button.**

   What type of file did you delete? A text file? WordPad or Word document? Bitmap file from Paint? Clicking on the Type button makes the Recycle Bin sort deleted files by their file type. When all the text files are grouped together, for example, spotting the one you deleted is easier.

4. **Click on the Original Location button.**

   The last hope — this sorts the files by the folders where they were deleted. For example, the files deleted directly from your desktop are listed in the C:\Windows\Desktop area.

By making Recycle Bin sort through your often-unwieldy lists of deleted files, you can usually find the file you're after.

Restoring Your Original Windows Colors and Menus

It's hard to restrain yourself when faced with all the decorator colors Windows presents in the Display Properties box. Not only can you choose between color schemes like Eggplant and Rainy Day, but you can design your own color schemes, as well.

And that's where the problem comes in. If you find that your fonts have somehow become hard to read — and you've been fiddling with the Display Properties box — you may have set your menus to "white on white." White letters on a white background won't show up well, no matter how big they are.

To fix things, follow these steps:

1. **Right-click on a blank part of your desktop.**

   A pop-up menu appears.

2. **Press the letter R.**

   That selection brings up the Properties dialog box.

3. **Hold down Shift and press Tab, and then press the right arrow twice.**

   You arrive at the Appearance box, ready to restore Windows 98 to its former glory.

4. **Press Tab, and then press the down arrow.**

   The Scheme box immediately begins cycling through its other schemes, from Brick to Windows Standard Large. When you push the down arrow, the preview window displays the schemes.

5. **When you see a color scheme that's visible, press Enter.**

   Windows switches to the new, visible color scheme. The new scheme may not be as Andy Warhol-influenced, but hey, at least you can see it.

Now, if you feel it's worth the effort, go back to the scheme that you had before and take a good look at these entries: Icon, Inactive Title Bar, Menu, Message Box, Palette Title, Selected Items, and ToolTip. Those all use fonts, and if you've chosen fonts that are the same color as their background, you won't be able to read them. Try sticking with plain old black on white.

Whenever you change settings in a display scheme, use the Save As button to save them under a different name. That way you can easily return to the original settings if your new ones don't work right.

Changing Your Name and Company

Remember when you typed in your name and company name while installing Windows 98 for the first time? Well, Windows remembers it. To see who Windows thinks you are, click on the My Computer icon with your right mouse button and choose Properties.

A box pops up, as shown in Figure 22-2, and Windows lists the name and company you originally typed in.

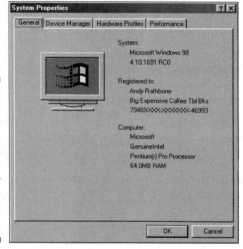

Figure 22-2: The My Computer icon's Properties page lists a computer user's name and company.

But what if you change jobs? Or change names? Simply reinstalling Windows won't do the trick; Windows always sticks with the first name and company you've entered.

You could delete Windows from your hard drive and then reinstall it, typing in the new information as you go. But I describe a quicker way next.

The file you're about to fiddle with is hot stuff. If you make a mistake while editing it or edit the wrong portions, you can seriously confuse your computer or its programs. Be very careful.

1. **Click on the Start button and choose the Run button.**

    A box appears.

2. **Type** regedit **into the Open box and press Enter.**

    The Registry Editor program appears.

3. Press F3.

A box appears.

4. Type the word you'd like to change — your name or your company's name — in the Fi_n_d what box and press Enter.

The Registry Editor searches through its internal secrets, looking for what you've typed. When the Registry Editor finds your name, it displays the line of text containing the name.

5. Double-click on the icon next to your name.

A box pops up, ready for you to edit the name.

6. Change the old name to the new name and click on OK.

7. Press F3.

The Registry Editor keeps searching for the name you typed in. If you've installed several programs, you can probably find the name listed several times. Each time, repeat Steps 5 and 6 to change the old name to the new name.

8. When the Registry Editor no longer finds the name, close the program.

Like any other program, the Registry Editor can be closed with a click in its upper-right corner.

9. Check the My Computer icon's Properties page to make sure that the change took place.

Your new name should now appear, as shown in Figure 22-3.

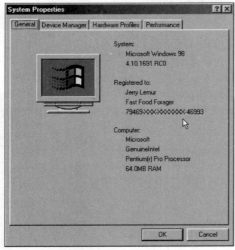

Figure 22-3:
By editing the Registry, you can update your name or organization.

✔ Don't type too long of a name for your organization, or the Properties page won't have room to display it: The name runs right off the edge.

✔ Once again, be very careful when fiddling with the Registry Editor. That's where Windows stores all its settings, and Windows may stop working if a crucial setting gets unset.

Always Hold the Right Mouse Button When Dragging and Dropping

Windows 98 enables you to do things in a zillion different ways, with no right way. That offers you more chances to stumble across the task that you're trying to accomplish. But it also makes it harder to remember the right way to do something. Does holding down Ctrl while dragging and dropping a file *move* the file, *copy* the file, or create a *shortcut?* Who knows?

Well, Windows 98 knows, and you can make it remind you whenever you drag and drop something across your screen. Simply hold down your right mouse button as you drag and drop. When you release the mouse button, Windows 98 brings a menu to the screen that lets you choose between moving, copying, or creating a shortcut to that particular object (see Figure 22-4).

Figure 22-4:
Holding down your right mouse button while dragging and dropping makes it easier to see what you're doing.

Opening a Recently Opened Document

Ready to open a file you used yesterday? Chances are, you won't need to start clicking your way through an endless chain of folders to find and open it. Instead, head for the Documents list on the Start button menu. Click on Documents, shown in Figure 22-5, and Windows 98 lists the last 15 documents that you used.

Click on the document's name, and Windows 98 loads that file into the program that created it, and then brings them both to the screen.

Sending to Simpler Times

Right-click on most icons, as shown in Figure 22-6, and a menu pops up, containing, among other entries, the words Send To. This seems easy enough to understand, given the items that pop up when you click on the Send To command: With a single click you can send your object to your mail program, fax card, floppy disk, or if you're a laptop user, your Briefcase program.

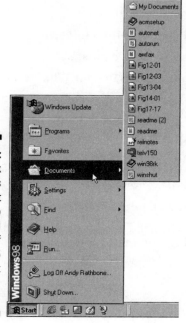

Figure 22-5: Click Documents on the Start button to see and load any of the last 15 files that you worked on.

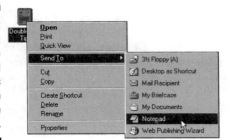

Figure 22-6:
Customize
the Send To
command
to send files
to your own
favorite
places.

But to really take advantage of the Send To command, you need to start adding your own items to the Send To menu. For example, wouldn't it be convenient to put Notepad on the list so that you could send any file to Notepad with a simple click? Or you could list a folder named Temporary on the Send To menu, making it easy to send files quickly to a folder for temporary storage.

Best of all, adding your own items to the Send To command is easy. Just follow these steps:

1. **Right-click on the My Computer icon and choose Explore from the pop-up menu.**

   The Windows Explorer program appears on-screen.

2. **From drive C, double-click on your Windows folder.**

   The Windows folder opens, displaying its contents.

3. **Double-click on the SendTo folder that's in your Windows folder.**

   The SendTo folder opens, displaying a shortcut for every item that appears on your SendTo menu (see Figure 22-7).

4. **Drag and drop shortcuts into the SendTo folder for items you want to appear on the menu.**

   For example, drag and drop a shortcut for Notepad into the SendTo folder, as well as a shortcut for any often-used folders or programs.

5. **Close the Explorer program and any open folders.**

   Any shortcut that you place in the SendTo folder shows up in the Send To menu that appears when you right-click an object.

Figure 22-7:
The shortcuts listed in your SendTo folder are shown as menu items in the Send To area that appears when you right-click on an object on your desktop.

Getting Rid of the Seedy Stuff

Sometimes Windows 98 goes overboard with its level of friendliness, especially when you insert a compact disc into your CD-ROM drive. If you've slipped in an audio CD, for example, Windows 98 automatically starts blaring the first song on the album. Or if the CD contains a Windows 98 program, Windows looks for a special "AutoPlay" program on the CD and starts loading that, as well.

If you just want to grab a file off the CD, however, this friendliness turns into an obstacle: You have to wait until the CD's "automatic" program runs before you can shut it down and use Windows Explorer to fetch your file.

To disable this CD friendliness, follow this trick: Hold down the Shift key while inserting the CD into your CD-ROM drive. That keeps Windows 98 from playing your audio CD or looking for the CD's AutoPlay program.

To permanently keep Windows 98 from automatically fiddling with your CDs, follow these steps:

1. **Click the My Computer icon with your right mouse button and choose Properties from the menu.**

2. **Click the Device Manager tab and find the CDROM drive entry.**

3. **Double-click on the CDROM drive entry to open it up and click on the CD-ROM driver that appears directly below it.**

4. **Click the Properties button at the bottom of the page and, when the new Properties page appears, click the Settings tab.**

5. **Click in the Auto insert notification box to remove the check mark.**

This disables the AutoPlay feature. To restore the feature, simply repeat the process and put the check mark back in the box.

Chapter 23

The Secret Credits Screen

● ●

In This Chapter

▶ Hidden little doodads in Windows

● ●

*W*hen artists finish a painting, they place their names in the bottom corner. But when a programmer finishes a program, where does the name go? Many companies won't let their programmers stick their names on their programs.

So because programmers are such a secretive, sneaky bunch, they often hide their names in the program itself. These hidden initials, sometimes called *Easter eggs,* have been popping up for nearly 20 years.

Computer history buffs point back to the late 1970s; back then, savvy players of Atari's 2600 game console discovered a secret room with the programmer's initials hidden in the ADVENTURE game cartridge.

Today, programmers are hiding a lot more than their initials. Here are some of the goodies you can uncover in Windows — as well as the secret keystrokes you need to discover them.

Riding the Clouds of Windows 95

Windows 95's hidden patronage to programming makes your eyes sorta get misty. Sorta.

1. **Click on a blank portion of your desktop with your right mouse button.**

2. **Choose** <u>F</u>**older from the** <u>N</u>**ew menu.**

3. **Name the folder** and now, the moment you've all been waiting for.

   Just type in those words, exactly as you see them.

4. **Click on the folder with your right mouse button and choose Rena<u>m</u>e.**

5. **Rename the folder** we proudly present for your viewing pleasure.

6. **Click on the folder with your right mouse button again and choose Rena<u>m</u>e.**

7. **Rename the folder** The Microsoft Windows 95 Product Team!

8. **Double-click on the folder to open it.**

   Sit back and watch as the show begins, seen in Figure 23-1. (And listen, too, if you have a sound card.) And prepare to sit for a long time. A l-o-t of people worked on Windows 95, and they seem to have listed all of them. (In fact, you may have to push your mouse around a few times during the display to keep your screen saver from kicking in!)

   If the trick doesn't work, you've probably spelled something wrong or capitalized a letter somewhere you weren't supposed to. Keep trying, using the exact order spelled out in these steps.

Figure 23-1:
Windows 95
comes with
its own
multimedia
secret
credits
screen.

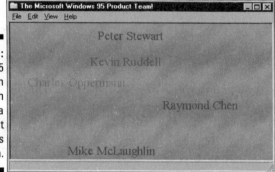

Still Using Windows 3.1?

Don't be ashamed to admit it. In fact, Windows 3.1 comes with its own secret credits screen, described next. Tell your friends, although it's pretty much old news by now.

1. **Hold down Ctrl+Shift throughout the next two steps.**

2. **Click on Program Manager's <u>H</u>elp menu and choose <u>A</u>bout Program Manager.**

3. **When the box pops up, double-click on the Windows icon.**

   The icon is in the box's upper-left corner.

4. Click on OK.

5. Repeat Steps 2 through 4.

The Windows icon turns into a waving flag.

6. Repeat Steps 2 through 4 again.

This time, you've hit it big time, and the show begins.

- See the man pointing at the chalkboard? As you keep trying the trick, over and over, you spot four different guys.

- The guy with the glasses is Microsoft's CEO, Bill Gates.

- The bald guy is Microsoft's Steve Ballmer.

- The bearded guy is Microsoft's Brad Silverberg.

- The bear is The Bear, the Windows 3.1 team mascot.

Yet another secret: The Windows 3.1 credits screen isn't limited to Program Manager. It works in just about any program that comes with Windows 3.1: Cardfile, Calendar, Paintbrush, Clock, and others.

And Now for Windows 3.0 . . .

Still using Windows 3.0? (I won't say anything if you won't.) All this fancy credits stuff doesn't work. But this trick does:

1. Hold down F3 and type WIN3.

2. Release F3 and press Backspace.

Surprise — new wallpaper!

Appendix

Should I Upgrade to Windows NT?

•••

*1*f you read Chapter 4 of this book, you know that Microsoft perpetually releases new versions of Windows. (And why not, seeing as how each new release brings oodles of cash into the corporate coffers?)

The newest release is Windows NT 4.0 — soon to be Windows NT 5.0. That leaves a big question: Who should upgrade from Windows 98 to Windows NT 4.0 or 5.0? After you're through reading this appendix, you'll be able to make an informed decision.

What Hardware Does Windows NT Need?

Each new release of Windows requires a more powerful computer. Windows NT 4.0 currently requires a machine with the guts listed in Table A-1.

Table A-1	Windows NT 4.0 Hardware Requirements
What Microsoft Says	**What Microsoft Means**
A Pentium	A *fast* Pentium, Pentium Pro, Pentium II, or ultra-fancy RISC computer (explained later)
VGA	Super VGA or better
Hard drive with 110MB free	2 gigabyte hard drive or larger
CD-ROM drive or network access	Fast CD-ROM drive
16MB of memory	32MB of memory
Mouse	Mouse
Optional network adapter card	Mandatory networking

The chart needs a little bit of explanation. First, Windows NT is a real hog. Unlike Windows 98, Windows NT needs a *lot* of room. You need a fast computer with a huge hard drive.

Next, Windows NT can't be installed from floppy disks; you need a CD-ROM drive, or access to one over a network.

Here's something new: Windows NT can run on more types of computers than just Intel's 486/Pentium/Pentium Pro-type of computers. Windows NT can run on computers that use RISC (Reduced Instruction Set Computer) technology: The system runs on a MIPS R4x00, Digital Alpha AXP, or Power PC computer. However, most of these computers cost megabucks in comparison to plain-old desktop PCs, so you probably won't be picking one up at your local computer superstore.

The fact that Windows NT can run on so many different types of computers is a bonus: If you're moving from one company to another, you may still be able to work on the same Windows NT operating system, even though the new company uses a different type of computer than the one your old company uses.

Windows NT comes in two versions: *Workstation* and *Server.* Windows NT Workstation, the less-expensive package, runs well on small networks of less than ten computers. Windows NT Server usually runs on a computer that controls networks on larger setups; it routes information to copies of Windows NT Workstation that run on the individual computers.

What Can Windows NT Do Best?

Windows NT 4.0, shown in Figure A-1, looks almost identical to Windows 98, shown in Figure A-2. But beneath the skin, Windows NT is completely different. Windows 98 is more like a family car, designed for daily driving. Sure, you can stretch it for maximum performance. And if you stop by a garage sale and see a big piece of rattan furniture that you can't pass up, you can probably fit it into the backseat and get it home.

On the other hand, Windows NT is like a powerful truck built for heavy loads. It's as easy to drive as a family car (provided that you don't have to get under the hood and try to adjust the transmission), but it has the power to carry large pieces of furniture on a daily basis without tearing the uphol-stery in the backseat.

To cut away from this goofy car analogy, Windows NT is basically made for networking in large environments, where large chunks of information need to be moved around reliably, securely, and at top speed. Windows NT lets you customize the network to a fine degree, allowing wide varieties of access.

Figure A-1:
On the surface, Windows NT looks a lot like Windows 98, shown in Figure A-2.

Figure A-2:
Windows 98 looks a lot like Windows NT, shown in Figure A-1.

Windows 98, too, offers networking capabilities. And for a small-office setting, it's probably all you need. (Chapter 17 shows you how to set up a network in Windows 98.)

But Windows 98 can't offer all the networking options needed by corporations that may string dozens of computers together.

Why Not Switch to Windows NT?

Windows NT may be powerful at networking, but that doesn't mean it's a winner in every category. Here's where Windows NT drops a few notches in esteem.

No Plug and Play

When you stick a new piece of hardware into your computer, Windows 98 makes an effort to recognize the incoming piece of gadgetry and automatically install the right piece of software to make it work. Known as *Plug and Play,* this technology has smoothed wrinkled brows all over the world. For once, computers have made a giant step toward greater ease of use.

Windows NT 4.0 doesn't use the Plug and Play technology. Microsoft, still behind schedule in releasing Windows NT 5.0, left Plug and Play technology out of Windows NT 4.0 in order to make its production deadline. Look for Plug and Play in Windows NT 5.0, due to hit the shelves sometime in 1999.

Lousy game support

Because Windows NT 4.0 is used primarily in a networking environment for large corporations, games weren't a high priority in system design. Don't be surprised if some of your favorite games won't run under Windows NT. (In fact, you won't even find support for many of your multimedia gadgets. No Virtual Reality helmets here, unfortunately.)

Large and hard to configure

Finally, Windows NT is huge, requiring gobs of hard disk space just for itself. Also, because it offers so many options for networking, Windows NT is much harder to configure. You'll probably have trouble when plugging new parts into your computer or trying to get your latest piece of software to run correctly.

So Should I Upgrade to Windows NT 4.0?

If you're in a corporation running large networks where dozens of people log on daily, Windows NT may be what you've been waiting for. First off, it's probably more robust than any previous version of Windows: It won't crash so darn often. If you've been using older versions of Windows NT, you'll find Windows NT 4.0 easier to use — because it now uses the Windows 98 interface, it's finally been brought up to speed in the Windows world.

But unless you're running a large network, you probably won't find much advantage in upgrading to Windows NT.

The operating system takes up too much space on the hard drive, it's terrible for game players, and the lack of Plug and Play support makes Windows NT much harder to use.

The verdict? Windows NT 4.0 is not for home users, or even small-office users. Unless you're running a large network, stick with Windows 98.

Index

(continued)

(continued)

IDG BOOKS WORLDWIDE BOOK REGISTRATION

Register This Book and Win!

We want to hear from you!

Visit **http://my2cents.dummies.com** to register this book and tell us how you liked it!

- Get entered in our monthly prize giveaway.

- Give us feedback about this book — tell us what you like best, what you like least, or maybe what you'd like to ask the author and us to change!

- Let us know any other *...For Dummies*® topics that interest you.

Your feedback helps us determine what books to publish, tells us what coverage to add as we revise our books, and lets us know whether we're meeting your needs as a *...For Dummies* reader. You're our most valuable resource, and what you have to say is important to us!

Not on the Web yet? It's easy to get started with *Dummies 101*®: *The Internet For Windows*® *95* or *The Internet For Dummies*®, 5th Edition, at local retailers everywhere.

Or let us know what you think by sending us a letter at the following address:

...For Dummies Book Registration
Dummies Press
7260 Shadeland Station, Suite 100
Indianapolis, IN 46256-3945
Fax 317-596-5498

BUSINESS AND GENERAL REFERENCE BOOK SERIES FROM IDG

COMPUTER BOOK SERIES FROM IDG